This Unfriendly Soil:
The Loyalist Experience in Nova Scotia
1783-1791

Following the American Revolution, more than 20,000 loyalists fled to Nova Scotia, doubling the population in a single year. Neil MacKinnon provides the first detailed account of this great wave of immigrants, their exodus and settlement, their adjustment to the new land, and their effect upon its people and institutions.

Loyalists in Nova Scotia hoped that their anticipated prosperity, to be achieved with British aid, would show that the American rebellion had been a terrible mistake. But prosperity was elusive. The loyalists were disappointed not only by their treatment at the hands of the British government, their reluctant benefactor, but also by the apparent unwillingness of the government and people of Nova Scotia to recognize their sacrifice and encourage their advancement. This sense of opposition from the existing community made their experience different from that of loyalists elsewhere and contributed to the intensity and longevity of Nova Scotia's loyalist tradition.

The early period of loyalist settlement came to a close shortly after Britain granted portable pensions and withdrew free provisions, a turn of events which led many of the exiles to return to their homeland. By 1791 relations with the old settlers and the provincial government, conflict among themselves, and changing attitudes toward the United States had modified loyalist opinions and expectations in ways they would never have imagined a decade earlier.

Neil MacKinnon is a member of the Department of History, St Francis Xavier University.

This Unfriendly Soil

The Loyalist Experience in Nova Scotia
1783–1791

NEIL MACKINNON

McGill-Queen's University Press
Kingston and Montreal

© McGill-Queen's University Press 1986
ISBN 0-7735-0596-2

Legal deposit 3rd quarter 1986
Bibliothèque nationale du Québec

Printed in Canada

Printed on acid-free paper

Canadian Cataloguing in Publication Data
MacKinnon, Neil, 1938–
    This unfriendly soil
    Includes bibliographical references and index.
    ISBN 0-7735-0596-2
    1. United Empire loyalists – Nova Scotia.
    2. Nova Scotia – History – 1784–1867.* I. Title.
    FC2321.4.M24 1986   971.6′02   C86-093782-8
    F1038.M24 1986

To the memory of my brother

HUGH CHARLES

Contents

Preface

The study of literature on the loyalists often tells us as much about the historian's values and times as it does about the loyalist himself. When not expunged from the record, they were treated by most American historians simply as a foil to the triumph of the new republic. Such an attitude, prevailing among scholars of the revolution since its conclusion, seemed at no time so firmly entrenched as in the 1960s with the dominance of the "consensus" school. Much of the scholarly attitude towards the loyalists was summed up in Bernard Bailyn's belief that "we have not yet made it clear why any sensible and well-informed person could possibly have opposed the revolution."[1]

That the pendulum might have reached its point of suspension with this dismissal is indicated by Bailyn's later work. In *The Ordeal of Thomas Hutchinson* he sought to understand just such a "well-informed person." This sympathetic study of the governor of Massachusetts is a great distance removed from Bailyn's earlier studies in its acknowledgment that there was another side to the question of independence.[2] Although Hutchinson and the other loyalists emerge as misguided, obdurate, and out of step with the desires of America, such a study by such an eminent scholar could only give greater legitimacy and impetus to the study of the loyalists and their ideology.

Many of the recent studies that have shed new light upon the revolution are those looking at it from the perspective of the Americans who opposed it. In the last two decades the number of studies concentrating on the loyalists has increased dramatically. Perhaps the most influential of these studies is Robert C. Calhoon's *The Loyalists in Revolutionary America*.[3] A big book, it describes the changing loyalist perceptions and policies in the wide, shifting sweep of the years from 1760 to 1781. In a remarkable integration of a huge variety of sources the work brings a subtle understanding to the complex and varied factors shaping loyalist motivations and decisions. After reading Calhoon's study and other recent literature one accepts the loyalists not simply as foils but as people who also confronted the momentous issue of allegiance, and from their own perspective found continued allegiance to the crown to be the proper decision.

In Canada, the interpretation of the loyalist's role was markedly different. In Canada's loyalist tradition, the best of America, remaining faithful to the British crown and institutions, refused to accept the new republic, abandoned home and fortune, and at great sacrifice followed Britain's rule into the wilderness. There at considerable personal cost they were to found a new society and imbue it with their own distinctive character. Because of its excessive hagiography, the Canadian loyalist tradition found itself easy prey for twentieth-century scholarship, and the loyalist myth of elitism, their motives for leaving the United States, and even their claims of sacrifice came under strong attack.[4] One product of this fierce and somewhat fashionable assault upon the accuracy of the loyalist myth was a tendency to dismiss the loyalists themselves, their experience in Canada, and their contribution to this nation. There seemed a grave danger indeed of the baby disappearing with the bath water.

However, as Jo-Ann Fellows aptly remarks, "it is hardly fair to blame the excesses of the Loyalist Myth on the Loyalists. The Loyalists would be as surprised as many historians have been to see the picture of themselves and their beliefs that has come down to the present time."[5] With the dragon of the loyalist myth safely slain, with the controversy over the tradition's accuracy exhausted and grown stale, with new methods and approaches being introduced by a new generation of historians, an interest was renewed in these people, who they were, what they had experienced, and what they have left us.

This reawakened interest was augmented by the dissemination of Louis Hartz's "fragmentation" theory of the development of colonial societies, and the application of that theory to Canada.[6] Briefly, Hartz argued that colonial societies differed from that of the mother country because they were founded by only one fragment of European society and that such a fragment, dominating the empty new environment of the colony, would mould the values defining that society through the years. Historians influenced by this thesis claimed that the loyalists were responsible for either our liberal tradition or our Tory touch, for our acceptance of interventionist governments and our "mosaic" society.[7] Such arguments were both sweeping and challenging, and, in their sweep, vulnerable, but the ensuing debate helped to rekindle interest in the loyalist contribution and legacy to English-speaking Canada.

It is hoped that this study will be an additional contribution to our knowledge of the loyalists. It is less concerned with the loyalist legacy than with the actual loyalist experience in the early years of exile. It is a study of the refugees who came to Nova Scotia at the close of the American Revolution, of their exodus and settlement, their adjustment to the new land, their impact upon it, its people, and its institutions, and the manner in which the new circumstances and the simple passage of time altered the refugees themselves. It is an attempt to understand the manner in which the heritage of these exiles changed, and was changed by, the new environment, and what was both lost and gained in this transformation. These early, formative years were a time of settlement, adjustment, and dependence, a phase that came to a close shortly after the granting of portable pensions and the cessation of free provisions. It ended with the return of large numbers of loyalists to the United States and the acceptance by the others of the conditions of their life in Nova Scotia.

Theirs is a remarkable saga. In one year this flood of immigration doubled the existing population of the province. In one sense they came as a cohesive body, a particular people descending upon Nova Scotia during a particular period of time. They came with the shared experience of the war years, which gave them to some degree a common bond, a sense of being "ourselves alone" in an alien land among an alien people. And their history is a history of the weakening of that bond in the transition from American exile to Nova Scotian.

The uprooting of any people is a traumatic event. It could be no less than that for these people because most had been driven from America. However, they differed from other loyalists in British North America who were occupying empty territories that would soon be loyalist provinces. In many respects those in Nova Scotia had more in common with Mary Beth Norton's loyalist exiles in England who found themselves under a government and among a people that not only failed to recognize the extent of their sacrifice but apparently wished to hinder their attempt to regain a place in the sun.[8] Nova Scotia already had a sizeable, entrenched population. This was a major factor in shaping the distinctive experience of the Nova Scotia loyalists and it would affect the intensity with which the loyalist tradition would be held and passed on.

For such loyalists the final resolution of the war was not forth-coming until almost a decade after the fighting had ended. On leaving

New York the loyalist was unable to accept his defeat. Thus Nova Scotia could not be simply a haven; it must also be a vindication. Encouraged by their great numbers swelling the population of this infant province, by Britain's promises of aid, by the potential strength of the postrevolutionary empire, they hoped to prove, by their anticipated prosperity and freedom from discord, that the rebellion had been a terrible mistake. However, it was yet to be seen whether Britain would fulfil her promises, and whether Nova Scotia would have the capacity to give these refugees much more than a hard-scrabble living. Their relationship with the old settlers and with a non-loyalist government, the struggles among themselves, their changing attitude towards the United States, the alterations that the passage of time would bring about made the loyalists' world in Nova Scotia very different from the one they had anticipated, and by 1791 would leave them, their attitudes, and their expectations more changed than most would ever have imagined.

I am indebted to various librarians and archivists for the assistance they have given me in preparing this study and wish to thank in particular the staffs of the Public Archives of Canada, the Public Archives of Nova Scotia, and the Douglas Library of Queen's University, Kingston. St Francis Xavier University has been of great help in terms of both services and financial aid supplied. The Canada Council has been very generous, particularly in granting me a Leave Fellowship. This book has been published with the help of a grant from the Canadian Federation for the Humanities, using funds provided by the Social Sciences and Humanities Research Council of Canada. For this assistance I am most grateful.

Among the individuals I would like to thank are Bev MacIsaac, Frances Baker, and Deborah Murphy, all of whom contributed to the typing and revising. Dr Phyllis Blakeley of the Public Archives of Nova Scotia initially suggested the topic and encouraged the attempt. Christina and Murray did not hesitate to spend evenings at that same archives checking sources for a brother far way. Professor J. Murray Beck was kind enough to read the manuscript and offer thoughtful, helpful advice. And my former supervisor, Professor George A. Rawlyk, shepherded the manuscript through to completion. Although he is in no way responsible for any faults, he has given much of his knowledge and time. As important to me as his judgment and criticism has been his encouragement. And finally I would like to thank my wife, Barbara. Although she might never read this, her patience and fortitude have sustained me at all times.

This Unfriendly Soil

*When you are informed that fifty dwelling
houses besides Mills Barns and other Outhouse are destroyed – which belonged to the
Loyal Industrious Husbandmen who have
for nine years been contending with this
unfriendly soil – to gain a subsistance – to
have all these labour and prospects blasted
in one hour ... you may form some faint
idea of Shelburne.*

Gideon White, White Collection, PANS

CHAPTER ONE

The Evacuation

It was during the last years of the American Revolution that the terms, the promises, and the expectations with which the loyalists came to Nova Scotia were formed. These years also defined the cast that their values and emotions, attitudes and rhetoric, would assume in Nova Scotia. They came fresh from the trauma and humiliation of the war's end, and the memory of that experience had a marked influence on their lives in the new settlements. To understand the loyalist in Nova Scotia it is necessary to be aware of the events that overtook him in the closing years of the revolution.

On October 19, 1781, Lord Cornwallis surrendered at Yorktown. With this defeat, Britain decided to discontinue the war, thus shattering any lingering loyalist hope of an eventual triumph. There had always lain below the surface of loyalist confidence in their cause a muted fear of a lost war and their abandonment by Britain. Yorktown gave such fears substance.[1] Many outside the lines simply gave up hope, accepted the new order, made their peace, and advised others to do likewise.[2] Desertions rose alarmingly, far outpacing the rate of recruitment and replacement. "The Provincial Corps seem to be crumbling fast to pieces," reported one observer.[3] Yorktown had buried not only loyalist hopes for the war's outcome, but also much of the loyalist faith in their cause.

On February 23, 1782, Sir Guy Carleton formally accepted command of the British forces in America.[4] He was instructed to make his objective the withdrawal of the troops from New York, Savannah, and Charlestown. As for the loyalists and their possessions, the king's servants left them to Carleton's tender care. The instructions reiterated that the removal and preservation of the king's troops was "the *immediate* object to which all other considerations must give way." His next objective was to impress upon the Americans Britain's desire for reconciliation. He was, in effect, encouraged to take almost any step which would demonstrate Britain's desire for peace and reconciliation.[5] Such primary objectives could not augur well for either the loyalists' claims or their future.

By the time of Carleton's arrival, on May 5, 1782, most of the loyalists had accepted the bitter fact that the war was not to be won. Their concern, in the confusion of "the uncommon close of the war," was how badly the war was to be lost. As peace approached, they found themselves experiencing a series of jolts, each of which they had barely confronted and accepted before being struck by another, in what the refugees could only have considered an escalation of appeasement. Having accepted the cessation of offensive war, the loyalists were stunned by the announcement in August 1782 that independence would be recognized and were despondent over what many considered their desertion by the king.[6]

The fate of the loyalists in an independent America appeared uncertain and unpromising. Many now began to contemplate the inevitability of exile, and make plans accordingly, with many of the plans centring on Nova Scotia.[7] As the summer passed Carleton also came to look more and more to Nova Scotia as a refuge for the loyalists. In June 1782 he had received a favourable report on the colony, its forests, climate, available land, fish and game, and the potential value of its harbours. After the August announcement Carleton sought to channel loyalist anger by stressing the alternative of evacuation and the creation of new homes, "if the most reasonable Expectations should fail them here."[8]

Carleton's plans for the loyalists and the colony were being made under the combined difficulties of sketchy instructions and sparse communication from Britain. In September he transmitted letters to the secretary of state, "without knowing whom in particular I have the honor to address."[9] The pressure of events, however, and the discretionary powers of his instructions set Carleton to preparing a sanctuary for the loyalists in Nova Scotia. In the same month he wrote to the lieutenant-governor of Nova Scotia, enclosing a list of families wishing to emigrate to the colony. Carleton also recommended the agents of those coming, asking that they be aided in exploring the country.[10]

The agents referred to represented the major organization of loyalists planning early immigration to Nova Scotia. It was based on Long Island and the Jersey shore where meetings were held and agents chosen. Proposals were then drawn up for Carleton in which the members of the association requested transportation to Nova Scotia for themselves, families, and livestock, provisions for the journey and a year's subsistence, the tools necessary to establish mills and farms, land clear of title, well situated, surveyed, and ranging from 300 to 500 acres a family.[11] Equipped with detailed instructions, the agents departed with the early loyalists in the fall fleet, arriving at Annapolis on October 19, 1782.[12]

Another association of loyalists was created in the fall of 1782, which was to give birth to one of the most fleeting urban centres in Canadian history. About 120 families had decided to settle at Port Roseway, a sheltered harbour on the southwestern shore of Nova Scotia. This long, narrow harbour was the chief and almost only attraction of the spot. It had been visited briefly by the French who had named it Razoir, by Alexander McNutt who had a conditional grant of 100,000 acres there,[13] and otherwise had been ignored by all but these desperate people in New York. The harbour and a spirit of optimism born of despair seemed to blind them to any of the location's faults. This group, of which many of the movers were mercantile, had experience, knowledge, and some money. They now had a harbour, and seemed not to notice that they had neither a hinterland nor, with Nova Scotia's long coastline, rugged terrain, and lack of roads, and with Port Roseway's poor timber and agricultural resources, much chance of developing one.

Nevertheless, an association was created "for the purpose of Settling at Port Roseway in Nova Scotia, as early as possible Next Spring."[14] On November 16 a committee was chosen to transact the general business of the Port Roseway Association.[15] With Carleton's approval, Joseph Pynchon and James Dole were chosen to go to Nova Scotia at the first opportunity and place before the governor the association's instructions and requests. On the same day that the instructions were drawn up a memorial was written to Governor John Parr of Nova Scotia emphasizing the immigrants' past loyalty and introducing their two agents.[16] There is little trace anywhere in the instructions or the memorial of the humble supplicant. They had been loyal, and they were now seeking part of their compensation for that loyalty, as much as they could get.

On April 5, 1783, Carleton received the articles of peace and the king's proclamation ending hostilities.[17] Under Article Five, Congress was to recommend to the state legislatures the restitution of confiscated properties and the rights of British subjects, and those within the lines who had not borne arms. Congress was to recommend to the states that "Persons of any other Description" should have liberty to go or remain in the various states, and be unimpeded in their attempts to get restitution for confiscated property. Article Six precluded future confiscations and persecutions, freed existing prisoners, and stopped prosecutions. Article Seven stated that there was to be peace between Britain and the United States, that hostilities were to end, prisoners were to be freed, and British troops and ships withdrawn from the United States "with all convenient speed."[18]

By April 8, when Carleton read the treaty to the loyalists in New York, the other shoe had fallen and the defeated found themselves dealing with what seemed to them a very harsh settlement. What broke the loyalist heart was that Britain allowed Congress the freedom to simply recommend restitution. Congress had neither the power nor the desire to do anything else. The patriots knew that, the loyalists knew it, and most assumed that Britain knew it. She placed great emphasis, however, on the conciliatory effect of her gestures and of the ending of the war. Perhaps it could look that way from London, but those in America were certain of the benefits of Article Five.

"Our fate seems now decreed and we left to mourn out our days in wretchedness," Sarah Winslow had written on hearing of the peace. "No other resource for millions but to submit to the tyranny of exulting enemys or settle a new country."[19] She was perhaps too sanguine about the option of submitting to the enemy's tyranny. Few loyalists were to be allowed to do so, for the rebel response to Britain's hope for mutual conciliation was a fierce and widespread drive to prevent the loyalist's return. Resolutions were followed by legislation to this effect, and legislation was followed by unchecked violence inflicted upon those who attempted to return from behind the lines. "The rascally acts that are daily established," wrote one embittered loyalist, "will prevent us from ever being subjects in either of the thirteen Provinces."[20]

The chief target of loyalist anger was not really the rebel. He had been the enemy and was now a victorious enemy. The target was the government that, as they believed, had handed them over to the enemy, forgotten the promises made, and used them as a sacrificial pawn in the peace game. "Was there ever an instance, my dear Cousin," asked Sarah Winslow, "can any history produce one, where such a number of the best of human beings were deserted by the government they have sacrificed their all for?"[21]

And yet among many there was also a sense of acceptance. They knew their fate and now could take concrete steps to meet it, a situation differing from the bitter mixture of hope and despair that had accompanied their waiting. For those in the provincial regiments, many for years in arms, the war would be over and defeat somewhat compensated for by the laying down of arms, the return to family, the picking up of the threads of one's life, and the laying of plans for the future, a concrete if somewhat bleak future. For the civilian refugee, exile in a new land could not be much worse than life in war-torn New York. Moreover, Britain had made many promises and to secure peace had been forced to abandon some of them. They hoped that there would be consequent recognition on her part of the need to compensate the loyalists for that unjust settlement. "I am heartily tired of the war," wrote Ward Chipman, "I wish to be placed in a situation where I can form my prospects for future life without the continued apprehension of having them all deranged."[22]

The peace meant exile, and for most the exile was to be to Nova Scotia. To many in this traumatic period it was not so much a case of exile to Nova Scotia as of exile from the triumphant states, and there was many a brave allusion to quitting "this damned country with pleasure," and "the pleasing prospect of soon Emigrating to the Regions of Port Roseway."[23] The loyalist rhetoric spoke of any fate being better than that of remaining among rebels, yet the rebels insisted upon drawing their attention to that fate. The *Connecticut Journal* reflected with glee on their desperate future in "the wilds" of Nova Scotia where snow lay on the ground for six months of the year.[24] Even friends and fellow loyalists who had a choice took a very cautious and negative view of their place of exile. "I am sorry," a friend wrote to Ward Chipman, "to hear your Prospects are such as to induce you to think of a Retreat to Nova Scotia, and confidently hope that something better may happen."[25]

But since many of those going to Nova Scotia had little other option, they could not look ahead with such pessimism or with much objectivity. Many must have seen in Nova Scotia what they wished to see, a land of promise where they might recoup their losses and prove their cause not wrong. They were aided by the favourable accounts which Carleton was receiving from those sent by him to scout the area. They were also encouraged by the agents' accounts that were coming back to New York in the spring and summer of 1783, for these were strong on potential and promise. And they must have devoured printed letters from early loyalists in Nova Scotia, like the one in the *Pennsylvania Packet* which stated that the loyalists "may here find a safe and advantageous asylum." Roseway, one of the most natural harbours in America, would, with the accession of affluent and energetic immigrants, be one of the great ports of America. Even the much discussed fog went hand in hand with a remarkably rich fishery.[26] Another letter spoke highly of the helpfulness and kindness of the provincial officials. "I think," the letter went on, "from several corroborating circumstances, that the settlements eventually must be ranked amongst the first in America."[27] In the cold awareness of defeat and exile such optimism was a needed balm, and within it lay the fantasy that with the swift rise of a rich and loyal Nova Scotia, and the inevitable decline of a republican America, the loyalist might still win his war. Occasionally the advance upon a poor and barren colony could take on the trappings of a crusade. "We shall all soon be with you – everybody, all the World moves on to Nova Scotia."[28]

Meanwhile, throughout 1783 Carleton was immersed in the myriad details and decisions of a mass evacuation. To complicate it, the British government had given him sweeping general instructions to withdraw from America, without informing him how he was to evacuate and, worse, whom and with what. One of his chronic worries was the lack of transports. By January 1783, with the evacuation of the south completed, with the 26,000 tons of shipping he had on hand, and with the expectations of more tonnage in the spring, Carleton felt the evacuation of New York was at least possible.[29] On the very eve of the departure of the first fleet, however, Admiral Digby was taking a different tack, contending that the tonnage on hand fell far short of what was necessary.[30]

The Port Roseway Association's task in New York was now drawing to an end. On April 15 the board wrote to Sir Andrew Hamond, the former governor of Nova Scotia, thanking him for his aid there and his representations to the secretary of state while in England. They mentioned having recruited over 400 families, "among which are some very respectable Persons, who we trust will add dignity to our Settlement." They expressed great disappointment that Carleton had declined their request for more than six months' provisions, and predicted that their sufferings in the approaching winter, owing to the lack of these materials, would be immense. They were in effect asking Hamond to do what he could for them in England.[31] They also wrote a memorial to Carleton expressing their gratitude for his efforts and referring to their own fortitude in facing this great challenge in a new land.[32]

And that was it. The board had herded its members into a tight, aggressive little organization in New York, had lobbied, quite successfully, for land and favours from those in power in New York, Nova Scotia, and England, and now, except for the last-minute scramble of tasks on embarkation, its work was done. "As no material business was left for the Body to transact at New York A Motion was made that the meetings of this Association do adjourn until the body arrived at Port Roseway."[33]

In comparison with such civilian refugee groups as the Port Roseway Association, the provincial regiments seem to have got off the mark very slowly. It was not until March 1783 that a memorial was drawn up and presented on their behalf to Carleton. It went through the familiar recitation of zeal and sacrifices for the British cause, adding the certainty they felt that despite Britain's intentions they would not be able to remain in America. With homes, properties, and incomes all lost, they were now asking for land and aid in settling elsewhere, pensions for the disabled and dependents of those killed, permanent rank for the officers and half-pay upon reduction. Carleton quickly sent their petition to the British government, asking that serious and generous consideration be given to their requests.[34] Agents were sent to find tracts of land extensive enough for the thousands of soldiers and with the promise from Carleton of six months' pay and at least one year's provisions and clothing, those responsible began to drawn up returns of the provincials planning to settle in Nova Scotia.[35]

Now began the job of listing, providing for, and embarking the loyalists of the first fleet, which departed in April. The refugees were permitted to take with them every article considered necessary for their labours in the new land. Much of this went aboard the ships carrying them, the remainder being carried by smaller vessels bound for Nova Scotia.

During the organization of the second fleet Carleton continued to pursue the difficult task of balancing the demands of Britain, General Washington, and the loyalists. The loyalist problem was one of logistics, of gathering, organizing, listing, victualling, and otherwise providing for the refugees. Washington, of course, simply wanted him to evacuate New York as quickly as possible with as few negroes and other American "property" as possible. Carleton's letters to Britain were filled with references to the need for transports. It is always surprising to find how little guidance he received throughout this period.[36] Moreover, the instructions he did receive he found overly concerned with the foreign troops and their swift return to Britain, perhaps to the detriment of the loyalists.[37] He feared too swift a withdrawal of troops would denude the loyalists of both transport and protection.[38] The transport on hand was utterly inadequate to the task of removing both the troops and those seeking asylum under new circumstances.[39]

The new circumstances playing havoc with Carleton's plans and Britain's wishes were the unexpectedly large number of loyalists now clamouring for refuge from American violence.[40] The ships that had carried the loyalists to Nova Scotia in April were drifting back to New York and being revictualled for return trips. On June 17, 2,472 refugees sailed for Nova Scotia.[41] In early July a smaller fleet was prepared and on July 8 three vessels sailed for Port Roseway, with a much larger group for the St John River.[42] Another return showed 1,615 going to Nova Scotia on August 5.[43]

In August Carleton received final instructions to evacuate the army "and such of the Loyalists and their Effects, as they can."[44] Admiral Digby was to use the transports repeatedly on the circuit between New York and Nova Scotia. Additional ships were being sent and he could also use prizes and hire trading vessels or employ whatever else he could get, as long as New York was evacuated as quickly as possible.[45] The result was a great increase in the number of private vessels used to carry the refugees to Nova Scotia.[46] The earlier "fleets" were thus being replaced by a more constant flow of individual ships and companies from New York.

There were still a surprising number of loyalists seeking escape. The chief reason why so many decided on exile late in the season was the continuing risk of persecution. "The mob alone rules," a fact which produced an astonishing exodus.[47] In a letter to Governor Parr, Carleton drew attention to the refugees yet to come, both those of the Civil Department and those who had found late in the season that they could not stay. He hoped that transports for this evacuation would be ready by mid-September, although the date "must greatly depend on the number of Refugees who shall be obliged to fly from hence."[48]

On September 9, several ships sailed for Annapolis and Port Roseway. On the 15th a fleet of British regulars and provincials sailed, seven hundred of them bound for Halifax, most of the others for the St John. From the notices in the newspapers it appears that a large fleet of refugees was intended to sail on September 20, but it is difficult to say whether the fleet sailed on the date set. A Philadelphia paper reported a fleet sailing on the 28th from New York. The Admiralty papers listed a large fleet leaving on the 24th, with fourteen vessels for Port Roseway, three for Annapolis, and many others for the St John.[49] By late November all that remained were those British and foreign troops destined for England and awaiting sufficient transport, the civil departments and those loyalists still required for the administration, some late refugees for Nova Scotia, and Carleton, eager to complete the evacuation, awaiting the promised transports and a fair wind.[50] The numbers he had dealt with had been immense, the logistical and emotional problems imposing, and yet it had been a well-planned, well-executed, and remarkably successful evacuation of refugees from a great port.

On November 25 the city of New York was abandoned.[51] It was reported that "everything remained quite quiet when we came away."[52] Arrangements had been made for the remainder to proceed to Staten

Island to await the last transports, and on December 3 Admiral Digby wrote that he had fully embarked the army "and every Loyalist that has applied for a Passage."[53] On December 5 these, and the commander in chief, Carleton, sailed away from the new America.

Some loyalists had come to Nova Scotia before the great flood at the war's end. With the evacuation of Boston by Howe in the spring of 1776 Halifax became a depot for the dispossessed, but Nova Scotia treated their presence less as a vanguard than as a wartime aberration, a cargo to be found in, and limited to, a wartime port. The arrival of the Boston loyalists did not affect the outports. In Halifax the occasion seems to have been one of overcrowding, soaring prices, and for many Haligonians fat profits.[54] The question of the Boston loyalists, however, was hardly raised in either council or assembly.

By June, General Howe had sailed away with his army and by the fall of 1776, owing chiefly to the cold and the high price of provisions, most of the refugees were also gone.[55] Other refugees drifted into the province during the revolution, but since they were few in number and came as individuals intermittently throughout the war, they made little impact. Rarely is the refugee mentioned in either official correspondence or the newspaper.

The reaction of this vanguard to Nova Scotia was a mixed one. On the one hand, it had to be better than the land of bondage from which they had fled. On the other, there was the reality of this fog-bound land where prices were high and yet life was primitive. One could survive in Nova Scotia, but one could hardly live in it.[56] To many of these early refugees this cold, barren land with its cold, smug inhabitants was less a sanctuary than a stop-over. They would leave when opportunity allowed them, perhaps to return to the Thirteen Colonies when the war was won.

By the summer of 1782 the people of Nova Scotia were beginning to realize that the war was coming to an end. Among officials, and apparently also among the people, some form of reconciliation with the American colonies was anticipated. Such an attitude tended to preclude any thought of a refugee problem.

As the war wound down, the British government appointed a new governor of Nova Scotia. John Parr, the son of an impoverished Irish officer, had been born in Dublin in 1725.[57] He was a professional soldier who had joined the 20th Regiment of Foot as ensign at the age of nineteen, and had been wounded at Culloden and later at the battle of Minden.[58] By 1771 he had purchased the rank of lieutenant-colonel and command of his regiment. He was major of the Tower of London from 1778 until July 1782, when he was superseded and appointed governor of Nova Scotia.[59]

Parr arrived in Halifax on October 5, 1782, a short, bald, and fat career officer delighted with the plum he had pulled from the pie.[60] On October 23 he wrote to General Grey that oft-quoted letter of complacent pleasure at the supposed sinecure and haven he had found for his twilight years.

I have found every thing here to exceed my expectation, have met with the greatest civility and attention from all Ranks of People, a most excellent house and Garden, a small farm close to the Town, another of 70 or 80 Acres at the distance of two Miles, where I propose passing two or three months in Summer a snugg little farm house upon it, a beautiful prospect, with good fishing, plenty of Provisions of all sorts except Flower, with a very good French Cook to dress them, a Cellar well stock'd with Port, Claret, Madeira, Rum, Brandy, Bowood Strong Beer & a neat income (including a Regim't of Provincials which I am Colonel) of £2200 Ste'g p Annum, an income far beyong my expectations, plenty of coals & wood against the severity of the Winter, a house well furnish'd, and Warm Cloths, that upon the whole my Dear Grey, your friend Parr is as happy and comfortably seated, as you could wish an old friend to be ... and I am determined to be happy, and to make every one so who comes within my line, that is as far as good humour and society will make them.[61]

He also wrote to the prime minister, Lord Shelburne, to describe his arrival and reception, thanking him again for the sinecure. Once more there was that air of smug delight at the material advantages of the situation, little mention of the difficulties of the province, and less of his plans for its future.[62]

During his first days in office the loyalist problem seemed but a small cloud on Parr's horizon.[63] In a letter to Carleton he promised to give the loyalists all the government assistance possible, and then proceeded to hedge on just what was possible.[64] Having been made aware of the coming deluge, however, he soon made the home government aware of the unprepared state of his province, lacking the necessary lumber and firewood, lacking soldiers for protection, and with most of its land held by absentees in England. He informed Shelburne that 300 of the "unfortunate Refugees" had already arrived at Annapolis and that more were to follow in the spring. "They must be for some time uncomfortable."[65]

There was ample reason, as the autumn wore on, for Governor Parr and his officials to begin to feel the enormity of the loyalist problem press upon them. There were Carleton's urgent reminders from the confusion of New York.[66] There were the loyalists already arrived in the colony and 500 more on their way from Charleston. There was also the threat of a food shortage to be met, a threat serious enough to induce Carleton to order a thousand barrels of flour to be issued from the king's magazines at Halifax.[67] In this situation, the officials took what action they could for the loyalists, and tried to cover themselves for any lack of action. In September, Richard Bulkeley, the provincial secretary, had written to Joseph Durfee of the Loyalist Association of New York, mentioning their request for land around Port Roseway, and assuring him that inquiries had been set in motion to ascertain the available land in this and other areas, and that all possible aid would be provided.[68]

Parr informed the secretary of state, Thomas Townshend (shortly to become Lord Sydney), of Carleton's estimates for the number of loyalists arriving that fall, and his requests on their behalf regarding land and exemptions.[69] Worried that Carleton's recommendations differed from his own instructions, Parr sought Townshend's direction.[70] Reporting the arrival of the Charleston loyalists, he was concerned to underline General Paterson's responsibility for them.[71] With little concrete advice from the government, with great fear of precipitating its anger by overly bold moves, Parr was intent upon deflecting what responsibility he could to others, and where he could not, delaying until he received explicit approval from Britain. Such concern for his own position led to delay and procrastination where speed and decisiveness were demanded.

By January Parr was writing to Britain of the loyalist presence, and already feeling, if only slightly at this stage, the squeeze between the loyalist demands and his fear of the government's wrath at excessive generosity. To Carleton, he expressed his own conviction of the importance to the province of the loyalist coming, and stated that he had already made provision for a much larger tract of land than had been applied for. Moreover, he had asked the secretary of state for instructions which would allow him to grant the loyalists land in such quantity and under such conditions as they wished. Once he received such authority, they would not meet with any impediments whatsoever.[72]

By April 22, when the preliminaries of peace were published in Halifax,[73] notices of escheats were appearing in the *Gazette*. It was not simply a matter of placing the refugees on vacant land, for in this small province over 5.5 million acres had been granted away by the government since the founding of Halifax.[74] To ensure there was sufficient land for the great numbers anticipated, it was necessary to initiate an active recovery of some of those millions of acres.

From January 1783 to December 1784, 1,179,220 acres were confiscated.[75]

Charles Morris, the surveyor general, had been at work securing land for the loyalists since the previous year. Pressured by the demands of refugees already in the province and fearing the consequence of delay, he had already employed twenty-three deputies, and was now petitioning the government to honour these extra expenses.[76] Parr in a forwarding letter found the expenses "just and reasonable," and reported that much progress had been made in laying out and surveying lands for the newcomers.[77]

The coming of the loyalists in the spring of 1783 set off a flurry of memoranda in and instructions from Whitehall to cover most contingencies and to supplement Parr's general instructions. The governor's task had been made more difficult and disturbing by the absence of instructions from England dealing specifically with the loyalists. He could be damned, in this vacuum, for either boldness or timidity. He had promised to do all that was in his power for the loyalists, "notwithstanding I am disagreeably circumstancd in not having had any Instructions from Government, to regulate my conduct to them."[78] By May 1783, however, Whitehall began to issue directives on the amounts of land to be granted, and to whom, differing little from Parr's revised instructions on granting land.[79]

Many of the instructions were again summed up and clarified in a long letter to Parr on June 24, touching upon land grants, naval reserves, escheating, the limitation of speculation, and quick sales, absentees, and special favours.[80] Because speculators in the past had locked away huge tracts of land, no grants were to be made to those "who do not mean to become immediate settlers and actually improve the Lands they apply for." Parr was also warned against those who would seek extra land because of connections, influence, or affluence, and asked to "observe the most impartial conduct upon every application of that nature." And finally the letter reiterated the demand that would so frequently close dispatches on the fate of His Majesty's loyal refugees. Parr was to watch his expenses and to avoid any unnecessary charges upon the treasury.[81]

By the fall of 1783, Parr and his officials had been given both the instructions and the intent of the home government concerning the loyalists. "The King has been graciously pleased," wrote Charles Morris in October, "to order the Charges of Surveying for Loyalists to be paid but then the greatest frugality is to be observed."[82] The government had thus, in instructions, memoranda, and letters, laid down its policies and occasionally sung its own praises concerning the forthcoming settlement of Nova Scotia. The loyalists, in their despairing state, would perhaps have snapped at any hand. Many snapped at the British hand for offering too little too late.

As well as the advice and instructions, however, there came the loyalists, over 16,000 of them, and the plans and preparations had to give way to the actuality of settling. Surveying and laying out of land had been going on for over a year. It was now time to put the refugees on their own land and ensure their survival.

CHAPTER TWO

The Great Wave

In the fall of 1782 the agents of the associations were joined in Nova Scotia by a vanguard of early loyalists. In October about 500 had come from New York to Annapolis.[1] Jacob Bailey vividly described the overcrowding, each house being shared by several families, many unable to procure lodging at all. He stressed the shortage of necessities and the destitution of the refugees. Yet he still placed the scene closer to inconvenience than catastrophe.[2] It was a strange and disconcerting winter for both loyalist and Nova Scotian in Annapolis, people tumbling over each other in a community too small to hold them, strangers sharing overcrowded homes, the court-house, stores, and every private building packed with refugees, others unable to find shelter at all, and the old settlers, taking advantage of supply and demand, raising the price of rent and provisions to levels regarded as extortionate by the refugees.

It was no better for the 500 refugees from South Carolina who arrived in Halifax with the heavy ordnance after the evacuation of Charleston, "coming almost naked from the burning Lands of South Carolina to the frozen coast of Nova Scotia."[3] As if this were not enough, these early refugees were also cursed with a particularly cold winter.[4]

The immediate necessities were food and shelter. Carleton, in the spring of 1783, advertised in New York for flour to be sent with the loyalists to Nova Scotia.[5] Parr informed the secretary of state that he had promised the refugees boards for building, and hoped that the expense, £1,000 so far, would be defrayed by the government.[6] By spring Richard Bulkeley was ordering mills in the province to deliver thousands of boards to Shelburne and the Bay of Fundy.[7] As already noted, Charles Morris, the province's surveyor general, was busy seeking out and gaining knowledge of the lands available, trying to strike a balance between the lands available and a flexible estimate of the number of loyalists expected, between the urgent presence of the associations, with their organizations, agents on the spot, and vast demands, and the possibility of later waves of loyalists, less organized and vocal, but still requiring to be settled.

It was not until April 21 that Benjamin Marston, a former merchant and magistrate of Marblehead, Massachusetts, was appointed by Morris as deputy surveyor in charge of Port Roseway;[8] a week later Marston sailed with William Morris for the port, arriving on May 2, two days before the fleet.[9] One of the major reasons for this tardiness was Britain's failure to instruct and guide her governor. John Parr was caught in the crossfire of righteous loyalist demands and growing British parsimony. To spend without authority, as he did, took some courage, but it was a very limited and timid courage, leaving little ready for the loyalists when they came.

On May 4 there arrived at Port Roseway "upwards of thirty sail in all, in which there are three thousand souls."[10] It was not until the seventh that the surveyors and agents chose a location for the town, one quickly rejected by "the multitude" on the following day in favour of another location on the eastern side of the northeast harbour.[11] "Friday, 9. According to the determination of Thursday, laid out the centre street of the new town, and the people began very cheerfully to cut down the trees – a new employment to many of them."[12]

In the days following the arrival of the initial fleet, loyalists continued coming in small but steady numbers. The good weather held with only three rainy days in May.[13] Despite a serious brush fire and the grumblings of those who had chosen bad lots, the work went steadily on, and by the end of May Marston could turn to placing the newcomers.[14] Once the lots were drawn, huts and tents blossomed. On Sunday, July 20, Governor Parr finally arrived at Port Roseway, and seemed impressed by both its progress and promise.[15] On Tuesday, amid cannon salutes and with the streets lined with loyalists in arms, he landed to view the town and attend a reception and exchange of speeches with the principal inhabitants. It was then that Parr named the town Shelburne, a choice which struck at least some as bitterly ironic, and appointed the justices of the peace and other officials. Having exchanged toasts, he retired to his ship with the leading citizens for "an elegant dinner."[16] On Wednesday evening he attended a supper and ball given by the town which did not cease until five in the morning, when Parr returned to his ship "as highly pleased with the entertainment as the company appeared gratified and delighted by his presence."[17]

Much of this was a minuet for public consumption because both the loyalists and the governor had to be circumspect concerning their true feelings. The refugee seeking to represent loyalty to the crown was committed by extension to offer loyalty to his governor. And the governor, no matter how frustrated by their ceaseless demands and underwhelming gratitude, was caught up in the rhetoric required for these people. Beneath the surface, however, lay loyalist resentment of the tardy surveying, the confusion and ineptness of official actions towards them, and even, on the day of speeches, the governor's failure to incorporate the new centre.[18]

The centre seemed to take root quickly. Many of those who received their town lots in the summer of 1783 began work on their houses. Some brought the building materials with them, including house frames and bricks.[19] Others, especially latecomers, raised rough shelters, lived aboard the transports, or spent the winter under canvas.[20] Reports spoke of over fourteen hundred dwellings of one type or another built by the coming of the first winter.[21] Not enough lumber could be imported, despite good government prices, so that John Wentworth, surveyor general of the king's woods, allowed the loyalists at Shelburne "to cut such pine timber, growing upon their respective Lots, as were not fit for public Service."[22] They had also set up sawmills to "cut boards eno' to cover from Six to Ten Houses in a week."[23]

Despite such efforts, for most refugees in Shelburne it was a winter of cold, scarcity, and discomfort. A man of Colonel Buskirk's rank was happy in that first year to find shelter for his family in the basement of Marston's house.[24] Deborah Smith described the primitive conditions of that first winter: "The snow was about two feet deep ... There were a number of houses building, but none finished; plenty of marquees, tents and sheds for the people to shelter under, which they greatly needed at that season of the year. It looked dismal enough."[25]

On mainland Nova Scotia, Shelburne was the focal point of interest in that spring and summer, simply because of the concentration in that one spot of so many refugees. Yet throughout the summer loyalists were being funnelled into the Bay of Fundy. Most of those not going to the St John landed at Annapolis where, despite the extreme overcrowding, there was some shelter until the land was granted. The New York Loyalist Association was still undecided on which side of the Fundy to settle, or was delaying the decision as long as possible in order to secure the best terms and land. It was common practice to "solicit grants on both sides of the Bay and to take up whichever lot circumstances or fancy dictated."[26]

The New York agency was both optimistic about the numbers who would come under its guidance, and concerned about the land it would receive, feeling already that the acres being discussed would be too few.[27] James Peters, the new agent, had written to Botsford and Hauser of the fleet's departure on April 27, with 5,000 for Halifax, Port Roseway, and the Bay of Fundy.[28] A June fleet, which the agency felt would be the last, was also in preparation, transporting over 1,600 people.[29]

Already the agency's carefully laid plans were being turned awry by the confusion of embarkation. Storms had scattered the fleet. Supplies, which were not to have been distributed until the landing, had been passed out aboard ship, with consequent discrepancies. Botsford and the other agents were criticized by the agency for the apparent mess in which the group found itself.[30] The agency was angry because of the lack of preparation for the arrival of its charges, the lack of progress concerning the land grants to the group, the number of loyalists who preferred Port Roseway, and the progress of, and cooperation extended to, Port Roseway compared with their own fortunes. Whereas the Port Roseway Association, with its officials at Shelburne to guide its members and cooperate with the officials there, made visible progress in developing its centre, the New York agency, its officials still in New York, its agents in Nova Scotia, many of its charges still in New York and others scattered between the St John and Annapolis, its agents still undecided on what land to take, seemed to lose control of the emigration. Nevertheless, it was a major presence and the government was busy seeking and laying out land for it in the Conway district.

Through the summer and fall of 1783, the loyalists continued to pour into the province, although not in such marked waves as experienced in New Brunswick.[31] There was, however, a flow and ebb to loyalist arrivals, its first peak occurring in May, with lesser numbers coming through the summer, and then another peak at the beginning of fall, succeeded by a brief lull, and then another rush with the evacuation of New York. In the steady flow into Shelburne, there had also been two major waves, that of the initial fleet and a later contingent arriving on June 19. Late in September Nova Scotia received "the Fall Fleet" with perhaps 8,000 refugees.[32]

There was a distinct commercial flavour to the later waves. Merchants had waited and watched the struggle in Britain between those interests wishing to continue trading ties with the new nation and those seeking to exclude Americans from the empire's trade. By the fall loyalists in New York, hearing that the mercantilists had won, and that America was to be excluded, saw that Nova Scotia might take over America's carrying trade to the West Indies.[33] Large numbers of this commercial class would of course make their way to that glittering star, Shelburne, others to Halifax. Some, however, realized that both were almost saturated with commercial types, enterprises, and ambitions, and sought other, less crowded spots.[34]

Although prominent, the commercial men formed only a minority of the fall arrivals. A large number of disbanded soldiers began arriving in September, and by the end of the year Shelburne had received over 1,300 soldiers and dependents.[35] With the impeding evacuation of New York, many loyalists who had earlier misjudged its inevitability, or their chances of returning to their former homes, finally grasped the reality of the situation and joined the exodus to Nova Scotia. There were also among them the opportunists, neither really patriots nor loyalists, who, with the loosening of identification as the rush to evacuate overcame them, simply saw a better opportunity in Nova Scotia, with its free provisions and land, than New York offered. Many of these fall loyalists, far removed from the myth of the selfless gentleman, managed to induce in Benjamin Marston both anger and contempt. "These people are the very worst we've had yet, They murmur and grumble because they can't get located as advantageously as those who have been working hard these 4 months. They seem to be the riff-raff of the whole."[36] Businessman and soldier, the disillusioned and the "riff-raff," all were part of the influx of refugees arriving in Nova Scotia in the fall of 1783.

Despite the great number crowded into Shelburne, land was being laid out and taken up in most other known regions, and thrusts being made in areas not as yet known.[37] Like Shelburne, other loyalist communities in 1783 displayed a combination of hope and hardship, public promise and private despair. Annapolis, according to many, had made remarkable progress. One traveller felt that it "must in Time be the Grand Metropolis of this part of the Country."[38] Although the rents were exorbitant, the loyalists at Annapolis were somewhat better off than those in other areas. As in Halifax, they did not face the forest, for at least there were buildings.[39] Isaac Browne, however, found prices three times as high as in New York, and could not afford to build even "a small Hut, such as other unhappy fugitive Loyalists generally creep into." Moreover, food and provisions were limited, and growing more scarce with each day. Jacob Bailey wrote of the 1,500 men, women, and children just arrived that fall, "in affecting circumstances, fatigued with a long and stormy passage, sickly and destitute of shelter from the advances of winter.... Several hundreds are starved in our Church and larger numbers are still unprovided for."[40]

Port Mouton was occupied, first by the southerners of Tarleton's Legion and their dependents, and then by the Civil Department from New York, some late refugees and free negroes, over two thousand of them in all.[41] The Civil Department had Brook Watson as patron, John Stuart as agent, and Major Molleson as driving force, but even with these advantages many spent the winter in huts.[42]

For loyalists throughout Nova Scotia the first year was one of hardship and uncertainty. The 38th and 40th Regiments hutted in the woods that winter and because of their late arrival had to take what lands were left over in the spring, rock gardens in Clements. The 60th Regiment spent the winter aboard ship off Falmouth until forced "to come on shore on account of the inclemency of the Season and no Firing allow'd Us on board the Transport, we are by this time in a poor and wretched Condition."[43] The Duke of Cumberland's Regiment spent the winter in the woods outside Halifax. The loyalists in Cumberland were also forced to exist in primitive circumstances when the government was unable to get any lumber to them.[44]

Halifax also received the refugees. In January 1784 Parr informed Lord North that, "in consequence of the final Evacuation of New York, a considerable number of Refugee Families are come here, who must be provided for in and about this Town, at some extraordinary expence, as at this Season of the Year I cannot send them out into the Country." To illustrate their distress Parr enclosed a list of those aboard the *Clinton*. "Destitute of almost every thing, chiefly Women and Children, all still onboard, as I have not yet been able to find any sort of place for them, and the cold is setting in very severe."[45]

The government had to strike a balance between its desire to lay out the land and get the loyalists upon it as quickly as possible, and the immediate problem of loyalist survival. The primary task was to ensure their survival through the first winter by furnishing sufficient provisions and shelter. The secondary but concomitant task was to give them roots in the country, to get them onto the land and into the economy as quickly as possible, while provisions lasted and could cushion them. Until his instructions arrived, Parr could move only in the direction he felt Britain would accept. With the clamour of the loyalists about him, this often meant acting first and hoping for British approval later.[46] Where it did not oblige him in any way to put his neck out, Parr was all for speed, wishing "all Expedition may be used in putting the People into Possession of Their Lotts."[47]

Surveyor General Morris's was the nightmare position in that year. As late as July he had no guarantee that the deputies could be paid and had already expended £500 of his own money for instruments and chainmen in the hesitant expectation that Britain would reimburse him.[48] And there was always a shortage of instruments.[49] He picked up his extra deputies in a haphazard fashion, many recommended by officials, some by the loyalists and others by their agents.[50] A strong recommendation from Carleton was sufficient proof of ability to get an appointment.[51] Chosen in such a fashion, some were not that good, competent, or honest.[52]

Shelburne was the most formidably difficult of the enterprises in terms of numbers and lack of preparation, but, once having accepted Marston, Morris seems to have given him his head; there is relatively limited correspondence with Marston, and several references to him as an example of frugality. In sending him a plan in August, Morris underlined one practice espoused by the government. Once Marston had made a return of land available, "you can then proceed to lay out the land for the People as they shall Judge best for themselves conforming to the Governors Instructions for laying out farm Lotts."[53] Water lots, however, were not for everybody, but only those "people of ability to Improve and who are in real want of Places for Stores Wharves &c &c."[54]

Size and numbers made Shelburne of principal concern. Yet because of personal rancour other undertakings seemed as difficult to Morris. "I cant help saying the Settling Pictou is one of the most troublesome Tasks I have had in hand since the first Settling the Colony."[55] Perhaps the most confusing to deal with was Amos Botsford, the New York Association's agent, seeking land for his charges both on the St John and in the Digby area, delaying in order to acquire the best land and advantage and retain all options. In doing so he caused endless confusion for the surveyor general.[56] Despite the confusion many of the association's members were settling in the Digby area. "The business goes on here but slow occasioned by bad weather and the Streets being filled with trees and Brush being fallen therein."[57]

Another characteristic that emerged as the year wore on and numbers became overwhelming was the tendency to leave land allotment to the loyalist associations. The arrangements by corps and, with the civilians, by associations, meant that land grants tended to take the form of blocks assigned to groups. The failure to put the people on their land by the fall only increased this tendency, for urgency often bordered on panic. It was simply faster and easier to lay out the land in large blocks and assign it to associations, which could more easily organize, deputize, and supervise.[58] But in the name of expediency a great deal of power had been thrust into the hands of the associations.

Another aspect of settlement was the degree of importance and use made of the military, particularly the navy. The commanding officer of the army was always diligent in meeting those requests he was authorized to meet. Commenting on the loyalist arrival in Nova Scotia, General Paterson wrote that he had "given every kind of assistance in my power."[59] But if the loyalists were grateful to any of their benefactors, they expressed this gratitude most frequently to the navy. It had been responsible for transporting them to Nova Scotia, and on orders of Admiral Digby continued to keep a very watchful eye upon the fledgling communities, seeing to it that the settlers reached their destinations, and that implements and provisions were delivered to them. An example of this concern was the care taken of the early loyalists in Annapolis by Captain Briggs of HMS *Amphitrite*, to the extent of parting with £200 of his own money.[60] *La Sophie* played a similar role: "She has been appointed for some time to convoy and assist the Refugees going to Cape Roseway and St. John's where Captain Mowat is particularly well acquainted and so much respected that I received a Memorial from the Refugees, begging that he may not be removed from the service to which he was appointed."[61]

During the first winter, the navy was the life-line of the loyalist in terms of provisions and the unexpected. The *Renown* was stationed at Halifax, the *Mercury* at Shelburne, the *Bonita* at Port Mouton, the *Atalanto* at Annapolis, the *Observer* at the St John.[62] Care of the loyalists was part of their standing orders, including "paying particular attention to all such New Settling Loyalists ... as many have established themselves, or any hereafter settle within the said Limits, in countenancing and in affording them all proper assistance and Protection."[63] Throughout the period of settlement, the attitude toward the settlers of the military in general, and the navy in particular, differed noticeably from that of the government and its officials, as did the degree of gratitude it aroused.

As the refugees arrived and were distributed in the summer and fall of 1783, reports and requests were dispatched to England. Parr was particularly concerned about the government's reaction to the greatly increased expenditure of funds made necessary by the influx.[64] In Charles Morris's attempts to get compensation for himself and his surveyors one sees the extent of the efforts put forth by the surveyors, and of Britain's demands for action on behalf of her unfortunate loyalists, as well as her reluctance to pay for it. As late as February 1784 Morris had not received any reimbursement for the more than £1,200 he had advanced from his own pocket, and he was suggesting to Marston and other surveyors that they inform

Britain "in a modest but pressing manner" that is was impossible for them to continue without getting paid.[65]

Throughout the summer and fall the governor was sending letters to Britain, expressing his fears concerning the weather and government support, reporting numbers arrived and progress made, and emphasizing his endeavour to carry out conflicting instructions to care for the loyalists while observing "the utmost Care not to incur any expence which can possibly be avoided."[66] Writing to North in October about the surveying, Parr again stressed the emergency, the numbers, and particularly the high costs in Nova Scotia in order to explain the £3,000 of expenses incurred for salaries and equipment.[67] The completion of this work had become imperative because of the harsh fall experienced in Nova Scotia that year, "for the oldest man in the Province does not remember such severe bad weather, as we have had for some time past."[68] Besides severe weather, and inadequate supplies, number of surveyors, and authorization, Parr also had to cope with the problem of loyalist grievances and complaints. In a letter to Evan Nepean, Lord Sydney's secretary, he explained that he was doing all that he could to alleviate their awful situation, "notwithstanding it is impossible to please some of them, who are most unreasonable in their demands and expectations."[69]

Although Parr continued to do all in his power for the loyalists, he was to remain very much aware of the limitations of that power. Despite agreeing to the expenses he had incurred and accepting their inevitability, Whitehall yet warned "that every possible degree of Oeconomy will be observed."[70] Parr was somehow to please the loyalists while managing not to displease the government in doing so. Britain could be equally righteous over the fate of her unhappy loyalists and the threat of squandering money on them, and it was Parr's delicate and unenviable task to satisfy both her pious rhetoric and her parsimony.

As the year turned, however, Parr's fears abated to some extent. The possiblity of disaster and death, and his responsibility for them, receded. To North he expressed his relief that all but a few of the late loyalists were under cover and safe for the winter. The lack of disaster he put down to both the liberty he had taken in supplying boards and the lucky winter of 1783–4, "the openest and mildest Winter, ever known in this part of the World." The coming of the loyalists he now painted not in the black shades he had used earlier but in the rose tints of opportunity and reciprocal advantage. Not only would they give the province, long lacking in population, an enhanced stature, but the province would in turn offer "a happy Asylum to an unfortunate People whose greatest Crime has been their Loyalty to the best of Kings."[71] The loyalists, and Parr, had survived the winter.

With the coming of spring the governor and the surveyors worked frantically to get the loyalists out of the crowded towns and onto their land in order to avoid arousing the ire of both government and refugees. Occupying the land was not the sole problem. There was also the issuing of lumber, which involved getting sufficient amounts to the refugees and determining the amount to be granted to each class of loyalist. Parr had, for example, limited the supply of lumber sent to the Digby settlements, believing they had received enough, but he then approved an allowance of 1,000 feet of boards and 2,000 shingles to each family, "which he understands to be the general Allowance made at St. John's River."[72]

By the spring of 1784, many of the lots had not as yet been assigned and there existed a strong sense of urgency about getting the refugees helter-skelter onto the land. Morris was instructing his surveyors to put the people where they wished as quickly as possible.[73] In Shelburne the frenetic activity of the first year was carried over to the second. Refugees continued to come. Much of the land had not yet been granted, much of it was not even laid out. By May close to 800 town lots were still to be located, the number available being far short of the number desired.[74]

As in 1783, the need for haste was tempered by the fear of expenditure.[75] Parr felt the cold wrath of disapproval in the fall of 1784, when Whitehall declared that surveying expenses were extremely high, and requested that the accounts be examined more carefully. Whitehall needed to say little more. "I have given the closest attention to economy in every expence," wrote Parr to Sydney, "and your Lordship may be assur'd that my attention to it, shall be unremitted."[76]

Despite such caution and the fear of offending the government, the work of settlement advanced. Parr witnessed and was responsible for one of the largest relocations of that troubled era. He and others were impressed by what had been undertaken, what had been accomplished, and what might be achieved in Nova Scotia. Quite often in the correspondence of 1784 one catches a reflective pause on the part of the officials. Large numbers of loyalists were actually settling in, and it was becoming apparent that the future of Nova Scotia might be radically altered. Despite difficulties, complaints, and defences against loyalist grievances, there was often expressed an optimism about the new Nova Scotia and its potential growth. In large associations or as individuals, the exiles had come by the thousands, the waves not ceasing until December. They had poured into the old centres of Annapolis and Halifax, and created the new centre of Shelburne. They filled these areas and overflowed into the woods beyond, awaiting land on which they could build and into which they could sink roots. They lived in churches and stores, aboard overcrowded ships, and in wilderness huts. Provisions and shelter had been organized for them, land was being escheated and laid out for them. To have survived the settling of the refugees without major catastrophe must have seemed, at least to the officials responsible, success in itself.

Opinion regarding the work of Parr and the officials, however, varied according to one's vantage-point. To the casual visitor the mushrooming of these loyalist settlements seemed wondrous, and criticism of the officials was muted by the instant presence of the communities themselves. The official would see how much had been wrought with so little. The landless loyalist would recognize the simple fact that he was not on the land, would remember the confusion and delays of the officials, and would be far more critical. The money expended, the walls raised, the provisions consumed in that first year were considered of little worth by many of those who were not yet on their own land. They were miserable, and it was difficult for them to nurture dreams of their community's future amid the harshness, scarcity, discomfort, and uncertainty of that first year. Lt.-Col. Robert Morse, chief engineer in America, gathering a general description of the province for Sir Guy Carleton, was as critical as were many loyalists.

I am sorry to add that a very small proportion, indeed, of these people are yet upon their lands, owing to different causes – First – their arriving very late in the season. Secondly – timely provision not having been made by escheating and laying out lands, in which great delays and irregularities have happened. Thirdly – a sufficient number of surveyors not having been employed, but lastly and principally, the want of foresight and wisdom to make necessary arrangements, and steadiness to carry them into execution, the evils arising from which, will be felt for a long time to come, not only by the individuals, but by Government, for if these poor people who, from want of land to cultivate and raise a subsistence to themselves, are not fed by Government for a considerable time longer, they must perish. They have no other country to go to – no other asylum.[77]

CHAPTER THREE

Provisions, Musters, and Mobility

The issue of provisions was a dominant one in the first years of the loyalist settlements. It loomed large because it was the key not to comfort but to sheer survival. The early years were filled with the scurry and worry of loyalist and official over the delivery and extension of the bounty. The desire for an efficient and fair distribution of provisions led to the musters of 1784 and 1785, which showed the distribution of loyalists throughout the colony. The lists also partly revealed the mobility among the settlements, the numbers still arriving, already departing, and frequently moving from place to place within Nova Scotia.

In New York the loyalists had requested provisions for both the voyage and a year in Nova Scotia. Carleton, lacking the necessary authority, could promise the agents only six months' provisions. At the time of their leaving, however, they were victualled for twelve months,[1] the provisions being the same as those given to His Majesty's troops.[2] With little on hand in New York or Nova Scotia, officials counted heavily on swift delivery from England, only to find that difficulties arose in gathering provisions from the scattered sources there.[3] By September 1783 the loyalists were petitioning earnestly for more provisions. A polite memorial from the leading citizens of Shelburne underlined their desperation. Mentioning both their past sacrifices and future zeal on behalf of Britain, the memorial pointed out that the harsh country, lack of materials, late arrival, and the "vast additional Numbers exceeding all expectation" made imperative the need for an increase in provisions. Otherwise they would suffer great distress and see their settlement "rendered in a great measure impracticable."[4]

There was little in Nova Scotia to give them, whether the government was willing or not. General Campbell wrote that the stock was "reduced to a very small quantity." The regiments on disbanding had received only half their bounty.[5] In February 1784 Parr wrote to North on the need for more provisions, citing both the memorials and the fact that too few were on their land as yet to give any hope of imminent self-sufficiency.[6] On the same day a similar letter was written by Campbell, questioning the ability of many to survive on the provisions allotted. With the communities "exceedingly crowded," the winter harsh, and the land rough, most loyalists would be "in the deepest distress" if further provisions were not allowed.[7]

Without word from England, and feeling the pressure of loyalist hardship, Parr took what action he could. Advertisements appeared in the *Gazette* for supplies to be sent to the settlements.[8] Parr was also admitting small craft from the United States "with Provisions only."[9] In March Campbell, on his own authority, issued a proclamation extending the bounty to those in need.[10] In explaining his actions to London, he stated baldly "That multitudes therefore will inevitably perish, unless the Royal Bounty of Provisions should be continued for some time longer."[11]

However slowly, Britain did move to meet the pressing needs of the loyalists. In the spring of 1784 the Treasury at Whitehall informed Governor Haldimand at Quebec that the king had extended the period for issuing provisions, at two-thirds of the regular supply, until May 1786 if necessary. Haldimand was also advised to send the surplus at Quebec to Halifax for the loyalists and disbanded soldiers in Nova Scotia.[12] It was not until June that Nova Scotia was told of the extension of provisions for a year.[13] By August Parr was writing of the "universal satisfaction" brought about by this action.[14] Now the problem was to get the supplies from Halifax distributed throughout the province. When Parr sought ships for this purpose, Commodore Douglas ordered all transports fit for duty to carry the supplies to the settlements before winter set in. By December he wrote with relief of the completion of this task and the return of the transports.[15] Thus the year ended. Although few in the settlements were living in a state of abundance, the attempt had been made to assure them through the king's bounty that they would be enabled to live.

The problem of securing adequate provisions, however, continued in 1785. The passing of winter found the loyalist communities once again anxiously awaiting supplies from England. Campbell explained that some of the distress was owing to the difficulty of communicating with the settlements during the winter. But it had also resulted from "the licentiousness of many of the Settlers who seized upon and dissipated the provisions sent them for their winter supply."[16] By June Parr was writing to Sydney to request additional supplies.[17] In

November he sought supplies from Campbell because many loyalists had already consumed the one-third rations given them. Parr cited both the fact that the governor of New Brunswick had recently authorized an additional supply of one-third, and the need of those in Nova Scotia "not in Circumstances to Maintain themselves through the Winter without such Assistance."[18]

One effect of the distribution of provisions was the mustering of the loyalists in order to estimate the amount of bounty required by each settlement. The muster of 1784 was prompted both by Campbell's desire to know the actual number eligible for provisions and by his desire to put an end to "the abuses which are daily gaining ground in the issue of provisions." Some abuse resulted from the act that the boards appointed earlier to see to the provisioning of the settlers had been weak and uncoordinated. Campbell had consequently appointed a new board with more extensive powers and general control than the old ones.[19] The principal abuse to be corrected was the collecting of bounty by a large number of people who were not entitled to it.[20] Examples were myriad. Timothy Hierlihy, who had indented for "116 people" in Antigonish, was found by the inspector to have only sixty-two,[21] and this was not an exceptional case. "By the exertions of this Board many abuses were corrected and all the idle vagrants who had been loitering about the streets of the metropolis & were daily committing irregularities, were by being precluded from the bounty of provisions forced to take possession of their lands, & on producing certificates of their being actual settlers they were restored to the enjoyment of their rations."[22]

Edward Winslow, appointed secretary of the board, was responsible for much of the coordination. His great task was eliminating the false returns from distant settlements, while avoiding excesses of zeal which might lead to "harsh and unequitable decisions." His answer was to parcel the province into districts and appoint responsible men to muster the people there.[23] The work of Winslow and his deputies resulted in a detailed accounting of the number of loyalists and of their location.

Although they could be found almost everywhere in Nova Scotia, the majority of loyalists were concentrated in a few well-defined pockets. There seemed to be so much land to begin with and little chance of running out of suitable tracts, but in fact earlier immigrants had settled on the more arable and accessible land, other choice areas were held by those with influence, and consequently "the best Lands in the Province bordering on Navigable Waters have been granted many years ago, & that very few tracts but such as are escheatable; are now to be obtained."[24] What remained were such empty areas as Digby, Shelburne, and Guysborough.

Shelburne held the greatest loyalist concentration. Halifax, as both established port and seat of government, drew many, and they spread out beyond the town into Dartmouth, Preston, and along the eastern shore to Sheet Harbour, as well as along the road from Halifax to Windsor and Truro. The Guysborough area was almost virgin land until the newcomers formed settlements at Country Harbour and on Chedabucto Bay. There were loyalist settlements along the north shore, in Antigonish and Pictou, Ramsheg and the Cobequid Road. Rawdon and Douglas were loyalist nodules. In Annapolis and King's County the loyalist presence was found in Digby, Clements, Granville, Annapolis, Wilmot, Aylesford, and Parrsboro.

In the general return, the total muster, larger than that of those entitled to provisions, came to 16,920 loyalists, disbanded soldiers, and dependents on mainland Nova Scotia.[25] This figure was less than the total number of those who had come to Nova Scotia. Some, by the time the muster was held, had already removed to New Brunswick, Prince Edward Island, or Canada, while others had returned to the United States. The muster would also have missed some scattered, small communities in isolated places along the difficult coast of Nova Scotia. There were others who did not put in a claim for provisions or who did not appear before the boards. Those residents of Ramsheg who had few qualifications for provisions would be unlikely to make the long trek to Cumberland simply to be enumerated. Halifax, where only a handful were mustered, had over 1,200 loyalists, according to John Parr. There were others, such as Robinson's "great numbers," whom the muster master, for one reason or another, refused to list at all. The people denied provisions fell chiefly into two categories: those who had no claims as loyalists, and those loyalists who had no claims as "settlers." Some of the former consisted of non-loyalists who had posed as needy refugees during the eva-cuation, and whose pose, accepted in the confusion of New York, was more easily detected in the close communities of Nova Scotia. There were also the non-loyalist captains, crews, and passengers of the ships continually shuttling between New York and Nova Scotia in the first years of settlement. Of those not listed, however, most were loyalists who were either too affluent or too indolent to qualify for the bounty. They were chiefly Winslow's vagrants, people making no effort to prove themselves as serious settlers, and thus not eligible for provisions. Nevertheless, the muster is a solid guide to the loyalist numbers and distribution throughout the province. It is also a brisk reminder that in two years the immigrants had come to outnumber the "natives."

On October 30, 1784, Campbell sent his general return to Lord Sydney, expressing confidence in the accuracy of the musters. "The great abuses which have arisen in issuing provisions to the Disbanded men and Loyalists, have by this measure been detected and checked; and such persons as were judged unworthy the Royal Bounty have been discontinued from receiving any further proportion thereof."[26] Because of further abuses in the distribution of provisions, however, Campbell, in 1785, ordered yet another muster of loyalists and disbanded troops. He found, for example, that over 160 had already left Chedabucto.[27] What concerned Campbell was the fraudulent use of the names of such absentees. But what was revealed as a result of his concern was the fact that many were leaving their grants, either to move to another part of the province or to leave the province entirely.

In November Campbell sent the completed muster to Britain.[28] It showed a total of 14,952 for mainland Nova Scotia. "Exclusive of the above numbers, 742 Loyalists and disbanded Soldiers have been struck off the Provision List in Nova Scotia, 129 in the Island of Saint Johns, and 71 in New Brunswick being considered as unworthy of a Continuance of the Bounty."[29] One thing that stands out is the disparity in numbers between those dropped off the list in Nova Scotia and their counterparts in New Brunswick, so many in the former, so few in the latter. Another is the fact that, within a year, while provisions were still being distributed, an estimated 1,968 had left Nova Scotia. Almost half of that loss came from the Shelburne area. Other areas of loss were Chedabucto and Digby, while some districts such as Antigonish, the Pictou and Cumberland area, and the Minas area towns had gained. If provisions were important enough to warrant loyalists moving from one district or province to another to gain a little more, and if, despite the fact that provisions were still being granted, Nova Scotia lost close to 2,000 loyalists in so short a time, there seemed little chance of retaining all these settlers in the province once the provisions had ceased.

The departures revealed in the musters indicated a marked fluidity within the loyalist movement. For the great mass of the loyalists, the experience of arrival and early settlement formed a distinct and solid whole. And yet within this apparently uniform experience there were movements in and out, comings and goings that do not fit the norm. The very nature of a muster freezes people at a given point in time and gives a static quality to their numbers that is misleading. At the time of the 1784 muster there were approximately 17,000

loyalists in Nova Scotia. Yet before, during, and after the muster there
was a great deal of movement among them. There were refugees
moving from one region of Nova Scotia to another, refugees still
coming in, and refugees already leaving.

A strong attempt was made by the proprietors and government
of St John's Island to draw loyalists away from Nova Scotia.[30] That
the move was having some success is indicated by the muster of
1784. In September 1784, sixty-nine loyalists left Shelburne for the
island. Several other vessels were reported to be carrying loyalists
from Shelburne to the same destination, and many more residents
were expected to follow in the spring.[31]

The migration to the island indicated early disillusionment with
Shelburne. Many loyalists throughout Nova Scotia, experiencing a
harsh land and life, remained only briefly. Many of the unfortunates
at Port Mouton made their way to New Brunswick.[32] More typical
of the very early departures were those who made the musters of
1784 necessary – the disbanded soldiers and dubious loyalists who
had come for what they could get and would leave as quickly as
they could get it. They were the ones described as "rice Christians"
by E.C. Wright, "those who came because transportation and provisions were being handed out, and who returned when the Royal
Bounty of Provisions was no longer distributed to them."[33] They
were leaving, however, long before the issuing of provisions ceased.

Despite these departures, emigration was exceeded by a continued
immigration which was not quite a part of the great loyalist wave
that had broken upon the province. There was a flow of loyalists
to and from New Brunswick. Many sought land on both sides, finally
choosing the better sites. There were also some who came from New
York via Quebec.[34] Another class of immigrant came from the United
States, many of them qualifying as loyalists but few as refugees.
Although accepted as the king's friends, they had kept a low enough
profile to be able to remain in the United States, tarred hardly at
all by the brush of Toryism.[35] A number of such loyalists, finding
encouragement enough in the land, provisions, and potential of Nova
Scotia, drifted into the colony during the first years of the postwar
settlement.

There were also the refugees who had fled America for England
only to find the streets paved simply with stone, opportunities too
few, fellow refugees too many, and the attitude towards them
disconcertingly cold. In August 1784, forty loyalists and dependents
were given berths on the *Fair America* for Nova Scotia.[36] Within
two weeks the numbers swelled to at least 150, the *Fair America*
was set aside for those loyalists emigrating to Nova Scotia, and Parr

was ordered to give them the usual provisions and materials granted to people "in their Situation."[37]

A number of very poor loyalists were sent to Nova Scotia less perhaps for their own betterment than to keep them off the dole in Britain. "There are Sir numbers of poor distressed Loyalists daily applying to us to assist them in getting to Nova Scotia," Thomas Miller informed Nepean. "They appear to be in a wretched situation and we would wish to give them all the aid in our power, we humbly conceive that Government wish to send all those poor distressed people to that Country where by industry they may earn their bread."[38] There were also border-line cases in Britain, those who could be proven neither fish nor fowl, but who were seeking transportation and supplies as loyalists. Major-General Campbell was caught in the quandary created by the "great numbers of Emigrants from the Mother Country" applying for lands, provisions, and other bounties from government, "but as I have no instructions relative to these people, and am not perfectly convinced in my own mind of the policy of encouraging such emigration I have not considered them as entitled to the Bounties."[39]

The question of the refugee as undesirable alien was raised by the arrival of the ship *Sally* with a cargo of emigrants from Britain. She had brought about 300, thirty-nine of whom had died at sea; twelve more died shortly after arrival, and the rest were quickly quarantined on the eastern shore, living under canvas until the disease was identified and controlled. They were reported to be "almost destitute of clothing and provisions."[40] To prevent any repetition of the incident, Parr beseeched Nepean not to let the lord mayor of London send any more of the sweepings of the jails as he had done with the *Sally*.[41]

Equally unwelcome were the non-loyalist immigrants from Britain who sought to cash in on the opportunities that existed in the wake of the loyalist influx and British largesse. Along with the new merchants and businessmen bound for Halifax came the pilot fish, young people emigrating to seek their fortunes somehow in a society experiencing a rapid increase in population and government expenditures, only to find – as most of them did – unemployment, poverty, and a desperate need to return home.

Perhaps the height of the unwanted immigration was reached when a brigantine from Liverpool dumped convicted felons upon the shores of Nova Scotia. North had requested of Parr that a group of convicts be allowed to land unmolested, ironically implying a double standard that treated Nova Scotia as a punishment for convicts yet a reward for loyalists.[43] The governor was predictably annoyed at the arrival of a group of people he felt to be of no use whatsoever to Nova Scotia, and ordered "That these people shall not be landed nor any others received that may come hereafter."[44] Enough was enough.

Along with the continuing departures and arrivals, there was also a great deal of loyalist movement within the province and even within the settlements. At Shelburne, where Marston and the other surveyors were busy trying to bring some order to the situation, the refugees were adding to the chaos, for one of the marked characteristics of the years 1784 and 1785 was the remarkable mobility of loyalists as land-owners, the buying and selling, switching and exchanging of land tickets and titles within the community. Many with poor land sought and bought better, many with good locations sold and left. "Few settlers at Shelburne were satisfied with their locations so that the shifting of land ownerships became almost universal," H.C. Mathews notes. One example from Mathews's handful of Scots is indicative.

On October 13, 1783, George Chisholm bought lot No. 110, Mason's Division, of fifty acres from the grantee Kenneth McKenzie for £30 "Current Money" and sold his town lot to one Alexander Fraser for £10. Two days later he bought Fraser's town lot (No. 14, Block letter N North Division) for £10, an equal trade, and immediately sold it to Kenneth McKenzie for £20 "Current Money." Four months later, on February 12, 1784, he acquired the adjoining lot, No. 111, Mason's Division, from the grantee, James Wilson, in equal trade for his lot (No. 6) on the Roseway River.[45]

Only one of Mathews's Scots stayed on the Shelburne side of the peninsula. The others, attracted by the better land and fishing grounds, the sheltered cove and the abundance of timber, found or bought land around Jordan Bay east of Shelburne.[46] Rev. William Walter mentioned several times the migration from Shelburne to the surrounding country. In the fall of 1784 he wrote of the town's decline "in reality," when many who finally received their farm lots moved onto them, emptying all the back part of the town.[47] He later mentioned "numberless little settlements" on the sea coast east and west of Shelburne.[48]

Other loyalist communities in the early years showed the same mobility, some of the newcomers moving onto farms or buying more or better land, others selling and leaving one area for a more promising, or simply leaving. The improved lands advertised for sale in the *Gazette* indicate that loyalists were not limiting themselves to their grants but that those who could afford to were buying good land.[49] Meanwhile the citizens of Sissiboo were advertising in the *Gazette* the advantages of the town in the hope of drawing loyalists and, one assumes, non-loyalists to the community. They seemed less interested in establishing a loyalist knot there than a prosperous town.[50]

One instance of the spreading out from the major dumping grounds such as Annapolis and Shelburne was recorded by Mrs Van Tyle, who arrived in Shelburne with her family in the fall of 1783, built a log cabin, and spent the winter there.

...but when the spring came and we saw nothing but rocks and moss, they made up their minds to look for a more favourable place. They had orders from the Surveyors to take up land where they could find it unlocated. On the 20th others set sail for Yarmouth, Joshua Trefry, pilot. There they found the land all taken up; were recommended to Tusket. Found the land there looked more favourable returned to Shelburne, took the family on board, and arrived at Tusket, 11th May, 1784.[51]

Some moved on to other areas because of surveying errors or prior refugee claims. Most were like the officers of the North Carolina Regiment, who wished to move from Country Harbour to New Philadelphia for better land and opportunity.[52] Others, like Gideon White at Chedabucto, Jacob Bailey, the Delanceys and Botsford at Clements, sought land in two or more areas, leaving the decision as to which area to settle until later.[53] In a proclamation of November, Campbell, pointing to the confusion caused by "the frequent removal" of loyalists and disbanded soldiers from the districts where they had been located, ordered that none should receive provisions "at any further place except the one where he has been located and mustered."[54]

By 1785, however, the "removal" of loyalists to other parts of Nova Scotia was becoming less frequent. Immigration had also declined, although there were still odd lots of loyalists coming in. The group arriving in April from St Augustine was one example of a late arrival.[55] Parr, appalled by their condition, assured the British government that he would do all that he could for "These Wretched people," checking his enthusiasm only to promise that he would do so if possible at no expense.[56] In July another group arrived at Shelburne from East Florida aboard the transport Spring.[57] In contrast to the preceding year, however, these arrivals were isolated, infrequent incidents. The major phase of loyalist immigration had passed by 1785, and Nova Scotia turned from reception to assimilation.

The rush was over, and the instruments used to cope with the rush were being put away. By December 1784 Parr had cut back drastically on the distribution of timber.[58] A feature of 1785 was the winding down of the land-granting machine. Notices still appeared in the *Gazette* of escheat inquiries, but at a lesser rate. Some land set aside for groups who were expected but who never appeared was now being unfrozen.[59] There seems also to have been a move toward earlier confiscation of land which was not being used. James Torrane's licence of occupation in Shelburne was for land forfeited by another, and dependent upon his making improvements within the month.[60]

In March Charles Morris was emphasizing that "The land in this Province will be given Out with a Sparing Hand in future."[61] Because the emergency had passed, and because of the "accumulating Expences Complained of by the Ministry," a circular letter went out from the secretary's office in May stating that since "the business he [Parr] trusts is now so far accomplished as to fulfil the promises of Government to them by passing Grants without any further Expence to the Crown, He has therefore thot proper to Order the Chief Surveyor to Reduce the number of Deputies as well in your District, as in every other part of the Province and to employ such only as are the most Capable and Active in the Business."[62] In July 1786 Bulkeley wrote to the Board of Agents at Shelburne that since the business was nearly completed, the governor "would not desire your former Constant attendance any longer," but asked that they meet once a month to handle any business arising.[63] The machine, having served its purpose, was being dismantled.

After so much activity, its slackening was like a pause in the heart-beat of the settlements. The surveyors and suppliers were gone, much of the government assistance ended, and the loyalist left on his own with his land and his future. The first years of settlement had been characterized by the frantic rush of officials and assistants to lay out land and put impatient loyalists upon it, by the extensive movement within the loyalist body, people occupying new land, moving on to other land, buying more property, selling and leaving, spreading out from the initial centres. All seemed in motion. That very motion, however, bred the confusion which permitted neglect of some loyalists and abuses by others. This in turn instigated the musters. Among other things, the muster rolls indicated that a surprisingly large number of loyalists were already leaving Nova Scotia. Even among those remaining, the urgent and continuing dependence upon provisions did not hold great promise for the success of the settlements. Free land, government timber and tools, and the king's bounty were insufficient in themselves to root a permanent settlement.

CHAPTER FOUR

Early Progress of the Loyalist Settlements

Comments on the progress of the loyalist communities during the early years varied with and depended upon the perspective of the observer. The overview of the settlements given by officials and others stressed the visible progress: the land granted, acres cleared, and houses built. Upon this was erected an optimistic impression of the future of the loyalist in Nova Scotia. The pace of settling, however, differed from community to community, depending upon the calibre of the refugees and their leadership, the efficiency of the surveyors, and the quality of the location. For the individual loyalist, moreover, the sense of overall progress was counterbalanced and often out-weighed by personal hardship and hunger, by present frustration and fear of the future.

From its birth Shelburne was impressive. John Parr was struck by the quality of the harbour itself, "about five miles long, and three and a half broad, the depth of the water from five to twelve fathom, a safe Bay without it for ships to Anchor in, a deep bold Shore without Rocks or Shoals, and good holding Ground."[1] Not all were so favourably impressed. The first impact of that wild coast and empty shore jolted many refugees, and made believable the story John Inglis heard of how "on their first arrival, lines of women could be seen sitting on the rocks of the shore, weeping at their altered condition."[2] Some took one look at their land and left. Parr had been informed of refugees selling their lots before they received their grants, and others selling who had not yet come to Shelburne. According to one observer, "Many who got Land sold it almost immediately and set off with the Cash in hand."[3] There was, however, a bravado about the loyalist landings at Shelburne born both of a psychic need and of the optimism stimulated by Sydney's promise to make Nova Scotia the envy of America.[4] Shelburne was taking root, a loyalist presence in that obscure region of an obscure province, and regardless of their private misgivings, both loyalist and official had to present their best face to a curious world. Among Nova Scotians and earlier loyalists there was some awe at the sudden emergence of this obscure harbour. It was clear that, with the arrival of vast numbers of loyalists, with the rise of new centres and sources of power and influence, Nova Scotia would never be the same again, though no one was certain of the exact nature or extent of the impact and its ramifications. "But all agree that it is one of the finest harbors on the Continent and exceeding well adapted for a fishery. Many of the settlers are people of great property and there is an unanimous spirit among them to render that place superior to Halifax – but to accomplish that will be a work of time."[5]

In settling the people on the land, Shelburne made more progress more quickly than other settlements. To a degree this was owing to the preparations of the associates and their leadership. It was also owing to the fact that Shelburne was the centre upon which, because of its concentration of loyalists, all eyes were turned, and consequently officialdom hurried to avoid censure. Other reasons were given by Charles Morris, particularly the importance of having a board of agents on the spot to handle details and decisions, relieving the surveyors of many of the local headaches.[6] In Shelburne, Morris made it his policy to ignore completely the individual grant. He wrote to Marston of the impossibility of granting by individual lots and asked him to draw up a grant for the whole district.[7]

Marston worked steadily on until the end of July 1784, when rioting by disbanded soldiers against the free negroes drove him out.[8] Despite the considerable effort made, the great number of loyalists settled and lots granted, by the fall of that year the job was not completed.[9] Nevertheless, although hardship continued, the loyalists at Shelburne were cushioned against destitution, for provisions were available, prices were regulated and, in comparison with Halifax or Annapolis, reasonable, game and fish were plentiful,[10] and transports were available "for the Relief of any Inhabitants of this place distress'd for the want of convenient Housing."[11] And yet by the time of the 1784 muster there had already been a loss of population. As a result of that muster 445 people had been struck off the provisions list, leaving a total of 7,478 eligible for provisions. No servants were listed in this total.[12]

The decrease can be accounted for. There were a good many deaths during the winter. Some of the poorer people went to Halifax for employment, others engaged in the fishery and made no attempt to settle their lands. Most of the early emigrants were disbanded soldiers who had removed to St John's Island and other areas. Some, even at this early period, returned to the United States, discouraged by the outlook. As all these were excluded from the muster roll, it is evident that it did not include all who, at one time or another, lived at Shelburne. The instructions issued to the muster-masters were to exclude from their rolls those who were not actually settled on the lands allotted them, or were not making preparations for settlement.[13]

Life in Shelburne was often crude and uncomfortable, but the achievements and expectations of the first years were impressive. "In six months time there were upwards of 800 houses built, and most of them of the very wood that grew where the town now stands, Here are at present from 1,400 to 1,500 houses, and some of them as good as any in the Province."[14] There was an air of pride in Marston's diary as he noted the number of houses gone up, and described a ball at McGragh's tavern on the queen's birthday, with dancing, tea, and cards, "in a house which stood where six months ago there was an almost impenetrable swamp – so great has been the exertions of the settlers in this new world."[15]

The refugees were getting onto their farm lots, clearing and planting. Fallen timber and moss, which gave them an immense amount of work,[16] concealed a land "very rocky & full of small stones – the soil exceedingly light, being a sandy loam."[17] It was a soil naturally productive of grass, of which a large variety grew.[18] Owing to the topography, however, few of the farms were capable of supporting sufficient livestock, a fact which led to the pursuit of extra pasturage for the cattle.[19] It was not good farming country and offered slim chance of supplying the local market, much less developing an export trade in agricultural produce. Perhaps the inhabitants counted on little else, for the future of Shelburne was not in agriculture but on the sea and in trade, and they believed a great port did not need good land.[20]

Whatever the precariousness of its infant economy, at this stage size alone made Shelburne a major centre. It was one of the larger cities in North America,[21] and as such it began to assert the pull and receive the attention of a major city. There had been talk and perhaps an assumption that it might become the capital of Nova Scotia. It was undoubtedly taking on some of the trappings of a metropolis. The *Gazette* of Halifax was soon receiving its foreign news from Shelburne.[22] Three newspapers had appeared, first the *Royal American Gazette*, followed by the *Port Roseway Gazetteer and General Advertiser*, and finally the *Nova Scotia Packet and General Advertiser*.[23] Private schools sprang up, such as that of W. Leary and E. Fogarty, which offered not only the three R's, the classics, and practical training, but also a dancing school meeting twice a week for "the young Ladies and Gentlemen."[24]

It possessed the trades and services of an urban centre, including "Charles Oliver Bruff, Goldsmith & Jeweller at the Sign of the Tea-Pot, Tankard and Cross-Swords,"[25] and a hairdresser who promised "Ladies and Gentlemen dressed, at their own Lodgings, on the shortest notice, and in the newest fashion."[26] There was a chamber of commerce by 1785, which at its meeting of May 2 approved plans for the establishing of a loan bank.[27] The by-laws passed by the Sessions and justices of the peace, from regulating the size of loaves of bread to the removal of wooden chimneys and the appointment of firemen and a town crier,[28] introduced regulations of a kind necessary for an urban centre. In the barren wilderness along the south shore of Nova Scotia, Shelburne seemed a strange urban oasis. "From the correspondence of my old Townsman Nash," George Thomas wrote, "I am happy to find that Shelburne affords so much acceptable company & so many scenes of unexpected pleasure and amusement."[29]

"Shelburne," wrote one loyalist, "is worth all the rest of the settlements put together."[30] Almost equalling in size all the other new communities, the town and its prospects were prepossessing, yet the others were going through a similar phase of promise and achievement in changing the face of wilderness country. Parr felt that all of them were, in general, getting on very well in establishing their economies. By the end of 1785 he was extolling the improvements in the fisheries, agriculture, and timber, ticking off the ninety sawmills in the province, twenty-five of them built since 1783, and stressing the province's ability to supply the West Indian market.[31] Parr was not alone in noting the extent of progress and change. One man spoke of the new towns starting up "as by enchantment."[32] Edward Winslow, after touring the province, also commented on the saw mills, finding nine built in Annapolis within a few months, and more planned in both Annapolis and Digby.[33] The potential development of the fisheries was spoken of in favourable terms by Parr and by such refugees as Jacob Bailey.[34]

A price is always paid. If doubling the population was to have an important impact on Nova Scotia's future, the issue of supply and demand had an immediate impact on the individual refugee, and throughout the province there was talk of the exorbitant cost of living. Sir Andrew Hamond estimated that necessities had doubled in price since 1775.[35] Yet discussion of prices, exorbitant or simply high, sometimes disguised the fact that many had neither money to buy nor goods to barter. Jacob Bailey felt it would be several years before the most industrious farmers could raise provisions sufficient for their families.[36] Parr underlined the continued loyalist need for and dependence upon the king's provisions in 1785.[37] The Winslow Papers testify to the complaints in many parts of Nova Scotia and the fear of starvation.[38] The people of Ardois Hill, in a petition to the House of Assembly, give a picture of the loyalist experience unlike that of the mushrooming towns and receding bush.

Your Memorialists can well assure the Honourable House that they have no Disposition of being idle and Sloathful in their Business but resolve to get their living by the sweat of their Brow. Resolved as we be to scrape a living from amongst the Stumps by the Dint of hard Labour and Toil of Body and many Discouragement of Minds, our Lands produce us very little Bread, the Staf of man's life; – far from a Sufficiency to keep Soul and Body together any Length of time as we have to go twelve Miles to mill and there wait two or three days ere we can return with Bread to our Wives and Children.[39]

And there were disasters, such as that which struck Port Mouton. The first winter had been a miserable one with lumber for shelter being sent too late in the season to protect many from the elements. In the closeness, enforced idleness, hunger, and despair of the community, bitterness erupted into violence, with brawls, the odd knifing, and a rash of litigation in Liverpool when the spring court opened.[40] Spring brought disaster to the community, "for a fire has there happened, so very dreadful, as to have reduced to ashes by far the greater part of their dwelling Houses, as also all the Storehouses of every kind insomuch that no more of the Provisions given by His Majesty for their Subsistance could be saved than barely sufficient to maintain them until the 14th instant."[41] After the fire the refugees dispersed to Annapolis and Passamaquoddy, to Liverpool, Digby, the St John, and Guysborough, some in such a hurry to get away that they were leaving "in boats of only four oars, ill built, and one for sails provided only with blankets."[42]

One of the more promising areas outside of Shelburne was the eastern shore. For Parr this area included not only the settlements at Ship Harbour, Sheet Harbour, Country Harbour, and Chedabucto, but also those at Antigonish, Pictou, and Merigomish. There were upwards of two thousand loyalists in these settlements, according to Parr, "and amongst them many reputable and hard working Families."[43]

The development of the Guysborough area seemed like an after-thought, resulting from the need for an empty area in which to place disbanded soldiers and loyalists arriving late in 1783. This settlement was one year behind other loyalist communities. Whereas other areas had received their refugees and made progress in laying out and allotting land in the previous year, Guysborough was receiving its first refugees and surveyors in the spring of 1784. The Duke of Cumberland's Regiment was one of the early groups on the scene. Having arrived from Jamaica in December 1783, 300 of these South Carolinians spent the winter in huts outside Halifax.[44] On May 16 remnants of the corps arrived at Chedabucto, and the surveyor began laying out their lots. They were joined by members of the Civil Department from Port Mouton.[45] Some of the 71st Regiment, a highland regiment, also took land there. Part of the British Legion, recruited in New York and active in most of the southern campaigns, was also there. The Civil Department, one of the largest groups, assumed what leadership there was among the Port Mouton-Chedabucto Loyalists. It was all a very mixed bag.[46]

The St Augustine loyalists, as pathetic a group as the revolution tossed up, also found their way to the area. They had been originally driven out of the Carolinas and Georgia to Florida. When Britain gave up Florida, however, they were exiled a second time, 880 of them seeking refuge in Nova Scotia. They were less rewarded than other loyalists and soldiers both in land and supplies, for they had come late upon the land and could take only what others had rejected. Lacking leadership and numbers, their cries of distress were unheard among the demanding howls of larger, more forceful associations. Eventually, several years later, they received a grant of 8,450 acres. There were forty-eight heads of family on the grant.[47]

The growing community at Chedabucto, initially christened New Manchester, had a total muster of 1,050 entitled to provisions. Since few of the Duke of Cumberland's Regiment remained on their holdings, and the men of the 60th soon concentrated on securing their livelihood from the sea, the members of the Civil Department became the most influential group in the town, to such an extent that the name Manchester gave way in time to that of Guysborough, after their chief patron.[48]

The affairs of Chedabucto were blighted by a fight over the surveyor, which led to "a great many Disputes amongst our Gentry, Brownrigg & Cunningham against McDonald & ye Doctor [McPherson]."[49] To McPherson the surveyor was an incompetent who "intends to push in as many people as he thinks proper to draw lots with us."[50] MacDonald and McPherson had voiced their complaints and grievances to R.F. Brownrigg upon his arrival, but he was rather suspicious of them. He found that those complaining, who had been first on the spot, wished to monopolize the best lots and an inordinate amount of the provisions. They were also openly obstructing and defying Nutting the surveyor.[51] At the request of the McPherson party, however, Nutting was recalled, but not before having a curious revenge. According to McPherson's memorial, the surveyor reported the presence of a good strip of white pine which, being reserved for the king's use, inhibited the ambitions of the group; the report prompted their memorial denying the existence of any such pine.[52] Nutting was replaced by the candidate of the McPherson party, Amos Chapman, who seemed to be inefficient, slow, and open to influence.[53]

Like the others, the settlements in the Guysborough area were compounds of hope and desperation. One of the more memorable of the petitions from the area was that of the Cumberland Regiment, declaring their desire to become useful members of the community, but pointing out that, with only ten married women in the regiment and few eligible females in the district, they required the assistance of the government in getting wives.[54] This was no prank, for one loyalist, writing to Gideon White of his efforts to indent carpenters for the new settlement, added, "I have also applied for some Women & I believe a few will come."[55] The more pressing concern in the Chedabucto area, however, was food and shelter, for although described as industrious, the settlers in general were poor and short of provisions.[56] The 60th Regiment, "having been almost starved during part of last Winter ... must unavoidably perish the Winter following, if no Relief is afforded them before then, as they have not got even their Lands Survey'd to them Yet."[57] Their isolation, combined with their inability at that early stage to support themselves, made the provision ships of vital importance to their survival. In September 1785, when a supply ship bound for Chedabucto was hijacked by the crew, the loss of provisions brought great hardship to many of the white and death to some of the black loyalists.[58]

A good number of their fellow immigrants were building a community at Stormont on the eastern side of Country Harbour, southwest of Guysborough. The muster return listed 289 refugees,[59] consisting of disbanded members of the late South Carolina Regiment, King's Carolina Rangers, and North Carolina Volunteers.[60] Because of their frugality and industry, the potential for farming, fishing, and commerce, and the good harbour, another visitor felt "Stormont (which was last year a wilderness) is likely to become a place of importance in a few years."[61] By the fall of the following year (1785) the disbanded soldiers at Country Harbour were less sanguine, being reduced to only twenty-five days' provisions, not, according to their memorial, through laziness, but through lack of seed, and were stating

"That your Memorialists are fully convinced that three fourths of these people cannot exist till next Spring without a further relief."[62]

In July and August, C. Stewart began a study of the North Shore. He spoke very highly of Pictou, Merigomish, and Antigonish.[63] Early settlers in the Antigonish region were the disbanded troops of the Nova Scotia Volunteers. A group of independent companies serving in St John's Island, lacking to some degree both discipline and morals, had been merged with Timothy Hierlihy's group into the Volunteers, and, with Hierlihy as commander, served in Halifax from 1782 onwards, where at the war's end they were disbanded.[64] It was not until the spring of 1784 that Charles Morris requested Daniel McLean to lay out land for them at Antigonish.[65] In May Hierlihy and eighty-six other officers and soldiers entered Antigonish harbour and established the village of Town Point, renamed Dorchester in 1786.[66] Hierlihy put in a provision return for 111 people. Stewart, after checking, certified only sixty-two, eliminating thirty-three men, six women, three children, "and eighteen nominal Servants." Despite those absent and dropped, Stewart speaks of the majority at Antigonish as building their homes, and clearing and improving their lands. Another fact given in the Antigonish census is the age of the men. Of the seventy-seven whose ages were given, twenty-two were in their thirties, thirty-one in their twenties, eight over sixteen, and there was one "man" of fourteen.[67] This was to be expected in a military unit, but as settlers this disproportionately large number of young men, fresh from barrack life, with little family or other hostages to fortune, their future before them, may have been averse to staying with the endless, brutal task of clearing and planting. The effects of comparative youth, single status, and limited commitment as settlers would have been experienced by many disbanded soldiers in Nova Scotia.

As in many other settlements, the lots in Town Point were separated from the farm lots by as much as six miles. Moreover, as shown by the muster lists, many of these ex-soldiers, unable or unwilling to adjust to a settler's life, sold their lands and left the community within a year of arriving. There was, however, an air of optimism about the settlement, indicated in Hierlihy's recommendation to his son that some of the unclaimed lots in town be set aside for "the encouragement of Tradesmen and Maccanicks to settle among us."[68]

At Pictou and Merigomish there were 266 entitled to provisions. One characteristic of Pictou was the rapid turnover in land and the shifting of population. The disbanded troops of the 82nd or Hamilton Regiment had been granted land in the area. Some, after looking at the land, simply returned to Halifax and reenlisted. Others sold their grants, often for a few pounds. In many cases the abandoned land was left unoccupied, or occupied without title.[69] With many of the 82nd leaving, other settlers and soldiers moved in. Most of the Second Battalion, 84th Regiment, the Royal Highland Emigrants, a group which one historian found both sober and industrious, made their way to Pictou in 1784.[70]

The number mustered in the district of Cumberland was 856, but with a startling 459 struck off the provisions list. The area of Cornwallis and Horton also had more people struck off the provision rolls than were retained. Many of those eliminated were loyalists who, discouraged by the tardiness of land granting, had already departed.[71]

Because of the large number of loyalists at Annapolis, the failure to get many on their land before winter, and the immense overcrowding in the town throughout the winter of 1783-4, priority was given to getting those lands laid out and allotted before the spring passed. Botsford's delay in choosing land for his association in the area was still giving the surveyor general trouble.[72] Despite the delay, such rapid progress was being made on the farm lots that tobacco was being grown, more than enough for the "old smookers from Connecticut and the Massachusetts."[73]

In Annapolis, Grenville, Wilmot, and Clements, 1,830 had been mustered.[74] The Annapolis valley was extravagantly praised for its natural fertility and the improvements made by the loyalists. There was even some talk that it might become the seat of government.[75] A naval visitor in the summer of 1785 judged it the most productive country he had ever seen.[76] Jacob Bailey found in 1785 a very successful winter wheat crop and noted that "A spirit of Industry prevails among the emigrants.[77] At Granville, Edward Winslow was living "snugly" and Edward Howe, a farmer, "speaks with rapture of the Country."[78]

Yet mingled with the reports of progress and promise were the anguished cries for aid. Bailey mentioned the high price of food.[79] Concerning the loyalists, he wrote that "most of them have expended all their subsistance in building and clearing a little spot on the ground." Several, fearing starvation, returned to the United States.[80] In May 1786 a petition signed by 577 was sent to Parr, outlining their situation as "deplorable and alarming – most of them without Provisions or abilities to purchase them."[81] Parr, in a letter to Sydney, confirmed their need.[82] Bailey explained the paradox of hard times in a fertile valley by pointing out that no people, no matter how frugal or industrious, could be comfortable in a new country until they had lived there for seven or more years.[83]

Digby was almost pure loyalist. There John Robinson had struck twenty-eight from the provisions, leaving a total of 1,267. Although he cut few off the rolls, he did note "that a great number applied for Provisions whose Claims I thought so very unreasonable that I rejected them without inserting their names in the Rolls." He found the inhabitants very industrious and the settlement already flourishing.[84] Many questioned their "flourishing Condition," for what money they had went into building their homes, and "we are but just entering upon Business and the Cultivation of Our lands."[85]

Digby's difficulty stemmed from the discontent that had arisen over land grants and confused surveys. Robinson castigated the surveyors for their failure to settle the loyalists and their land problems more quickly and intelligently.[86] The grant for Digby was approved on February 20, 1784, for three hundred heads of family, although more than one-third of the grantees did not occupy their land. Groups other than the New York Association were also moving into the area seeking land.[87] The expected confusion and discord attending the surveying and settling of the land was compounded by the efforts of Botsford and his charges to monopolize the area while still casting their eyes over other parts of the province, and by the refusal of other loyalist companies to accept either their monopoly or hegemony.

Robinson had done the muster from beyond Digby to the Annapolis area, beginning with the southwestern regions and working his way toward Annapolis. There were small loyalist communities at Bear River, Nine Mile River, Gulliver's Hole, St Mary's Bay and Sissiboo. Although not optimistic about the settlement at St Mary's Bay, he was quite cheerful about the prospects of the others.[88] Stephen Jones, who had first settled on the St John, found the Sissiboo area very attractive. He had already cleared twenty acres. "I raised this Summer two Acres of Wheat and as much of Oats & Potatoes and in a few days shall put into the Ground four Acres of Wheat and Rye."[89]

There were loyalist clusters scattered along the Bay of Fundy coast of Nova Scotia from Digby to Cumberland. Men of the 84th Regiment under Colonel Small were settled in the Kennetcook region.[90] Wentworth's certificate of June allotted 81,450 acres to over 700 soldiers and dependents in an area extending roughly from the Kennetcook to the Shubenacadie.[91] The two settlements to be founded by the regiment were Kennetcook and Gore.[92] The officer in charge of mustering them held little hope for their success as settlers. Most of the men had not as yet settled on their land and were being employed by the old settlers as servants and labourers. Many were selling their provisions to these old settlers. The reason they gave for their sad plight was that most of them had not yet received their land grants, and those who were settling were being threatened with eviction by an earlier claimant, "a Mr. Halliburton an Attorney."[93]

Windsor was given a total muster of 278, of whom only 219 were entitled to provisions, most of them either loyalists from South Carolina or disbanded members of the 84th. The returns for the Windsor Road and Sackville also showed a marked disparity between the total muster and the number eligible for provisions. One hundred and thirty had been mustered but only thirty were eligible for provisions. One problem in the area around Windsor was that much of the best land was held by absentees, especially in Halifax. The loyalist was faced with accepting an inferior piece of land, working as a tenant for others, or buying. Stewart's remarks on the prospective settlers were not encouraging. Many, not having received their land, had already sold their provisions and were working as day-labourers in the surrounding community.[94]

Rev. George Gillmore's experience indicates how disheartening the loyalist experience in the Windsor area could be during those early years. He mentions in one letter walking to Halifax in 1785 and offering his land, house, and improvements as security for one barrel of flour and one of pork. He was refused. "Three winters I have bought Hay at a great price and carried it on my back four miles through the woods, where there was no path, or road, to keep alive two cows, which were the support of my family, with the help of potatoes."[95] Parts of the 60th Regiment were settling at Falmouth, although in January 1784 they were still aboard the transports, hungry and cold.[96] Land was being laid out for refugees on the Tusket River.[97] Disbanded soldiers of various British and American regiments, along with some civilian refugees, were to be found in the area around Cornwallis and Horton. As in several other cases, the officer in charge of the muster cited the failure of the surveyors to assist these people in getting on their land and stated "that many of them (from not getting their Grants compleated) have been obliged to leave the Lands they were Cultivating, and the Improvements they had made on them."[98]

There were other smaller pockets of loyalists along Nova Scotia's long coastline. Those along the coast from Halifax to Shelburne, where only nineteen were stricken from the provisions rolls, numbered 632. "The Commissary of Musters observes that the Harbours of Prospect, Margarets Bay, Chester, Lunenburg, La Hevre, Port Matoon & the Ragged Islands are well situated for Fisheries and that the Settlements of Loyalists at those Places, will afford a respectable Defence of the Coast."[99]

Between Halifax and Guysborough there were several small villages among the many bays and harbours. In the Dartmouth area, across the harbour from Halifax, 480 loyalists were mustered. "This settlement from its vicinity to Halifax and some other good Harbours promises to be a place of importance soon."[100] The Musquodoboit area had but sixteen loyalists, most of them from North Carolina, although the inspector considered it a "very promising Settlement." Another thirty or so were located around the Bay of Jeddore. One hundred and twenty-two loyalists, chiefly of the Royal Garrison Battalion, were mustered at Sheet Harbour. They had not yet been granted their land,[101] yet reports from the community indicated that, contrary to the norm, the old disbanded soldiers there were doing very well as settlers and pioneers.[102] At Ship Harbour there were 151 loyalists, chiefly refugees from South Carolina and disbanded soldiers of the Nova Scotia Volunteers. Because their land had not yet been granted, many others had already left the community.[103] "This causes much discontent among those who remain, and if not soon remedied, will drive the whole away," William Shaw informed Edward Winslow in June 1784. "It is indeed astonishing that so many good Settlers should until this day be left in this State of uncertainty."[104]

Halifax as a loyalist depot differed from other areas. For one thing, loyalists were coming to an already established port. For another, it tended to draw not so much those seeking land as those seeking an established urban existence. Consequently, the extremes of the loyalist spectrum are evident here. One finds the affluent, the influential, and those enterprising enough to anticipate affluence or exploit influence through government appointments. One also finds the other extreme, disbanded soldiers and questionable refugees, with little intention of seeking land to clear, simply waiting out the free provisions and amenities of the British government. Since the one class was prosperous enough not to appear on the provision musters and the other class was largely denied enrolment, because of their refusal to seek and settle on their land, the muster lists show relatively few loyalists in Halifax. Whether merchant or miscreant, however, there were far more than indicated on the lists. And among the sizeable number of black loyalists who had been landed in Halifax were many who chose to remain and offer their skills and labour for hire in this urban area. In time they were joined by others who, failing to gain any farm land from the government, drifted into the port in pursuit of employment, so that as much as one-tenth of the population of Halifax may have been black refugees.[105]

Halifax was also the depot for loyalists awaiting placement elsewhere, serving as a funnel and holding station for many of the refugees. In the first two years the inundation led to the crowding of public buildings and the blossoming of tents and temporary shacks. Most of these loyalists remained only until they could move onto their land.

The crush of so many people upset the balance of supply and demand, making the city a seller's market. Trade was brisk and demand great, with a very good market for British goods.[106] Lady Wentworth complained of the high prices, attributing them to an increase in population which "renders every article and necessary supply to be at a high rate."[107] Joseph Peters commented on the number of new merchants in town and the consequent increase in building, "yet, I am much mistaken, if a number of what are called merchants here don't embrace a Nocturnal opportunity of evacuating the Town before next Year at this Time: I wish not, but I cannot see how it is possible for so many of them to swim in so shoal water."[108]

Many of the mercantile class remained. And, to the dismay of the city fathers, so did many of the unemployed and unemployable. The overseers of the poor described the many "Disbanded Soldiers [who] are Daily & Nightly picked Up in the Streets in a perishing state & sent to the poor House afflicted with various Disorders." They estimated that one-half of their expenditure would be occasioned by the disbanded soldiers, and requested that Campbell help to provide for them.[109] According to a British army officer, much of the other half may have gone to assist those non-loyalist "adventurers from our country going about the streets almost starving . . . I wish a stop was put to this sort of emigration."[110]

There were thousands of black refugees in Nova Scotia, most having come as free loyalists, others as slaves brought by their masters on the evacuation of the American ports. To incite a counter-insurrection the British, with quite remarkable success, had been inviting blacks in America to join the royal cause since 1775. Estimates of those who joined run as high as 100,000, and they had been used in a variety of roles, from fatigue duty to active combat in the army and navy.[111] With the coming of peace and the necessity of evacuating New York, Carleton decided to embark those blacks who had joined the British before 30 November 1783, to compensate the American owners, and to keep a record of those leaving, his "Book of Negroes." From April to November 1783, approximately 3,000 free blacks were listed as embarking for Nova Scotia from New York.[112] Other blacks would embark at New York as slaves and "servants," and still others would come from the southern colonies as they were abandoned.

All in all, more than 10 per cent of the loyalists who came to Nova Scotia were free blacks.[113]

The free blacks saw themselves as loyalists and expected to be treated by Britain as such. Their great hope, besides the retention and extension of their freedom, was to receive land and enough provisions to allow them to survive until they could clear and farm that land. In the great inundation of 1783, however, with thousands of loyalists arriving precipitately, demanding that promises be kept, and with a land-granting procedure that was too complicated and an administration too small and inept to handle such a crisis, the black refugee, possessing little influence, was relegated to a far corner of the official mind. It seemed inevitable that where so many were demanding so much from so few, and where white settlers often waited years for their land, black settlers would wait much longer for much less.

Black Pioneers under Colonel Blucke were among the earliest arrivals at Shelburne. They were organized into companies which helped to build that town and one of their own. This community, Birchtown, several miles northwest of Shelburne along the Jordan River, had according to the muster of 1784 a population of 1,521 free blacks. However, taking into account arrivals after the muster and the number of slaves living with their owners in Shelburne, the black population of Shelburne County was probably at least double that figure.[114] Only 184 of the Birchtown blacks received farm land. "This fortunate third had to wait two more years after their white colleagues were satisfied, and when their grants were finalized in 1788 they averaged only 34 acres."[115] Perhaps another hundred, working for wages, managed to purchase farms, but most of the Birchtown black loyalists remained landless.

In other parts of Nova Scotia the black refugees suffered a similar fate, being basically segregated and landless. There were two other all-black settlements, Brindley Town, not far from Digby, and Little Tracadie in what is now Guysborough County. Brindley Town, the second largest black settlement, had sixty-five families of free blacks by 1784. Because of the confusion and ineptitude that marked the surveying of Digby, few white settlers there received a secure title to their land before 1800, and far fewer blacks. Although seventy-six black refugees received one-acre town lots, none was ever put in possession of a farm lot.[116]

One group that did receive farm lots were the black loyalists under Thomas Brownspriggs at Little Tracadie. In 1787, seventy-four black families received a grant of 3,000 acres there, an average of forty acres a family at a time when the white settlers were receiving grants of 200 acres and more a family.[117] Little Tracadie was one of the few black settlements to receive farm land. Another was the mixed community of Preston, not far from Halifax, where fifty-one black families received such grants between 1785 and 1787. Again what stands out is not only the fact that the blacks there did receive farm land, but also the marked discrepancy between the amount of land granted to black and white settlers, the former receiving grants of about fifty acres, the latter of about 200, with many blacks receiving no land whatsoever.[118]

There were other pockets of black refugees throughout the province, more than four hundred in Halifax drawn by the labour market, at least seventy families in the town of Shelburne, a hundred individuals in the Annapolis region, perhaps fifty in Liverpool, others in Windsor and Digby, and families scattered throughout other communities in Nova Scotia, almost all distinguished by the fact that they had received no grants of land from the government.[119] Being black, most had to wait until the white refugees were serviced, and often by that time it was too late, since Britain had ceased paying surveying costs and the majority of blacks were either unwilling or unable to pay such fees themselves. Thus the promises made and expectations raised during the revolution were not to be met. The black loyalists were not to be equal.

Characteristic of almost all of the settlements during the first years were the feelings of fear and desperation experienced by many of the inhabitants. Few were comfortable and many lacked sufficient food, shelter, and security. The contrast between their life in these raw communities and what many had known and left behind them was inescapable. Compared with that of other pioneer societies, however, their lot was not excessively hard, and their continued dependence on the provisions sometimes diverts attention from the fact that they did have the bounty and the king's protection to fall back on. Collectively, with this great number starting to clear and plant, to fish, cut timber, and build ships, to build houses and with them new centres, their impact was impressive, for they were undoubtedly changing the face of Nova Scotia. All were overshadowed by the miracle of Shelburne, with its host of new homes, its swift thrusts into trade, and its naive assurance concerning the future. Yet throughout Nova Scotia, despite the privation and hardship, "the astonishing advances that have been made by the Loyalists since the evacuation of New York exceeds description."[120]

Echoing this note of accomplishment, John Parr, in November 1785, summed up the state of the loyalist settlements in Nova Scotia. He acknowledged that, despite their great efforts and progress, they were still dependent on the king's bounty. "But I have not a doubt my Lord, after a few years this Province from its many resources will become a rich and flourishing part of the Empire, a valuable appendage to the parent state."[121]

Glancing out and back from Halifax in late 1785, Parr could feel some relief at a crisis passed. The rush was over and the refugees settled sufficiently to allow the dismantling of the land-granting machinery. His administration had handled close to twenty thousand refugees on the mainland alone, if not well then without the catastrophes that might have occurred. Extensive new areas were being settled, a miracle port on the south shore was building its stores, wharves, and warehouses, and seeking its destiny in the West Indies, the Guysborough, Digby, and north shore thousands were promising much for the farming and fishing segments of the economy. With time and growth of population Nova Scotia could not help but rise to unimagined heights of prosperity and importance. Sometimes overlooked, however, was the fact that too many were leaving at far too early a stage, that through ineptness too few were on their land, that many of the refugees, disbanded soldiers and civilians, simply existing on and for the bounty, were being revealed as of little worth as pioneers. For the others there was still a continued and crucial dependence upon the bounty, and the question of how many would stay, and how they would fare, upon its termination.

CHAPTER FIVE

A Fragmentary Profile

In a study of the loyalists of Nova Scotia, what keeps intruding is the question of who these people were. Were they, for example, a cross-section of the society they left, or a peculiar fragment of it? How much did the loyalists of Nova Scotia, in background and motivation, resemble the profile of the loyalist in general, and in what particular ways did they differ?

On the 150th anniversary of the loyalist arrival in British North America, D.C. Harvey, the late archivist of Nova Scotia, wrote an article concerning these people and their contribution to Canadian development. Not all of those who came to Nova Scotia after the revolution were considered by him to be loyalists. As far as Harvey was concerned, "The loyalists proper were those who as Americans remained true to the British allegiance and, having lost their cause, were forced to emigrate to the colonies or return to England."[1]

Whether or not one accepts Harvey's narrow definition, one must accept the fact that these refugees were, in characteristics, background, and motivation, a decidedly mixed multitude. Rev. Jacob Bailey described those in the Annapolis Valley as "a collection of all nations, kindreds, complexions and tongues assembled from every quarter of the Globe, and till lately equally strangers to me and each other."[2]

There were those who had not found the war a great hardship and had made money from it, through salaries and contracts. Young Ward Chipman had found himself, through the fortunes of war, worth £500 a year.[3] "Your agreeable situation at New York gives me the greatest satisfaction, & I hope your felicity will continue uninterrupted thro' a series of Years."[4] Whether it was public office and influence, Ward Chipman's £500, or profits on a smaller scale in the shape of steady pay and contracts in New York, there were those identified with the crown who had found their loyalty profitable but who at the end of the war would have to leave. Whatever their original motivation most of those who had so identified themselves shared a common fate. They were exiles from America.

There were a great many others in Nova Scotia, however, who did not fit this mould. They could not be classified as exiles because either they were not American or they were not forced to leave America. The obvious non-loyalists would be the British regulars disbanded in the province, close to 2,000 of them accompanied by 1,000 women and children. There were also the foreign troops, several hundred in all, including wives and children, consisting of small numbers of Waldeckers, Hessians, and others at Shelburne, Chester, and Nine Mile River, more at Bear River and Clements in Annapolis County. Even the provincial corps was very diverse in origin. Most were Americans raised in the colonies. The 84th, however, was chiefly composed of Scottish immigrants "arriving at that time in the United States or Nova Scotia."[5] W.O. Raymond described some of the other provincial regiments that contained few men born in the Thirteen Colonies.

The Loyal Nova Scotia Volunteers were raised chiefly in Nova Scotia and Newfoundland. These corps were never out of Nova Scotia, and were disbanded there at the peace, but they are included among the Loyalists. Many of the men of the Queen's Rangers, the British Legion, DeLancey's first and second battalions, and other corps, were immigrants, chiefly Irish, enlisted at New York. The Royal Garrison Battalion was mustered as a Loyalist corps and disbanded in Nova Scotia; nevertheless it included comparatively few Loyalists, the majority being officers and soldiers of British Regulars who had been invalided and sent to Bermuda to recuperate. This will suffice to show the composite character of the British American regiments.[6]

There were many among the lower classes who must have regarded provisions and land in Nova Scotia as better than their lot in New York. Benjamin Marston implies that the September arrivals in Shelburne were largely made up of such people.

Some loyalists came from England to Nova Scotia as the lesser of two evils. At the war's end they chose Nova Scotia as being less expensive than Britain, and a part of their America. Mary Swords, with a pension of £40 a year found "that I cannot with the greatest Economy Support myself and family on that sum here, am therefore desirous of going to Nova Scotia."[7] Other loyalists from Britain looked at Nova Scotia with a more speculative eye. John O'Donnell, in Ireland with little employment, was "much inclined to go to Nova Scotia but will wait yr ansr, & advise, first to inform me whether there may be any hesitation in getting the proper patent for getting possession of the Land: & next whether it wou'd be adequite to the expence attending a voyage from this place."[8] John Lindsay wrote a similar letter from Jamaica, asking whether he could secure land in the province without a personal appearance, and to what advantage it could be converted if he should go to Nova Scotia.[9] These, although exiles from America, looked on Nova Scotia not as a last refuge but as a speculative option.

Other loyalists who could have remained in America looked to Nova Scotia as a better alternative. Nehemiah Strong observed in September 1783:

The Accounts we have received from Nova Scotia, have been somewhat various; Some people who have supposed themselves to be great Sufferers by the late Tumult; and who have no great prospects of being in a very agreeable Situation in consequence of the late American Revolution, would not be averse from looking out for a better country, tho they must commonly discourse of these matters *Sub Rosa*. People in these parts would be glad to have a more particular Account of the Country where you now are, and I fancy that great Numbers from these parts especially Connecticut would flock hither in case they could have a Satisfactory Account of the Country.[10]

John Ingersoll had a similar impression of Nova Scotia. Writing to Amos Botsford at Halifax, he expressed his fear that "Larger fees, and a better bred people will be great allurements for your stay. – Those inducements must be very operative on your Mind, & believe me Sir have their force on me for a removal thither. – I want much to live in a style above what may be expected in Connecticut."[11] After the war, William Donaldson, finding business bad in the new states and prospects worse, and, almost incidentally, expressing his wish to live under the British government, eventually left the United States and settled on the St John.[12] In his diary Captain Booth had commented on a Mrs N. who had come to Halifax in 1776, returned to New York, and then, upon its evacuation, came to Shelburne: "it seems as if the advantage of Trade in those troublesome times had been the object in View."[13]

There were many such who could qualify as loyalists, but who came to Nova Scotia as the result of a speculative choice. There were others who could not qualify as refugees but who saw in Nova Scotia a source of opportunity. Surrounding themselves with a cloud of anglophilia, they wrote of their desire to come to Nova Scotia in order to live under the crown and the British system of government.

In their letters from America they would write of the madness of the new experiment, the glory of living under the king's flag, and casually test the waters of economic opportunity in Nova Scotia by gentle hints and questions.

Danice Rindge wrote to John Wentworth that bad reports from Nova Scotia had prevented many from removing who had planned to go.[14] The New York agents mentioned the many applications from friends outside the lines who would to go Nova Scotia if they could only obtain grants of land.[15] To Thomas Hassara, the uncertainty of many of the Nova Scotia loyalists as to whether they would receive their land grants would "Drive thousands of them out of This country," and moreover discourage thousands of Americans from coming. Their motivation for coming, according to Hassara, was their desire to live under a royal government, but more particularly to escape the high taxes and depressed economy in the United States.[16] Rev. Samuel Andrews planned to bring his Wallingford, Connecticut, congregation to Nova Scotia. He and his principal parishioners, having formed a group of adventurers immediately after the war, wrote to Parr asking for lands and rations. Parr granted them a warrant of survey for lands at Chedabucto, but receiving no word from Britain concerning their request, could not help them with provisions, a fact which discouraged most from coming, "as many of them were unable to proceed without the Aid of Government."[17]

Free provisions, which were looked upon by the British government as a means of preventing disaster among refugees who had no choice but the cold shelter of Nova Scotia, were looked upon by these late loyalists and non-loyalists as the *sine qua non*. They would come to Nova Scotia only if they could do better in Nova Scotia. Mary Peters, writing from New Haven, exhibited the ambivalence, and the tendency to place an economic price upon patriotism, of such immigrants. She spoke of the collapse of commerce in New Haven and the ensuing hard times, and added, "If we go to N. Scotia meet we must the difficulties that always attend Settlers in N Countrys if we stay where we are we can but only Starve."[18] Nova Scotia was less a refuge to these people than a possibility of greater opportunity, and if it was not that, it was nothing.

These prospective immigrants at least paid lip service to the crown, but beyond them were those who could be classified as neither loyalists nor sympathizers. They simple saw Nova Scotia as where the action was. Phelps Devenport reported in April 1786 that "Emigrations are talk'd of here to Nova Scotia and Cape Breton – whether any but Bankrupts will go I can't say."[19] Sir Guy Carleton, writing during the exodus, expressed the belief that Americans, not getting into the British trade and aware of the advantages in trade the people of the province would possess, "are now endeavoring to form connections with them, and numbers are desirous of settling among them."[20] So great was the number of applications and the sympathy of the local officials that by the spring of 1786 Lord Sydney had to chastise Governor Parr for the encouragement he had given to such groups as the Nantucket whalers, and to order him not to encourage any more such American emigration in the future.[21]

These were the non-loyalists, or if loyalists, those who had a choice and chose Nova Scotia because it appeared better than the place they were leaving. Because of the variety and complexity of their motives, their actions are not easily understood. They remained, however, a definite minority. The majority who came to Nova Scotia had to leave their former homes because of their commitment to the crown. Most of them were what Harvey would label as true loyalists, supporters of a losing side and casualties of a civil war. There is little difficulty in documenting the losses suffered by these people. There were many like John Swift, who had lost an estate, served in the war, been captured, and upon coming to Nova Scotia had the prospect of receiving only a plot of land and provisions.[22] The southern loyalists studied by Carole Troxler are remarkable for the similarity of their experiences. A large percentage of the North Carolinians, for example, fought at Moore's Creek Bridge early in the war, were consequently imprisoned or forced to go into hiding, had their property confiscated, joined the British cause in either the militia or the provincial regiments when the opportunity came, and, at the war's end, made their way to Nova Scotia where they received moderate grants of land.[23] Daniel Mathews of New York, who had held office and was therefore considered guilty of high treason by the rebels, appealed to Parr's "established Character for universal benevolence, but more particularly so Towards His Majesty's faithful Subjects who have risqued Their Lives and lost their property by their attachment to their Lawful Sovereign."[24] Thousands of similar refugees typified what would become the traditional image of the loyalist. Out of a sense of loyalty they had remained the king's friends, and had been driven from the land for this friendship.

It is apparent from the foregoing account that the motives of these immigrants, loyalist and non-loyalist, ranged all the way from pathetic necessity to naked opportunism. Yet they are all a part of this story for they were all brought to Nova Scotia by the war and its outcome. They were part of a single phenomenon, the loyalist wave tumbling over and altering the shores of Nova Scotia.

Their origins were as mixed as their motives. Shelburne's population, "bred and used to live in great towns," came chiefly from the major cities along the coast.[25] The loyalists of Annapolis, according to Jacob Bailey, came chiefly from New York, Philadelphia, the Jersies, and Connecticut. Of those in Annapolis whose place of residence was given in Captain Hunt's return, the majority came from New York state. Guysborough, like most loyalist settlements in Nova Scotia, was a mixed bag, containing the Carolinians of Cumberland's Regiment, the combination of New Yorkers and southerners in the British Legion, the Scots and Germans of the 60th, the few Scots of the 71st, the mixed group of the Civil Department, and the St Augustine loyalists. Digby, with a population more civilian than Guysborough, had a varied assortment from nearly all the states, but consisted "chiefly [of] natives of New York and New Jersey."[26]

Because of the lack of data on most individual loyalists in Nova Scotia, no authoritative analysis can be made of their places of birth. Information on them can be found in Lorenzo Sabine's study, in the published claims of loyalists in Nova Scotia, and in the land grant petitions. Each has dangerous faults. Sabine's study contains little more than a hundred names of Nova Scotian loyalists whose places of birth are given. The claims, although giving more information on more loyalists, still must be handled gingerly, for the claimants are not necessarily representative of the loyalists in general. The land grant petitions state or imply the origins of over 1,200 heads of family. Although they represent a substantial proportion of the loyalists, these numbers must be treated very cautiously. Over 500 of those named had settled in Sydney County, yet although Shelburne contained almost half of the loyalists in Nova Scotia, only five named in Shelburne indicated their former places of residence.[27] With so few from Shelburne represented, the figures derived from the land claims can lead to serious distortion. However, by studying the three sources in conjunction with each other and with the comments of contemporary observers, one can try to surmise, in very general terms, the origins of the Nova Scotian loyalists.

Since a few states produced many loyalists during the war, while others produced very few, the loyalists in Nova Scotia follow roughly, in terms of origin, the profile of those who remained loyal during the war. C.H. Van Tyne, in studying the loyalist claims, found that "Over one third, then, in a miscellaneous list of Loyalists, were from New York; and the next state in order was South Carolina, with only ... one third the number in New York."[28] The origins of those who made their way to Nova Scotia and New Brunswick conform roughly to this pattern, although varying from it and from each other in rather interesting ways. New Brunswick, for example, had a smaller percentage of southerners and New Englanders than that indicated by the loyalist claims in general. Nova Scotia had more southerners.

New York had the largest representation of loyalists in the province. Although only 28 per cent of the claimants filing in Nova Scotia, and the same percentage of Sabine's loyalists, were from New York, of the 469 petitioners for land who gave their place of residence, 41 per cent came from New York. A total of 769 men were identified simply by regiment, and many of these would have been from New York. The Shelburne loyalists would increase this New York presence, for both Parr and Benjamin Marston stress the preponderance of New Yorkers at Shelburne.[29] Jacob Bailey had also described the heavy representation in the Annapolis region, and hundreds of Westchester loyalists were settled in Cumberland County.[30]

Of the other middle colonies, Nova Scotia had fewer from New Jersey than the 22 per cent that E.C. Wright found in New Brunswick. In general the New Jersey provincials were located on the St John. Although 14 per cent of the claimants in Nova Scotia had come from New Jersey, only 7 per cent of Sabine's group were from that state, and only 2 per cent of the land claim petitioners. Yet many of the loyalists around Tusket and Yarmouth were from Elizabeth, NJ.[31] Wilson refers to the heavy New Jersey representation at Digby, as does Jacob Bailey in Annapolis.[32] And a sizeable number of Van Buskirk's New Jersey volunteers came with their families to Shelburne.[33] There were fewer from Pennsylvania. Of the claimants in Nova Scotia, 7.2 per cent were from that state. Only 5 per cent of Sabine's Nova Scotian loyalists came from there, while the land grants mention none.[34] There were probably some loyalists from Delaware, although none is found in the claims, land grant petitions, or Sabine's group.

The New England states seem to have been represented more by quality than quantity, leadership than numbers. The Lloyd's Neck group of Loyalists organized at New York to settle around the Bay of Fundy chose chiefly New Englanders to lead them. And Parr mentioned the troubles he had with the New England element in the province.[35] E.C. Wright suggests that Nova Scotia would have had more loyalists from New England than New Brunswick had, for some would have remained after the Boston evacuation to attract others. Most of the New Englanders, however, came with the evacuation of New York and would have been attracted less by the few survivors of the 1776 exodus than by the same motives as others clearing New York. The area is disproportionately represented in Sabine's sketches, much more weakly in the other sources. Of Sabine's group, 8 per cent came from New Hampshire. That state, however, is named in only 1 per cent of the claims filed in Nova Scotia and only 0.2 per cent of the land grant petitions mentioning residence. New Hampshire loyalists probably accounted for from 1 to 2 per cent of the loyalists in Nova Scotia. Rhode Island, with only 0.5 per cent of the claims, 1 per cent of Sabine's loyalists, and 0.6 per cent of the land grant petitions, made only a minute contribution. Although referred to by several observers, including Jacob Bailey and Samuel Peters, Connecticut loyalists in Nova Scotia filed less than 2 per cent of the published claims, 5 per cent of those mentioned in Sabine, and none of the land grant petitions, markedly less than the 13 per cent found in New Brunswick by Wright. The greatest number of New England loyalists in Nova Scotia were from Massachusetts, although the sources used vary widely as to the percentage. The land claims turn up only a tiny 1.3 per cent who mention coming from that state. A massive 44 per cent of Sabine's selection came from Massachusetts, a distortion almost as extreme on the other end of the scale as that of the petitions. Perhaps more acceptable are the published claims by the Nova Scotia loyalists, 14 per cent of whom came from Massachusetts. For all of New England, then, the sources used vary wildly from the 2 per cent of the petitions to the 58 per cent of Sabine's loyalists. As with Massachusetts, one is tempted to accept the percentage found in the published claims as more representative. Of the claimants 17 per cent came from New England. There is little reason to assume the proportion in Nova Scotia was as high as the 22 per cent that Wright found in New Brunswick.

One prominent feature of the refugee population in Nova Scotia is the considerable number who came from the Carolinas. Maryland was represented by only 1 per cent of the claimants and 1 per cent of Sabine's loyalists, while none of the land grant petitions mentions the colony. Virginia was named in 4 per cent of the published claims for Nova Scotia. Although only a fraction of 1 per cent of the land petitioners stated their origin as Georgia, almost 3 per cent of the Nova Scotia claimants were from that state. North Carolina, although contributing only 1 per cent of Sabine's loyalists and 3.6 per cent of the claimants, was mentioned in 32 per cent of those petitions stating a former residence. South Carolina, with only 1 per cent of Sabine's group, was represented by 23 per cent of the claimants and 24 per cent of the petitioners. What is even more marked is the fact that only 467 of the petitioners gave a former residence. Another 710 identified themselves by regiment, while 59 were listed as St Augustine loyalists. Many of these 769 refugees were southerners.

These figures are at least indicative that a sizeable portion of the loyalists came from the south. Carole Troxler states that the loyalists from the Carolinas and Georgia whom she could find and identify made up "at least 7.3 percent of the white Nova Scotia Loyalist immigrants."[36] This is a bedrock figure. If account is also taken of the Virginia and Maryland loyalists and of the figures found in the claims and land grant petitions, it appears likely that as much as 15 per cent of the white loyalists could have come from the southern colonies. One must add to this presence the black loyalists who made up at least 10 per cent of the total refugee population of Nova Scotia; almost all were southerners, and most of them came from Virginia and South Carolina.[37]

Another marked characteristic of the refugees in Nova Scotia is the number of non-Americans. Even among the Americans there appears to be a relatively high percentage of foreign-born. The claims reveal 22 per cent who mention that they were born outside America.[38] Of Troxler's Carolina and Georgia loyalists, a remarkable 72 per cent of those whose place of birth was recorded came from Scotland, Germany, and Ireland.[39] But a large number were not American at all, either by birth or residence. Of the 1,236 petitioners who gave some indication of their origins 20 per cent were regular troops disbanded in Nova Scotia. This figure is supported by the findings of W.O. Raymond.[40].

It is extremely difficult to estimate the origins of the loyalists in Nova Scotia, since the lack of information on so many makes extrapolation from the available sources a hazardous process. Nevertheless, from the sources available some broad generalizations can be made. Of those coming to Nova Scotia for land and a new life, about 20 per cent were not American loyalists or refugees at all, but rather disbanded regulars and their dependents. Of the American refugees it can be cautiously estimated that at least 40 per cent came from New York state, another 15 per cent from the other middle colonies. To put it another way, probably a majority of Nova Scotia loyalists, although a slim majority, came from just two colonies, New York and New Jersey. It is also estimated that no more than 20 per cent came from New England, and about 25 per cent, black and white, from the southern colonies. Since the strong representation from the middle colonies was to be expected, what stands out in Nova Scotia is the comparatively high percentage of regulars and southerners.

Numbers, however, did not necessarily represent influence. New Englanders, both in leadership and articulated protest, seemed far more visible in the early years than Carolinians. Moreover, there is a marked difference between those who came and those who stayed.

Many of the Carolinians in Guysborough and the regulars throughout the province soon drifted away. Since many of the New Yorkers went to Shelburne, the collapse of that centre would also have led to a decline in the numbers and influence of loyalists from that state.

Nevertheless, the question of origin is important, not only as an historical and genealogical problem, but also because of the influence it had upon these people while they were in the colony. Of importance to the loyalist was the identification of friend and enemy along old colonial or state lines. There was a sense of cohesion among those from the same colony, and of conflict with outsiders from other colonies. The identification by old colonial loyalties was to be a factor in the discord and lack of homogeneity within and among the loyalist communities.

It has now become almost a truism that the great majority of the loyalists in British North America were neither rich persons, Harvard graduates, professionals, nor commercial giants. The elite of prerevolutionary American society did not take up residence en masse in Nova Scotia, although there were certainly people of stature among the refugees. E.C. Wright observes that "Halifax may have attracted rather more of the governing, wealthy and professional groups than did the area north of the Bay of Fundy, though it is not easy to demonstrate that it had a larger share. The older settlements in the Annapolis Valley were also a drawing card for many, who, like Edward Winslow, found quarters there in 1783, and who, unlike that gentleman, remained where they first found shelter."[41]

Halifax as capital, hub, and established centre would draw many with money and influence, from the Sandemanians of 1776 who brought "substantial quality"[42] to the glittering social additions of the postwar years described in the Winslow papers. One indication of this affluence is the fact that despite the large number of loyalists mentioned in the sources as residing there, surprisingly few were receiving the king's provisions. There were pockets of gentility beyond Halifax. In King's County, for example, forty-nine of the 112 loyalists were commissioned officers, nine others received grants of at least 1,000 acres, and of the rest only seventeen were given less than 500 acres.[43] The loyalist additions to Annapolis included such "people of fashion" as the Delanceys.[44] David Seabury was a merchant there, "Brother to the Bishop of Connecticut, who w^t this Family are of the first rank, and very much respected in this place."[45]

Shelburne seems to have attracted an ambitious commercial class. The houses and mercantile establishments were both impressive and expensive in terms of capital outlay. There were men like Henry

Bolton who could spend £500 sterling on water frontage, buildings, and wharf without yet acquiring the water rights. He was seeking "a Grant of the water in the front of said Lott which will be the means of enabling him to support his young and tender family."[46] Shelburne's newspapers indicated that "the merchants and tradesmen catered to people used to a high standard of living. The long list of articles offered for sale would almost appear to have been stocked for a clientele in either New York or Philadelphia rather than for that of an isolated community in the wilds of Nova Scotia."[47] Benjamin Marston, condemning those whom he regarded as the ignorant, insolent masses at Shelburne, felt sympathy for "the distress of the sensible feeling part, who have come from easy situations to encounter all the hardships of a new plantation."[48]

That the loyalists of Nova Scotia, like those of British North America in general, were not simply an upper-class fragment is clearly shown by the land grants. Of the thousands of grants made, only 110 immigrants were considered of sufficient status to be eligible for the 1,000 acres given to field officers or civilians of similar standing. Very few of these were granted in Shelburne because the hunger there was for water frontage. In the rest of Nova Scotia, however, only 105 loyalists were considered of sufficient status to warrant 1,000 acres.[49] "The Loyalist Patricians," W.S. MacNutt notes, "for the most part went to England and remained there or found service elsewhere in the King's dominions."[50]

Shelburne, the loyalist hope, was marked by the prevalence of the lower class. Rev. William Walter described them as "mostly poor, & consist of persons of very various Characteristics, Dispositions & religious Sentiments."[51] Marston, whose diary is the most detailed source for the Shelburne loyalists, frequently criticized the people for lacking taste, energy, education, and leadership. "They have no men of abilities among them. Their Captains, chosen out of their body at New York, are of the same class with themselves – most of them mechanics, some few have been ship masters, they are the best men they have." These comments had been made during the summer of 1783. Yet the late arrivals of the fall of that year Marston found far worse than the early loyalists. Ultimately, after being driven out of Shelburne, Marston decided to go to New Brunswick where all his New England friends were. "Shelburne is composed of such a mixed multitude, so very few people of education among them, that it will take me all the rest of my life to get myself well accommodated to their ways of acting and thinking."[52] As chief surveyor in Shelburne, the man had been pushed hard and had found himself under great stress. There had to be friction between Marston and the settlers, and because of the rush of business, the confusion and frustration of all parties, he was inevitably on a short fuse. Aware of this, one accepts not the extreme nature of his comments but their basic premise, that Shelburne was not composed of an elite nor did it contain a larger core of such immigrants than the average port, but that it was in general the home of a working-class and lower middle-class population.

Like Shelburne, none of the other major loyalist communities was marked by the predominance of "the quality." Guysborough, with its heavy military population, had a very small group of officers and people of similar status. The great majority, however, were either humble refugees or men from the ranks. A similar situation existed in Pictou, settled by the 82nd and 84th regiments. Enlisted men lack status and money. Many of the 84th, in fact, had been immediately recruited upon arrival in America. "They were not only in poverty, but many were in debt for their passage."[53] Antigonish fared no better. Benjamin Marston had a very low opinion of the officers of Hierlihy's regiment. "Such another set of riotous vagabonds never were."[54] Nor was the Annapolis valley a mecca for gentlefolk. Bailey found that among the early loyalists there "only four or five ... either by fortune or education, have any pretensions to politeness."[55]

Evidence of the preponderance of a plebeian element in the loyalist communities is also to be found in the occupations of the refugees. Of Troxler's southerners, "almost all were small farmers before the Revolution."[56] Concerning the loyalists at Shelburne, John Sayre noted that "a very large proportion ... are Farmers and useful Artificers and among them a number of Merchants and Mariners."[57] Marston, less kind, did make an important point: the people of Shelburne were city people. "They are upon the whole a collection of characters very unfit for the business they have undertaken. Barbers, Taylors, Shoemakers and all kinds of mechanics, bred and used to live in great towns, they are inured to habits very unfit for undertakings which require hardiness, resolution, industry and patience."[58]

This observation is supported by an examination of the members of the original Port Roseway Association, the small and select group who planned to have Port Roseway for themselves, and whose plans were upset by the deluge of later loyalists. In the original group, of the 201 whose occupations are mentioned, approximately 75 per cent worked with their hands. There were fifteen listed under the ambiguous term mariner, seventeen merchants, four planters, three who combined the occupations of merchant and tailor, and one physician. This was the extent of the professional and entrepreneurial classes. Seventy-one farmers and only one fisherman were listed, both figures surprisingly low when one considers the eighteenth-century American economy. The rest were mostly urban skilled labour. There were three bricklayers, three bakers, a gunsmith, thirty-four carpenters, one stationer, five blacksmiths, one pumpmaker, three glaziers, two cutlers, one cooper, one bookbinder, one cabinet-maker, one wheelwright, thirteen tailors, one tallow-chandler, one tobacco-maker, one sadler, two grocers, one harness-maker, one shoemaker, four sawyers, two millwrights, one goldsmith, a hatter, a periwig-maker, a mason, and an engraver.[59] What stands out is that they were mostly craftsmen suited to an urban setting, and that a sizeable proportion of them were in the service trade.

The loyalists in and around Annapolis were described by Jacob Bailey in one letter as "chiefly Merchants and Mechanics from New York."[60] In another letter Bailey was more detailed and vivid, describing them as a very mixed bag of

disbanded soldiers and seamen, half pay officers, merchants, mechanicks, farmers, gentlemen formerly of independent fortunes now reduced to poverty – persons whose birth and education rank them among the lowest of the vulgar, suddenly enriched by spirited iniquity during the late commotions ... magistrates who heretofore served his majesty and their country, with fidelity, affection, honour and integrity, without support ... [and] multitudes advanced in life with large families and no prospect of obtaining subsistence.[61]

A return of Captain Hunt's company embarked for Annapolis Royal contains the occupations of thirty-eight of the men. Ten of them were listed as farmers, nine as yeomen, six as carpenters. In this small group, four were merchants. There were also three cordwainers, a shoemaker, mason, miller, butcher, mariner, and tailor.[62] Again one notes the relative weakness of agrarian representation in comparison with the colonial economy, and the strength of service trades dependent upon city or town life. Guysborough, Antigonish, and Pictou, on the other hand, were less civilian, with fewer tradesmen and more military, including disbanded regulars and remnants of provincial corps, the vast majority of whom were from the ranks with just a sprinkling of officers.

The presence in large numbers of the enlisted man in the more military settlements, the tradesman in the more civilian, simply confirms the fact that the loyalist communities in Nova Scotia were not preponderantly the home of an upper stratum of American society. The communities were for the most part cross-sections of the American social pyramid, and the weight of numbers existed at the base of that pyramid, in the lower and lower-middle classes.

In background, the Nova Scotian loyalists were noteworthy in several respects. They tended to be more urban than American society in general. They were also distinguished by the strength of southern representation and the comparatively high percentage of blacks. Another feature of the body of "loyalists" who received grants in Nova Scotia was the sizeable proportion who were not loyalists in the accepted sense at all, signifying those whose allegiance had led them into exile, either voluntary or enforced. On the contrary, many were disbanded regulars, while for others exile was not the price of loyalty but rather a response to the lure of opportunity.

What emerges as most important from a study of their background is perhaps the complexity of this people and the frailty of classi-fication. In status, occupation, origin, motivation, and wartime expe-rience, they were a markedly varied and divergent group of people, having little in common with each other but their abrupt presence in Nova Scotia and their fragile bond of "loyalism."

CHAPTER SIX

Loyalist Attitudes

Like their backgrounds, the reactions and attitudes of the loyalists in Nova Scotia were varied and complex. There were certain views common among them, for they had to a great extent shared a common experience. Most had lost more than a war. They had lost their homes and property, they had lost their birthright, and, long before the official peace, they had lost their faith in their cause. This loss of faith and sense of betrayal enveloped the loyalists as they set sail for Nova Scotia in "this hour of Darkness, Calamity & Confusion." There were brave epithets cast over their shoulders, about quitting "this damned country with pleasure," but they had not left because of an abhorrence for republican principles. They left because they could not stay. They were "wretched outcasts of America and Britain."[1] They reacted to the elements of their exile with a common instinct and a common rhetoric shaped in the crucible of revolution, and significantly tempered by this sense of desertion. But the bond of allegiance encompassed many types. These loyalists had fought the war for a variety of personal reasons. The postwar release from the centripetal force of their loyalty allowed the differences among them to emerge, and the harsh environment of "Nova Scarcity" accentuated them.

They had come to Nova Scotia because they had little other choice. It was the most accessible land in which to resettle. Canada was a distant interior wilderness, inhabited by people of a different faith and language. Some had gone to the West Indies, but most considered it an alien land of excessive heat and yellow fever. For different reasons, Britain was also an alien land. It was too complex a society, and without money and connections, wrote Jonathan Sewell, "the Man is lost – he is Nothing – less than Nothing and Vanity – & his Contemplation of his own comparative Littleness, is Vexation of Spirit."[2] Moreover, they were Americans, marked by the land in many subtle ways. To the northeast lay Nova Scotia, a short journey by sea, where rumour had it that good land was available. It was on the periphery of the world they had known, with the promise that only a young colony can have, a royal colony, moreover, within a temperate climate. They had little time to study this land of fog and exile, and yet because they were being expelled there was a certain bravado in their attitude to the land. Loyalists who had gone earlier, and agents of various groups who had come to scout the colony, sent back encouraging reports. The land was good, the cattle plentiful, the taxes few, the government cheap. The country was strategically located for the fisheries, the West Indies trade, and the British market, protected from the Americans by a royal government, and assured of rapid development. Joseph Pynchon, in his report as agent to the Port Roseway Association in January 1783, discussed in some detail the tremendous advantages of Port Roseway over both Halifax and the New England ports. "The Governor and Sir Andrew are both of the same opinion, that it will be one of the *Capital ports* in America."[3] There was, moreover, some small consolation in the fact that so many loyalists were going to Nova Scotia. Part of the promise of the land lay in these people who would settle it.

Letters from loyalists in England seemed to confirm their wisdom in choosing Nova Scotia. The disillusionment of two friends of Timothy Ruggles concerning their plight in England had induced him to come to Nova Scotia.[4] A friend of Jacob Bailey had written him concerning his appointment to the mission in Annapolis. "You are now on *good bottom* and must be much more happy than tho' you were here, dancing attendance for an uncertain pittance."[5]

To many Nova Scotia was a mixed blessing, with the present discomfort outweighed by the promise of the future. Timothy Ruggles, in the Annapolis Valley, was very much impressed with the fertility of the soil and boastful of the apples and other produce he was growing. Gideon White spoke as favourably of Chedabucto: "That situation is one of the best in this country." Edward Winslow found the country crowded and expensive, and yet a place of opportunity for a man – like himself – of talent and ambition. Jason Courtney was very discouraged on his arrival at Shelburne, yet again he perceived the considerable potential.[6]

The reality could be obscured by the promise of both the colony and the people settling it, and what sometimes emerged was a loser's wishful thinking that it would eclipse the republic they had left. They might be "laying the foundations of a New Empire" and establishing "a place chosen by the Lords elect."[7] But this sense of mission seemed limited to a few and threatened by the harsh reality of resettlement. Most loyalists were not so sanguine and would not have questioned the reference to "Nova Scarcity." "All our golden promises have vanished," one of them ruefully observed. "We were taught to believe this place was not barren and foggy, as had been represented, but we find it ten times worse ... It is the most inhospitable climate that ever mortal set foot on. The winter is of insupportable length and coldness, only a few spots fit to cultivate, and the land is covered with a cold, spongy moss, instead of grass, and the entire country is wrapt in the gloom of perpetual fog."[8]

The letters going back to the United States began to echo this assessment. A Philadelphia newspaper in 1783 noted the changing view of Nova Scotia. "Many of the refugees who have settled at Port Roseway have wrote their friends in New York by no means to come to that place."[9] Captain Callbeck could not congratulate Edward Winslow on his arrival in Halifax, for that would be "a very chilly and unmeaning compliment, the Country you have left is in every respect (but as to Loyalty) a Paradise in comparison."[10] Joshua Chandler, writing from the United States in July 1783, expected to see all of his people back within three months, for "Nova Scotia is not the place for Happiness, or I am greatly deceived."[11] And at Shelburne, especially, the dream of the loyalists was being shouldered aside by reality.

Nor was their opinion of the Nova Scotian any better. It was often contemptuous, patronizing, and self-righteous. The Nova Scotians were lazy, "languid wretches" who had been forced into some industry through shame at the loyalists' accomplishments and energies. A loyalist traveller through Nova Scotia in the summer of 1783 found that "the people seem to live and let tomorrow provide for itself. You see a sameness in the countenance of everyone except the Refugees who are quite a Different set of people." They were also shrewd to the point of greediness, and willing to turn the refugees' tragedy to their own advantage. To S.S. Blowers, they were "accumulating wealth at a great rate by the exorbitant prices which they extort from the Strangers."[12]

Occasionally, however, beneath this generalized dislike more immediate impressions of the Nova Scotian and his distinctive character can be found. In a journal kept by Mather Byles III, there is a description of a brief visit among some natives of Yarmouth "to see their manner of living," a description which tells something of both Bluenose and loyalist.

The houses, or rather huts, are very miserable, some thing like those inhabited by the French people on the road to Birch Cove – I stopped at four different cottages to see their manner of living, and amuse myself with a little *right down Yankeyism* – In one of them liv'd a New England shoemaker, who immediately after the first salutations began to question me *concerning the faith* – He told me he had been putting up his petition for rain "And I dare say" says he "we shall have a *spurt* before to morrow evening." – He asked my opinion of Allan's treatise, said he begun it: but finding it was not *right sound doctrine* he *hove* it by again. Allan, he says, died in New England last spring. His wife was receiving a visit from a young lady of about twenty, who had travelled from a back country settlement called Zebouge for her education – She goes to school, and learns all fine sort of work and siche-like.[13]

Byles's superior tone in amusing himself with a simple yet shrewd Yankee tells us less of the typical Nova Scotian than of those characteristics which the loyalist was beginning to classify as typically Nova Scotian. Yet this type of description is infrequent, for the loyalist at this time could not, without difficulty, measure anyone except by the yardstick of the rebellion and its tragic consequences. It was thought that because of the peculiar attitude of the Nova Scotian towards the rebellion, "their envy and malignity will induce 'em to throw every obstacle and impediment in your way. I am astonished that they have not art to conceal the principles by which they are actuated." As much as any of the rebelling states, they had been "King Killers" during the late war and had lived with "loyalty upon the tip of their tongues and rebellion in their hearts." Nor had the cessation of hostilities weakened this feeling, for they were still "inclined to favor the Americans in other words are Rebells," and Halifax was "that source of Republicanism" that nourished the rest of the colony.[14] "The people in this Country having catched the Contagion early and indeed I wonder it has remain'd in the stamp of Government as ⅞ths of the people are Bigotted to the American Cause ... The people in this country don't deny their principles and are in general like the same class of N. England from which they ransome for Debt."[15]

Yet the Bluenose Nova Scotian was merely an incidental factor in the early struggle for survival. The British government and its efforts were all-important and loomed far larger in the loyalist mind. The attitude of the loyalists towards the crown in these early years was one of utter dependence and great distrust. They feared not receiving what they would treat with contempt when received. Because of the repetitious petulance of many of their requests and comments it is easy to forget the prevailing mood of desperation. It was there before they left New York, from the time of the initial announcement that only six months' provisions would be issued. And it was there during the early period in Nova Scotia. Although there were complaints about receiving "nothing here but His Majesties' rotten pork and unbaked flour,"[16] the fear was in not receiving the rotten pork at all. Although provisions were continued for three years or more, the loyalists were never really certain how long the bounty would continue, and thus memorials such as that of the magistrates of Shelburne in January 1784, asking for a continuance, were common.[17] That it was often inadequate or unequally distributed was the crux of many loyalist complaints throughout the colony. Charles Morris, the surveyor general, writing to Amos Botsford of Digby in September 1783, referred to the discouragement resulting from the government's failure to send the promised supplies. And as late as 1785 Mather Byles had "an abundance of distressful stories from Shelburne, Passamaquoddy, St. Mary's Bay, &c, complaining of the shortness of provisions & the danger they are in of starving."[18] To a harried officialdom the loyalists appeared as insatiable ingrates. They complained loud and long about promises delayed in the keeping or not kept, and yet they met extra concessions with something bordering on disdain, as for instance on this occasion: "It is but a few weeks ago I heard of your Regiment being fixed on the British Establishment; I sincerely congratulate you on the event; Yet I confess it is no more than what equity and justice demanded."[19]

And yet their apparent ingratitude should be understood in the context of their claims, and their weighing of what they had sacrificed against what they had received for that sacrifice. If they were too grateful, they would be selling short the only marketable commodity they really had, their loyalty. The loyalists believed that Britain had sacrificed them for the sake of peace, and in Nova Scotia they were filled with a strong fear that she might therefore be moved less by gratitude than by guilt. If this were so, it would be necessary to keep before Britain the uniqueness of their loyalty and the price they had paid for it. Perhaps there was a trace of this pragmatism in their self-consciously strenuous celebration of such loyalist holy days as the king's birthday, and "the anniversary of the glorious and ever memorable TWELVE OF APRIL, 1782," the day on which Admiral Rodney had defeated a French fleet in the West Indies, an event celebrated, at least in Shelburne, "with all the Joyous mirth due, from every loyal subject, on so great an occasion."[20] Perhaps there was a slightly pragmatic as well as emotional basis for their hostility to the Nova Scotians, whose rebellious tendencies made an excellent foil for the loyalty of the refugees.

This stress was to be found in almost every letter to or concerning government officials, whether it was Charles Inglis's reference to "that sovereign for whom they had sacrificed everything but a good conscience," or the memorial to Parr from the Port Roseway Associates, "who have been great Sufferers in the present Unhappy Contest." The appeal was to be found most clearly expressed in the briefs drawn up for indemnification, in which the nobility of the loyalists stands in stark contrast to the quibbling of the British government over compensation for the loss of fortunes that "have been sacrificed by the State itself to the public peace and safety."[21]

If the loyalists' anger towards the crown had to be controlled, and expressed only indirectly through agents in London, their attitude towards local officials could be shown more directly. And it was. To the loyalists, the officials in local control of the king's generosity were indifferent to their plight or interested in it only as a source of exploitation. At quite an early stage, the spokesmen for the Port Roseway Associates were bitterly complaining of the treatment received and the obstacles placed in the way of settlement. Governor Parr was early accused of being unwilling to escheat, and faulted for both the shortage and the incompetence of his surveyors. In defending himself to the home government against such charges, he simply underlined the wide extent of them. There were constant clashes between surveyor and loyalist, in which "the Surveyors (poor devils we are) are reflected upon in the Grossest Manner."[22]

Moreover, government officials were frequently charged with procuring fees, specifically against the king's orders. Benjamin Marston, who rarely praised the loyalists of Shelburne, had as little use for Halifax officialdom. He commented on the arrival of a customs man from Halifax, "Mr. Binney was sent there to pick a little money out of the people's pockets under pretense of entering their vessels."[23] Even Guy Carleton was forced to complain to Parr that the surveyors and officials "are said to expect *presents* for the performance of their duty, which many of the settlers are not able to afford, but without which I am credibly informed, their applications are nevertheless neglected. Partialities in the general distribution of lands are also much complained of & attributed to the same unwarrantable conduct."[24] That few government officials were exempt from the hostility of the loyalists is indicated by Charles Morris's comment on the "unmeritted ungenerous complaints which have been made against all the officers of Government without Exception."[25]

Few loyalists felt that it was any part of their function to help the surveyor in any way, unless paid to do so. This refusal to help was a frequent cause for complaint in Marston's diary, and a regular litany in the letter-book of Charles Morris.[26] By 1785 the government was reduced to threatening the loyalists with the loss of their lots to more cooperative refugees if they did not furnish the necessary assistance as axe and chain men.[27] Moreover, there appeared to be a double standard among some of the loyalists. If the government was obliged to be honest and conscientious towards them, it did not necessarily mean that they in turn had to be honest and conscientious towards the government. Benjamin Marston was, from the earliest days of Shelburne, concerned with the threat posed by speculators and adventurers. One of the simplest and favourite ploys was for officers to have minors and servants included in the application for lots.[28] General Campbell was forced to set up a new board to check into the many abuses and frauds in relation to the provisions. Loyalists were claiming for families who had long since departed, and Campbell finally had to order a complete muster of loyalists and soldiers in the colony to stop such abuses. This did not solve the problem, for many refugees left in the following spring, the frauds increased, and Campbell had to order another muster.[29] Nor had the speculation in land been deterred, for in 1785 Morris noted,"we are well assured the People in every District are disposing of their land for much less than it cost Govt for laying out and never mean to settle in the country but to make the most of us."[30]

Behind the surveyor stood the shadowy presence of the government at Halifax, and the loyalists distrusted both its power and its motives. According to Joseph Aplin, "The town of Halifax is that Source of Republicanism from whence many Towns in the Province, occasionally, draw fresh Supplies. it not only sends members for itself, but for many other Towns in very distant Parts – The interest and safety of the Loyalists therefore consists in Stripping this Town of its Superfluous Advantages."[31] Aplin also expressed some reservations concerning its impartiality: "From such d---md G---rs, S---ys! Courtiers and brothers in Law God Lord deliver us." Edward Winslow referred to the Halifax clique which controlled government and anything else worth controlling as "nabobs," and Jacob Bailey dismissed them as "a few self-interested republicans at the Metropolis."[32]

The inhabitants of Nova Scotia could be dismissed as Yankees, but the power brokers in Halifax were a little more complex and a lot less American. Governor Parr, Chief Justice Finucane, Charles Inglis, and some lesser officials had been born in Ireland. "Our Chief Justice is gone the way of all Flesh," Joseph Peters wrote in 1785, "so that there will be an easy Birth for some other (I suppose) Irishman." Several years later he again drew attention to the Irish influence. "Wright is a Paddy, as most of our rulers are in Church and State."[33]

The focal point for much of the loyalist contempt was Governor Parr, and the criticism ran from the patronizing to the scurrilous. Thomas Barclay found him a man of little strength, dominated by the opinions of his officials, "to whose Arguments the *good, weak* man lends too credulous an Ear." Joseph Aplin saw the governor as a "man of real benevolent Heart, but from the natural Flexibility of his Temper and Disposition is liable to be drawn, imperceptibly, into measures foreign to the Decisions of his own unbiassed Judgment, which, at best, is not an object of Envy." Both at least attributed kindness to Parr. Neither was as malicious as the non-loyalist Joseph Peters on the subject of governors "sent out to rule the People with moderation and Justice Agreable to their Gracious Master's Instructions; when once arrived on the Summit of this Dunghill, become at once of more consequence than, and totally regardless of the King himself, and attend to Nothing but Arbitrary Sway, enhancing their fortunes, gauming of Beef, guzzling of Wine and Carrassing the Whores! ... Wo unto thee O Land when the Govirnors and Rulers Drink Brandy in the morning."[34]

What the loyalists considered Parr's incompetence would have ensured their hostility toward a man who was the protégé of the hated Lord Shelburne. They felt, moreover, that part of the land destined for them had been granted away by Parr to the old inhabitants, and that he had sold out to the Halifax faction, who, according to Bailey, "by artifice and profound dissimulation acquired an influence over the governor and directed him to dispose of honours and emoluments according to their sovereign pleasures."[35] Parr's great sin lay not in accepting the existence of a powerful clique, but in accepting one not dominated by the leading loyalists. He did not welcome them quickly into the seats of power. Moreover, he demanded their physical presence to claim the land, and limited the land allotments to a size suitable only for "peasants" or the humbler loyalist. Consequently, one of their most cherished objectives was to secure the recall of John Parr, and to see the Executive Council and the assembly then purged and replaced by "honest Loyalists."[36]

Hostility towards local officials, although not always as intense as among the elite, was nevertheless an emotion experienced by most loyalists. As with their contempt for the Nova Scotian and the view of their sacrifice as a debt outstanding upon the British government, the degree to which it was experienced varied widely among them. Yet to some degree it was felt by all. Such views, shaped by their recent past, constituted a common loyalist attitude.

As important as their common fears, frustrations, and resentments, however, was their attitude to each other, for next to the republicans and nabobs of Nova Scotia, what the loyalist feared and distrusted most was another loyalist. One can take the notion of a typical loyalist attitude only so far, for there was no typical loyalist. The great exodus involved close to 20,000 individuals, a complete spectrum of backgrounds, mores, motives, and ambitions. There were the very rich and the very poor. There were ex-governors and major placemen and there were the dregs of the port towns. There were those who had supported Britain because their livelihood or aspirations depended upon it, and there were those who supported her by reason of a simple concern for loyalty and the rule of law. Some would carve out a career on the basis of their past misfortunes. Others would turn their backs on the past, to build their houses and clear their two hundred acres. There were those who had left early in the revolution, and there were those who had left only when they had to. There were the loyalists who had spent the war in the womb of New York, and those who had spent it in the dirty, dangerous campaigns of some of the provincial regiments. There were the opportunists and the desperate. And there were the "niggers" with their "black wenches," who could be hanged for stealing a bag of potatoes, and whose frolics and dances could be prohibited by local by-law. Many of these came as servants, but within months reverted to their original status; some of them were free, to be rented out on five-year contracts, to be burned out when they became uppity and sold their labour more cheaply than the whites.[37] They were all loyalists, and the schisms among them were as marked as the attitudes they shared towards the non-loyalist world.

There was a world into which the common loyalist would never be invited, a delightful world of banquets and concerts and influence. Mather Byles's journal for his sister portrays a society marked by relative affluence and gentility. The writer noted the buying of "a magnificent carpet for my grand Parlor: & on the 23d had the Pleasure of entertaining Refugee Friends from N York at Dinner." He described himself, "sick, weak & dispirited, & grievously exercised with a troublesome Succession of sore Boils," dragging himself off, as a mark of true loyalist respect for the queen's birthday, "to dinner at the Governor's & to a public Ball & splendid Supper in the Evening."[38] There is a letter from Captain Brownrigg to Gideon White describing an assembly night in Halifax and such major crises as quarrels over a partner for a minuet.[39] Sarah and Penelope Winslow recorded the gay life of the privileged. On Sarah's trip from New York, for example, Brook Watson, the commissary general, saw to it that she had "a thousand advantages that no other family has had," including "an excellent Vessell without one passenger but those we chose ourselves."

Concerning the house she occupied in Halifax, "I leave you to judge whether the rooms are not very good when I tell you that this day week General Fox with sixteen of our Friends dined with us with great convenience." Penelope Winslow, in a detached fashion, described the life of her friends in Halifax, "pursuing pleasure with ardour. Feasting, card playing & dancing is the great business of Life at Halifax, one eternal round ... The new Imported Ladies continue to be the Belles." The fairest belle of all was a refugee, Mrs Wentworth, in her gown of sylvan tissue with a train four yards long, and her hair and wrist ornamented with real diamonds. Yet such an exciting life could not obscure the tragedy of the late rebellion, or the courage with which these individuals had met it. "With becoming firmness I supported our first great reverse of fortunes," Penelope wrote. "I bid a long farewell to an elegant house, furniture, native place and all its pleasures ... The banishment to this ruder World, you are a witness I submitted to with some degree of cheerfulness."[40]

The humbler loyalists were also affected by the banishment. Perhaps they were not as sensitive as Miss Penelope. They were, however, very hungry. The backdrop for the social life of Sarah and Penelope was a town where almost every church, shed, and outhouse was being used as a shelter for destitute refugees, and where bread lines were a prominent part of the street scene. In the first years thousands survived on a diet of codfish, corn, and molasses, and hundreds died from lack of sanitation, food, or shelter.[41] While some were "pursuing pleasure with ardour," the ship *Clinton* lay at anchor during that first winter, "crowded like a sheep-pen" with destitute southerners, chiefly women and children. Nor was Halifax isolated in its misery. A child's impression of early Shelburne was of a place in which "strong, proud men wept like children, and lay down in their snowbound tents to die." A Miss Van Tyne "called on some of our friends in their tents ... I thought they did not look able to stand the coming winter, which proved a very hard one." At Port Mouton, Tarleton's Legion was living in tents or huts of sod and log, with clothes too few and blankets too thin for the coming winter. Annapolis was more fortunate in that there were existing buildings in which the loyalists could seek shelter. Bailey mentioned that several hundred were packed in the church, "although larger numbers could not be provided for." Isaac Browne described "the daily increase of the number of distressed & Starving Loyalists" at Annapolis in the fall of 1783. Throughout the colony, for the great majority of loyalists, the overriding concerns were finding enough food and shelter to survive the first winter, and the gnawing fear that if the promised supplies were not forthcoming, "Numbers must and will inevitably perish."[42]

While some of the more fortunate were chiefly concerned with placement and position, most were concerned solely with survival. They were all loyalists, but, motivated by different fears and different ambitions, their attitudes towards many facets of life in Nova Scotia would vary widely.

Religious affiliation exemplified this diversity of attitudes. Rev. William Walter found that Shelburne consisted "of persons of very various Characters Dispositions & religious Sentiments," and that only with difficulty could one "systemize" them under the Church of England.[43] A great many of the loyalists in Nova Scotia were not members of the Church of England at all, but even among the large percentage who were, a slight Americanization had occurred, which struck the missionaries of the Society for the Propagation of the Gospel as foreign and perhaps dangerous. The outstanding example of how the American way might differ from that of Nova Scotia was to be found in the protracted struggle between Walter and Rev. George Panton for control of the Church of England community in Shelburne. It exposed an inherent conflict among the loyalists between Old World and New World attitudes.

Panton had been rector of Trenton, New Jersey, and later chaplain of the Prince of Wales' American Volunteers. He had been invited by some of the leaders of the Port Roseway Associates to be minister to the refugees at Shelburne. He indicated his interest, and received both blessing and salary from the Society for the Preservation of the Gospel. Because of confusion over his intentions and the state of his health, some loyalists had assumed he was not going to take the position. Dr. William Walter, rector of Trinity Church in Boston, and later a chaplain with Delancey's Brigade, had written to the SPG in July 1783, stating that the people of the proposed settlement had no clergyman, and that he was offering his services as minister.[44] The ministers arrived in the community within two days of each other, both claiming to represent the Church of England in Shelburne, and each seeking support for his claim from parishioners, governor, and the SPG.

Panton based his claim upon the invitation of the leading loyalists and the SPG's approval of him as missionary. Walter displayed petitions from Shelburne to show that he was the people's choice, and had no doubt that the society, "on knowing the affectionate agreement which subsists between the people & me," would see that his claim was recognized. When neither the governor nor the SPG showed any enthusiasm for his claim, he placed increasing emphasis upon the necessity for popular support, insisting upon "the Privilege and the Right of the Parishioners by Law to chuse their own minister." His supporters insisted that he had been chosen and accepted "by the unanimous invitation of the members of the Church of England in Shelburne." As for the claim that Panton was supported by the leading figures in Shelburne, it was obvious that they gave him such support "only because they conceive it will please the governor whose favour in grants of land & Public Offices they may wish." Emphasis was also placed upon the fact that Panton had been one of the fifty-five "who solicited for no less, I believe, than five thousand acres each."[45]

In response to these attacks, Walter was accused by Panton of "opposing public authority." He was also accused of encouraging a "dangerous Tendency, as Opening an Avenue for a Majority of *Sectaries* to introduce Clergymen of Obvious Principles equally dangerous to the Church and Government." Panton's supporters placed more emphasis upon the need to rally around "King and Country," and upon the fact that "no *genuine* member of the Church of England, and principled Loyalist, can, consistently and conscientiously, oppose a public establishment, by proper authority, which interferes with no person's rights and that such opposition must arise from sinister views."[46]

Eventually Panton gave up the fight and left Shelburne, but the struggle had revealed a basic cleavage between the appeal to democratic principle and the appeal to authority, between the right of the parishioners to choose their minister, and the duty to support a public establishment and public authority. It also illustrated another aspect of the clash between the elite and the masses, for Panton's supporters stressed the "respectability" of their members, and Walter's followers criticized both Panton's association with the fifty-five and his supporters' desire to please the governor. Moreover, the fight revealed a new connotation being given to the term loyalist. It was no longer simply a term associated with past deeds and sacrifices. It was also intended to suggest certain principles currently held, such as support for king, country, and authority.

Throughout Nova Scotia, the Church of England failed to make the inroads it should have made among the loyalists. Although no great number of adherents were lost to the Dissenters, the church, by failing to touch the masses, did not make the gains that might have been expected in these chaotic times. It did not change to meet the new demands of pioneering communities, and it had too many missionaries less interested in bringing the Word to isolated hamlets than in the infighting for posts and patronage.[47]

There were many Presbyterians among the refugees. The Shelburne Presbyterians had petitioned William Pitt for government aid, because they could not carry the expense of church and minister, "Numerous tho' they are." In Rev. Hugh Fraser they had a minister who had been acting chaplain to the 71st Regiment during the revolution.[48] However, although it would retain the loyalty of the Scots, the Presbyterian Church's emphasis upon a professional clergy and a more orthodox organization, and its lack of missionaries, would preclude it from winning many new souls among the poorer loyalists.

Baptist churches were organized under David George, a negro preacher who had arrived in Halifax with a body of loyalists in 1784. He began preaching in Shelburne, "but I found the white people were against me ... The black people came from far and near; I kept on so every night in the week, and appointed a meeting for the first Lord's Day ... and a great number of white and black people came."[49] The Baptists were not alone in preaching to the negro loyalists. Phyllis Blakeley, in her article on Boston King, describes the Methodist interest in Birchtown, and the conversion of both King and his wife to Methodism. William Black, the prophet of Methodism in Nova Scotia, won many adherents among the loyalists. A large number had been influenced by Methodist teachings before coming to Nova Scotia. Some, such as Robert Barry, had served previously as preachers. He had organized a "class" shortly after Black's first visit to Shelburne. Joseph Tinkham wrote to Gideon White about Black's preaching and hoped "he made some of you Shelburnites better by his Preaching there." Freeborn Garretson, a missionary from the United States, could write from Shelburne in 1786, "Blessed be God, there have been many as clear and as powerful conversions in this township, as I have seen in any part of the States."[50]

In a land peopled so quickly and with so few surveyors there were bound to be innumerable conflicts and legal squabbles over boundaries and ownership. These conflicts were widespread, but Shelburne was the major centre of strife, especially in the spring and summer of 1784. Because of the "Discontents and disturbances having arisen at Shelburne," the Executive Council was forced to appoint special agents to assign the land and to hear allegations.[51] But if such conflict was inevitable, it was also the source of stress among the loyalists, and this issue was of fundamental importance. The pent-up hostility and resentment resulting from their grievances, instead of being channelled to the outside world, turned inward, loyalist bickering with loyalist over questions of property, and the ensuing tension strained the common bond of loyalty.

In the White Collection of the Public Archives of Nova Scotia there is to be found a series of nineteen provisions for settling the land disputes in Shelburne, drawn up in August 1784. Perhaps most significant are the supplementary comments on town and water lots, comments permeated with charges of favouritism and unfairness. The land had been drawn for by lottery, and yet a favoured few had managed to subvert this fair policy by applying to the government for extra grants of three hundred acres. "And to this impolitic or rather inadvertent Conduct," it was observed, "is owing in some Measure the want of Lands in the Vicinity of Shelburne to satisfy the just demands of other Loyalists." The author also spoke of grave injustices concerning water lots where, by a legal technicality of definition, "Persons who had come but newly into the settlement" managed to nullify the rights of the owners and usurp the claims themselves. "Now, while these Instances of Injuries remain constantly before the Eyes of the people, their minds must be as constantly irritated, and till these injuries can be somehow or other redressed, many Subjects who would Scorn to be in the Breach of the Peace themselves, will nevertheless show much Reluctance at assisting the Magistrates when called upon, if they should even consent to assist them at all."[52] These injustices were being committed, not by Nova Scotian Yankees, but by fellow loyalists.

This too, in a sense, was inevitable. Close to twenty thousand loyalists had descended upon a poor and insignificant colony, seeking land, office, and security. It was apparent that the market value of their loyalty was hurt in such an inflationary situation, and that protests against the rebels and nabobs would succeed only to a certain degree, for there were twenty thousand other refugees with the same claims to the government's gratitude. There were simply not enough loaves and fishes, and often ambition had to be satisfied at the expense of other loyalists. There was an air of *sauve qui peut*, of taking care of oneself and one's friends, devil take the hindmost. "Keep this Hint to yourself," Charles Morris advised Dugald Campbell, "let the others do as they please." One could erase another loyalist's name from a memorial and insert one's own to get the land. One could claim land on behalf of his wife's loyalty, and demand the land of another loyalist to boot, for the latter "is a person every way unworthy of your favour and who in the place of being an acquisition, to our Province as [recommended] has proved himself to be nothing more than a nuisance." A man of slight influence could manage to take away the partly cleared land of a fellow loyalist and have it put under his servant's name.[53]

Many stories of loyalist abusing loyalist emanated from Shelburne. It was reported that at Shelburne "many unfair things have been practiced towards one another, in the Business of locating Lotts, and towards Government, in the wrong application of its Bounty: and that many of the Inhabitants who came late to the place, are about removing themselves to other parts of the province, being impell'd to it, by the unequal manner in which [business] is conducted there."[54] Benjamin Marston also described the conflict over land between the early arrivals and the late-comers: "The people yesterday drew for their 50 acre lots. They have left many out of the drawing who are equally entitled to a lot as those who have drawn. They want government, more knowledge, and a small portion of generosity. They wish to engross the whole grant into the hands of the few who came in the first fleet, hoping the distresses of their fellow-Loyalists, who must leave New York, will oblige them to make purchases."[55]

There was conflict and jealousy between the various groups into which the loyalists were organized, between the New York group, for example, and the Port Roseway Associates. These group loyalties and suspicion of outsiders tended to splinter the common front. When another group appeared to be receiving particular attention, "they cannot comprehend it, that others should have everything and they Nothing. The people for that Reason are discouraged and dispirited."[56] In Port Mouton there was resentment by the veterans of Tarleton's Legion towards Brook Watson's New York staff, who, having sat out the war in New York, seemed to be getting more material aid in Nova Scotia.[57]

The Botsford papers, revealing the resentment of the Digby group towards Shelburne, tend to underline the fact that personal loyalty and adherence were very weak beyond one's own agency or organization. Each agency and settlement appears to have been isolated, with little thought of the state of the other settlements. Concerning the Port Roseway group, "As they have declined being connected with us, we thought it right to give you this Notice, that you may act accordingly in fixing your location as soon as can conveniently be done, especially as their agents, Messers Dole and Pinchon are not probably in Nova Scotia."[58]

There were the inevitable power struggles within the groups, for these people had been lifted out of their environment and placed, often with acquaintances of a short time, into a new, alien, and fluid environment, where old forms and standards meant little, and status was in a state of flux. In his letters to Gideon White, R.F. Brownrigg described the jockeying for position among the loyalists in Chedabucto, where the community was split into two factions over such critical issues as land, provisions, and stores. The local Pooh-Bah, Dr McPherson, sought to monopolize for his own group the provisions and the best town lots. He also fought to replace the surveyor with a candidate of his own choice and "seems to wish to become Dictator to the inhabitants of Chedabucto." Brownrigg and his friends refused to extend such homage automatically. "Don't misconstrue me – we mean to live in perfect harmony – but to act with spirit." Apparently Brownrigg was too sanguine, for in July 1784 he wrote to White from Halifax, and in mentioning the clique in this rather muted letter, simply states, "they are very troublesome, and have partly drove me hither."[59]

The conflict which arose in Digby is indicative of the tensions which could split a loyalist settlement. A board of four had been appointed by the captains and heads of classes to divide the government material among the refugees. At the request of some discontented loyalists, the board decided to look into the accounts of Amos Botsford, the agent. When this was done, they should have ceased functioning as a board, but they apparently assumed the powers of a permanent committee, "powers which the people did not intend." What ensued was a contest between the board and the agents for political control of the community. As the struggle continued, the community divided behind either Botsford or the leader of the board, a Major Tempany. Both men sought aid in Halifax. Thomas Osburn stated that if Botsford had his way in Halifax, "he Osburn would head a mobb and Parade the Streets of Digby." Isaac Bonnell, on the other hand, stated that "It is fully thought by the Better kind of people here Should Tempany Return with any Power the settlement must be Broke up. I shall for my own lot leave it notwithstanding the great Expence I have been at."

The strain within the community created by the tardy surveying, and the conflict between the Botsford group and the newcomers, were heightened by the delayed arrival of provisions in 1785. The disturbances which broke out were serious and extensive enough to require action from Halifax. By the time order was restored, many loyalists had already left Digby.[60] Although the incident was not necessarily typical, it does illustrate the divisions, animosity, and bitterness that such a conflict could create within a loyalist community.

It was at Shelburne, however, with its large, mixed population in concentrated surroundings, that the problems of social interaction were magnified and mob violence erupted to pose a threat to civil authority. As early as May 16, 1783, Benjamin Marston found "people inclining to be mutinous, They suspect their leaders to have private views, and not without some reason." A month later he wrote, "Our people much at variance with one another, a bad disposition in a new settlement. Two of the Captains oppted to fight a duel this morning, but were prevented by friends who thought better of the matter."[61] The community was restive throughout 1783 and 1784. The magistrate, Pynchon, writing to Wentworth on the survey of timber, described the pervading atmosphere: "The Spirit that at present prevails sets not only the Effects of this office at Defiance – but Almost every other." Pynchon had advised Wentworth against marking the king's timber. It would be not only dangerous but without effect, "as no attention would be paid to it – And no prosecution practicable for want of Information – The Effects of this kind of Anarchy proceeds from the want of Support to the civil authority."[62]

In late July 1784 the state of anarchy described by Pynchon erupted in a massive riot involving an attack by the disbanded troops upon the negroes. There is a terse description of the riot and its causes in the diary of Benjamin Marston.

Monday, 26, Great Riot today. The disbanded soldiers have risen against the Free negroes to drive them out of Town, because they labour cheaper than they – the soldiers.

Tuesday, 27, Riot continues. The soldiers force the free negroes to quit the Town – pulled down about 20 of their houses. This morning I went over to the Barracks by advice of my friends, who find I am threatened by the Rioters, and in the afternoon took passage for Halifax. By further advice from Town, find I have been sought after. Arrived in Halifax Thursday 29th.[63]

Shortly after Halifax heard of the riot, the 17th Regiment was ordered to Shelburne to restore order.[64] Apparently the regiment was not successful, for on August 31, over a month after rioting had erupted, General Campbell was asked to send a reinforcement of four complete companies to Shelburne.[65] Governor Parr also requested that a frigate remain at Shelburne in order to prevent the outbreak of more violence and to lessen "the great danger to which the Inhabitants of Shelburne are hourly expos'd from the Turbulence & unruly disposition of a very considerable number of disbanded Soldiers with Arms."[66]

Besides sending troops and ships to quell the riot, Parr also dismissed the surveyor, Benjamin Marston, and appointed a board made up of leading residents to straighten out, and to have responsibility for, the land grants.[67] Parr's actions were ineffectual, for rioting continued throughout August, and in April 1785 fresh disturbances involving large numbers occurred.[68] What had started with the rioting of disbanded soldiers against the free negroes was too widespread and complex to be ended by the firing of a surveyor. Thus part of the character of Shelburne, as marked as the ringing vows of loyalty or the mushrooming of houses and commercial plans, was this undertone of conflict, violence, and the threat of anarchy.

There was a tendency in the summer of 1783 for a harassed and overworked government to give scant attention to the individual loyalist. Under pressure from the associations, Charles Morris conceded "that I will to the utmost of my influence prevent any *Separates* carrying their Points, whatever Pitifull Plaints they may make." By taking this attitude, the government was allowing each organization to assume responsibility for the stray loyalists in its area, and at the same time permitting it to assume more authority over land distribution than it had a right to. The government was in effect placing the fate of the individual loyalist in the hands of a partial and competing body, and allowing that body to assume an almost monopolistic control of land grants in the area. When seven families asked for land grants in the Conway area, Charles Morris ratified their request but Amos Botsford, the local agent for the New York association, evaded the issue. This action prompted a stern order from Morris and the governor to place them on the land, "Provided it does not materially Interfere with the General Settlement of Conway." A captain who came to the Conway area to draw a lot found that the new corps had usurped all the lots not yet drawn for.[69] Concerning another band of loyalists, Morris demanded to know of Robert Gray in 1785, "why these people have not had a common chance of drawing Lands with others."[70] Benjamin Marston referred several times in his diary to the almost dictatorial power of the Port Roseway Associates at Shelburne. "The Association from New York are a curious set," he observed, "they take upon them to determine who are the proper subjects of the King's grant. They have chosen a committee of sixteen who point out who are to be admitted to draw for lots." A short while later he wrote, "They wish to engross this whole grant into the hands of the few who came in the first fleet, hoping the distresses of their fellow-loyalists, who must leave New York will oblige them to make purchases."[71] Together with the struggle to survive, these conflicts among and within the groups dominated their early days in Nova Scotia. These loyalist clusters provided the immediate sources of tension and discord over land, provisions, and position. Under such circumstances, the native of Nova Scotia, frequently separated from the newcomers by miles of bush or coast, was often a rather nebulous enemy or rival, known of only at second hand.

Sometimes a part of this struggle, sometimes apart from it, but always a major factor, was the schism between the elite of the loyalists and the so-called "rabble." The members of the elite were basically those who had been or had known someone of influence before or during the revolution, and hoped to be someone of influence again. The rabble were all those who had been nobody and had little chance of being anything else. There were various shades of grey between, people who could not easily be fitted into either category, but an attempt was made to categorize by the two extremes, dividing the loyalists into the elite and the others. Strangely, the levelling factors of a bankrupting war and a province that was almost a frontier had not lessened the awareness of status. In a fluid situation, with neither guide-lines nor assurances of influence, the elite, in their desperate scramble for position, wrapped their exclusiveness about them like a mantle. With their sense of class, status, and privilege, and their contempt for the lower classes, these loyalists were far closer to the oligarchy in Halifax than to the common refugee. The only major difference between the two elites lay in the extent to which they possessed office and influence. But between the elite and the masses, there were far too many barriers, and the only thing they had in common was their loyalty, a tenuous cord, frayed by many basic differences.

There was the aura of the snob in the announcement of the death of Lord Charles Montague by Mather Byles of the red carpet and boils. Montague had led a Carolinian regiment to Nova Scotia, where he died on February 3, 1784. "He died suddenly at a little hut in the Woods of Nova Scotia," Byles writes, "& was Committed to the Earth with much military Foppery & ridiculous parade." It is difficult to judge which Byles held more in contempt, the "ridiculous parade" or the death of the man in a common hut in the woods of Nova Scotia. James Gautier called the people of Shelburne "banditti." N. Ford wrote of his delight in the fact that Isaac Wilkins "has got into an office now, that puts it out of the power of the rabble of Shelburne to remove."[72] Perhaps the best illustration of the gentleman's contempt for the rabble is, as we have seen, the journal of Benjamin Marston. The loyalists in Shelburne he found indolent. clamorous, and mutinous. Their captains "are a set of fellows whom mere accident has placed in their present situations ... Real authority can never be supported without some degree of real superiority."

They are like sheep without a shepherd. They have no men of abilities among them. Their Captains, chosen out of their body at New York, are of the same class with themselves – most of them mechanics some few have been shipmasters, they are the best men they have. Sir Guy Carleton did not reflect that putting sixteen illiterate men into commission, without subjecting them to one common head, was at best but contracting the mob.[73]

Marston found pathetic the attempts of these captains to play the role of gentleman, while their wives and daughters were ladies "whom neither nature nor education intended for that rank."[74]

In Halifax Mather Byles III wrote of his sister that she never went out because "there's nobody in the place worth making an acquaintance with – never goes to see a stranger that arrives because she supposes they are like all the rest." Ward Chipman received a letter from Gregory Townsend in Halifax congratulating him "if it is worth it on your getting the better of the Lower Lovers, it must be better for any country new or old to have their Public Concerns Conducted by men of Science & principle rather than illiterate or bad men of any Class." This attitude towards the masses could come out even when their aid was sought. Samuel Seabury, writing on the choice of a bishop for Nova Scotia, stressed that such a man should be a loyalist who had suffered much and knew the loyalists, both gentlemen and the masses. "I am personally acquainted with the principal persons who have gone thither to Settle, and with the temper and disposition of the inferior Classes; and I flatter myself that I have their confidence, and that no person would be more acceptable to them."

The select few believed that their compensation should be greater than their sacrifice or sufferings might warrant. They implied that the distribution of the spoils of defeat should be based more upon what one had been than what one had done.

The Merit of an American Loyalist consists, according to the Terms of the foregoing Resolves in a Compliance with the Laws, or much more in Assisting in Carrying them into Execution ... Where thos Principles are found to have been uniformly profess'd and acted upon they Constitute a degree of Merit which independant of all Consideration of Loss of Property gives the Persons who have thus acted a fair Claim to Attention and to a Support proportion'd to their Situation in Life and the disadvantages to which they have been subjected in Consequence of such their Conduct.[75]

Moreover, true reimbursement was to be found not so much in official claims and compensation as in position and appointments, and here merit was barely incidental, connections everything. The Winslow Papers, for example, are replete with instances of the wielding of influence for family and friends, portraying a seemingly parasitic coterie trading upon one another's favours. Mather Byles III, in referring to his father, summed up their expectations: "as every mortification and suffering which he has undergone, has been the effect of the purest principle, he has every reason to hope that his future prospects will brighten as they unfold, and the evening of his life be gilded with the rays of prosperity." To the mass of the loyalists, the outcome of the rebellion was a loss to be compensated. To the elite, it appears to have been at times an opportunity to exploit. The petitions for land grants strengthen this impression. Most of the memorialists, although emphasizing the services rendered and the losses sustained, seek little more than "such proportion of lands ... as may be most consistent with his Majesty's most gracious intentions."[76] Memorialists like James Benvie and Thomas Lockwood, "having served during the late war in The Regiment Late, the Royal Fencible Americans," were granted a hundred acres each. However, one finds James Twaddle, a cripple owing to a wound received in the revolution, receiving fifty acres, and Nathaniel Thomas, "late one of the members of His Majesty's Council for the Province of the Massachusetts Bay," 1,200. Stephen Skinner, who was among the fifty-five loyalists who felt themselves entitled to especially large grants, also applied as an individual for an extra "quality of land as is generally given to Gentlemen in the like circumstances." The New York agents could write to Amos Botsford for special allotments, for "the People will not object to our having an exclusive Choice of Lands."[77] Among his other grants, Isaac Wilkins managed to gain for himself ten of the town lots in Shelburne, and a public rebuke by the humbler loyalists. When General Ruggles was granted his 10,000 acres in Wilmot rather than Annapolis, so that it might not "prove very Injurious to the Settlement in General and very much Disgust the People," he was terribly put out by it all.[78]

The awareness of the many of the privileges of the few did not strengthen the fraternity of loyalism. The petition of the fifty-five gentlemen, and the counter-petition rebutting it, exemplify both the demands and the philosophy of the elite, and the resentment stirred up among the majority by such demands. In July 1783 a group of fifty-five gentlemen petitioned Sir Guy Carleton for approximately 275,000 acres in Nova Scotia. They requested to be put on the same footing as field officers, have the land chosen by their own agents, surveyed at government expense, "and the Deeds delivered to us, as soon as possible." Their claim to this land rested upon the fact that they were no longer living in the manner to which they had been accustomed, and "that the Settling such a Number of Loyalists, of the most respectable Characters, who have Constantly had great influence in His Majesty's American Dominion – will be highly Advantageous in diffusing and supporting a Spirit of Attachment to the British Constitution as well as to His Majesty's Royal person and Family."[79]

Carleton obviously was impressed by such a claim, for he recommended it to Parr, who actually began the survey.[80] The less respectable loyalists, however, were not as impressed, and they reacted quickly and angrily. They had come to Nova Scotia, "little suspecting there could be found amongst their Fellow sufferers Persons ungenerous enough to attempt ingrossing to themselves so disproportionate a Share of what Government has Allotted for their common benefit." Those particular gentlemen demanding such claims were "more distinguished by the repeated favors of Government than by either the greatness of their sufferings or the importance of their Services."[81] This rift increased the mutual resentment that existed between the "most respectable" loyalists and the others.

Although the refugees varied greatly in occupations and social strata, political and religious views, the fact that they had supported a common cause and suffered a common fate conditioned their response to a new environment. This experience permitted the caricature of the Nova Scotian and his government, and shaped the love-hate relationship with Britain. It found expression in the election of 1785, when lines could be drawn, the enemy defined, and the cry of loyalism brought forth and exploited. But the intensity could not last, and the common bond could not continue to dominate. There was much conflict with the Nova Scotian, yet it was neither constant nor intense enough to supply the cohesion necessary for a dynamic loyalist attitude. Land squabbles, opportunism, and group loyalties broke down attachments, while the basic conflict between the elite and the masses strengthened the fragmentation. The danger from without was too weak, while the dissension within was too strong, and the many refractory elements among the loyalists inhibited the growth of a common front.

CHAPTER SEVEN

Reactions to the Loyalist

There were perhaps as many reactions to the loyalists as there were non-loyalists in the province, making it futile to seek a common attitude. What one finds is a wide mixture of views running from those almost obsessed by the loyalist presence to those who felt hardly at all the impact of those great numbers. And, as might be expected, these observations tell us as much about the observer as they do about the loyalist.

Britain, for example, was caught in past rhetoric and promise, in the image she had helped create of the loyal subjects who had decided for the crown. The rhetoric remained basically intact. William Knox wrote of their having "sacrificed every thing, but a good Conscience, for their Attachment to this Country." Lord Sheffield felt that everything should be done so that any encouragement to Canada or Nova Scotia "be given in a great Measure to the Loyalists, who may settle there, and who so well deserve it."[1] In general those in positions of authority in Nova Scotia were told to do all that they could for the refugees.

But sentiment had to jostle with reality. That mercantilism was not dead is attested by a document in the Colonial Office records.

The permanency of their Connections with this Country should therefore be the Ground for every measure respecting our Colonies; The advantages to be derived from them should be the Second object of our Attention, and their prosperity to be encouraged, only, in so far as it would be much better to have no Colonies at all, than to have them in competition with this Country, or Revolt from it.

In the dispute over the St Croix boundary, Lord Sydney, although insistent upon the protection of the king's subjects in the area, did stress that "the King is equally disposed to cultivate that Peace and Harmony which for the mutual advantage of this Kingdom and the United States, ought to subsist." Moreover, in the issue of West Indies trade, pressure was immense from both the islands and the United States to open the area to American commerce, and in the debate the refugees were aware that they could be sacrificed again to appease other and more influential interests.[2]

Britain's contribution in aid of the refugees was impressive. "Altogether for surveys, lumber, tools and seeds, not less than $100,000 was spent in Nova Scotia. For transportation, clothing, provisions and government expenses, probably $4,500,000 additional was required. Two-thirds of this expenditure was in behalf of Loyalists from New York." And yet it was done grudgingly. Lord Sydney saw to it that the loyalists survived in Nova Scotia, that they were given aid and time to put down roots, but he did little else to meet his promise of making Nova Scotia "the envy of all the American states."[3]

Instructions to the colonial administration, when they did come, insisted that the officials do all that they could for the poor refugees while spending as little money as possible, and as time passed more and more emphasis was placed on the latter injunction. Parr seemed to spend as much time in explaining surveying expenses as in reporting the condition of the loyalists.[4] After Britain had disallowed Morris's accounts of £353.2 in 1784, Parr was forced to enclose them again, stressing that they were "founded in truth." "I inspect minutely into every charge, and act with as much economy, as if the payment came out of my own pocket, which does not give that satisfaction I could wish, however, I shall continue acting upon the same principle."[5] Charles Morris also felt and explained the dilemma. "His Excellency the Governor is fully authorized to draw for the expence of Surveys but at the same time is very pointedly injoined to frugality." A year later he was still writing of the "very pointed Letters from home" demanding economy.[6]

Britain was within her right to caution and hold responsible the officials. Colonial affairs had been a history of officials padding their purses with public funds, and it was only prudent to impress upon them that this was not their licence but loyalist aid. Moreover, the government was staggering under great war debts and increasing demands for economy. "The National Load is Immense already," Rev. Thomas Wood noted, "& where are the resources to gratify the American claims & to support & protect the Loyalists in their Province?"[7]

Under these pressures the British government did what it had to do, but moved to cut expenses as soon as it felt its duty in establishing the refugees had been sufficiently met. By the spring of 1785, although expressing the hope that Nova Scotia would "become the Envy of the Subjects of the ... Neighbouring States," Lord Sydney stated that timber was no longer "a measure of necessity," and urged that in this and every other form of aid to the loyalists, Britain "in future be put to the least possible Expence." When the citizens of Annapolis appealed desperately for more aid, Sydney refused them, fearing that further assistance "would consequently produce other applications which, considering the immence expence already brought upon this Country for supplies of Provisions and other articles issued to these people, could not be attended to."[8] To Britain the loyalists were an unfortunate burden, to be carried, like most such burdens, grudgingly and for as short a distance as decency permitted.

To John Parr the loyalists appeared as a threat to his political survival, for it was the refugee situation which changed a lucrative and easy posting into a nightmare of responsibility. He was required not only to administer the frightening logistics of settling these thousands but to walk between their demands for aid and Britain's for economy. Nor was he particularly well suited to carry out such a demanding task with either energy or authority. Physically he was elderly, greatly overweight, and often plagued by the ailments of age and good living. Joseph Peters commented on his recurring troubles: "Cousin *Parr* is bad with the *Gout* and Piles."[9]

Moreover, Parr was haunted by the impact upon his position of affairs in Britain. He had been appointed as a protégé of Lord Shelburne, the man hated by the loyalists for concluding the peace treaty, and when Shelburne fell, Parr's enemies expected the governor would fall also. By the spring of 1784 Lord Sydney had taken over as secretary of state for the colonies, an event which left Parr uncertain. "I begin to be very impatient," he wrote, "to hear how matters have gone since the Dissolution of Parliament, I have not a doubt but that they are consonant to the wishes of My Lord." By the fall he was still concerned with "what turn the dissolution of parliament has taken, if my Friend is in Office &c." While uncertainty concerning the British situation was bad enough, there was also the rumour circulating, particularly in the fall of 1783, that Parr was to be succeeded by General Fox, and the consequent glee of Fox's loyalist supporters.[10] Such a situation, with his champion in Britain out of power, his enemies in Nova Scotia anticipating his fall and seeking out any weaknesses which would help precipitate it, forced upon Parr a policy of caution and inoffensiveness, a desire to allow nothing to occur which would give his enemies a target.

Because of his awareness of the vulnerability of his position, there was an aura of persecution about Parr. He was strongly on the defensive against loyalist charges, feeling that "malignant representations would have been made against an Angel sent here by the man who sent me." In May 1784 he defended himself against reports concerning his actions that he feared were being sent home. He had always acted impartially towards the loyalists, simply because he knew none of them, and he had acted cautiously "knowing their Eyes were upon every action." In August he was countering accusations of taking large land grants. He had set aside for himself only 500 acres outside Shelburne, thinking that some day that centre would be the capital. To Parr such an amount was trivial compared to the amounts taken by his predecessors. Moreover, the unfair land allotments complained of were owing to the luck of the draw or to false representation by the refugees, not to his partiality. " 'Tis true I have had several Rascalls acting under me, principaly Surveyors, but am turning them *out* as fast as I find them *out*. I have also been deceived in the Characters of some Men, time will set me right here." In October he received some solace from Whitehall's assurance that they had heard only good reports concerning him, and that dissatisfaction was natural among a people uprooted and reduced in standing and position.[11] In these circumstances, Parr was concerned more with the loyalist assault upon him than with the loyalists themselves. His defence left him little time for impartial, objective assessments, and the attacks themselves moulded his judgment of the refugees.

By the end of 1784 he was more secure, for his faction was victorious in Britain, and this security encouraged him to take action against loyalist agents and patricians, such as Edward Winslow on the St John.[12] But governments change, alliances alter, and there were influential parties among the loyalists who would benefit by his fall. They included John Wentworth, surveyor general of the woods, a loyalist and former governor of New Hampshire who had been demoted by Lord Shelburne. Wentworth was supposed to have written a letter branding the government of the colony as proud, ignorant, and inept, and, according to Parr, "as disgracefull to Britain, as was the conduct of the American War, or what is still worse the American Peace." Parr described the letter in order to awaken his masters to Wentworth's motives, for "Mr W had a Government in View for the one he had lost."[13]

Parr's attitude, however, was shaped by more than his fear of loyalist antipathy and influence. Since some of their demands were exorbitant, some of their acts not quite honest, some of their accusations unfair, in this atmosphere of shrill complaints and shifty practices Parr was most often confronted by the worse side of the refugees' character, and formed his opinions accordingly. He was informed, for example,

that Sundry persons at Shelburne have not only drawn Lots for themselves, but have contrary to the intentions of Government introduc'd their Children or young men under Age to the same priviledges. Also Transcient Captains of Vessels and Seamen as well as other persons, have introduc'd themselves to draughts of Town Lotts as well as other Lotts in Shelburne, under pretence of being Settlers, but with intention of selling what they obtain to Advantage, to the Detriment and Exclusion of honest Settlers.[14]

Parr had little respect for the people of that centre, and complained several times of the lack of educated, talented, and well-bred settlers in Shelburne. Much later he was to describe them as "composed of the Dregs and Benditti of that Town [New York], of Boston of other Sea Ports with upwards of 1000 Disbanded Soldiers ... The generality of those who came here, were not much burthened with Loyalty, a spacious name which they made use of." In the early days of the settlement he had complained that despite his efforts the loyalists there refused to allow the government the time to plan and work for them. The magistrates he found squabbling among themselves and jockeying out of self-interest for as much land as they could get. "At Shelburne the Magistrates are divided among themselves, and also against the Surveyors, and the People are Inimical to the Magistrates." He even found Parson Walter actively plotting against him. "There never was a Plot without a Priest," he observed. By 1785, however, his establishment of and support for a board of agents had eased much of the conflict and confusion over authority.[15]

Parr's actions towards the loyalists were often better than his attitudes. Both on the St John and at Shelburne, although attacked fiercely by leading loyalists, his actions often prevented or limited the exploitation of the masses by the elite. Except on the issue of expense, his instructions to the surveyors stressed the need to accommodate the refugees as well as possible. When the military proposed laying aside great tracts of timber and land in Shelburne, Parr tended to side with the refugees, for the reservations planned "would deprive the Inhabitants there of the means of Erecting their Habitations, in time sufficient to Shelter them from the severity of the Approaching Season." Alarmed by the steeply escalating wages resulting from the scarcity of skilled labour, Parr threatened that "all persons making Exorbitant demands of that Kind and on this occasion will find themselves depriv'd of the Advantages which they would gain by a different behavior." When a widow in straitened circumstances, facing the curtailment of provisions, appealed to Parr, he ordered their continuation, "she appearing to me an Object deserving that Indulgence." Of the aid granted to his group, Thomas Miller wrote, "governor Parr received us with great Politeness and Humanity; He has done all a good man could to accomodate our Situation, And I have particularly felt his attentions."[16]

There were occasions when he would condemn them all. He complained of them en masse for not aiding in the surveying, unless paid for their activities. "I have to be sure a most troublesome, discontented, disappointed over expecting Race of Mortals to deal with." He had written earlier to Lord Shelburne of having found "some honest Men" among the refugees. "I stood in great need of them."[17] By inference, there were not many around.

To Parr, however, all loyalists were not bad, and he did try to make a distinction between the solid refugee, sincerely intent upon settling, and those causing trouble. He acknowledged that "there are many worthy good Characters among the Loyalists, to them I pay every attention in the power of man and have lately been able to distinguish them, at first it was impossible, every Settlement has two or three turbulent Spirits, who keep the rest in hot Water, I am afraid to attack them lest from persecution they might become second Wilk's. The Germans and Highlanders make by far the best and quietest Settlers." In a letter to Lord Shelburne he again contrasted the attitude of the majority with that of a minority of trouble-makers.

notwithstanding that I have used every exertion, have done every thing in my power for them, some few discontented Rascals, at the most distant Settlements, begin to be clamorous and seditous, expecting more than possibly can be done in so short a time, jealous that more is done for one Township than for another, which is not the case, &c, &c, they threaten, and I am told have wrote complaints home against me, without having them made known here, whatever they may be, I am thoroughly well prepar'd to meet. their ungenerous disposition soon shewd itself, upon a late unfortunate change in Administration, which they thought might change their Governor, if he did not comply with every request they made, some of which were highly unreasonable, they gave themselves some airs, but they had no effect with me. there are several Sufferers among them, but at the same time, there are many who have been enriched by the late War, and are in far better Circumstances, than they would have been, had there not been a War. Tho they plague me with complaints, and quarrels among themselves &c, I shall continue to render them every good office in my power, and may venture to assert with great confidence, that a *very great*

Majority indeed, approve of my Conduct, but there are some not to be pleased or satisfied.

A little later he could write that, although he found "some of them the most unreasonable and expecting upon Earth," nevertheless "by far the greater part are happy and Contented."[18]

Interestingly, he saw them less as loyalists than as Americans, commenting at one point that "they inherit a deal of that Liver, which disunited the Colonies from their Mother Country." He also commented on the divisions among them caused by old loyalists in the former colonies. The most troublesome were the New Englanders: "They want a Man of their own Country to be Governor." In the same letter he declared, "what an expecting, troublesome Being a New England Refugee is." He came back to the issue of nationalism and colonial loyalties in a letter to Lord Shelburne.

... it will be a difficult task, to bring about a good understanding, between a Refugee from one of the four Northern Colonies, and those from the Southern, to make them think they are one and the same People, and that their Interest is mutual, this is one of the great cause of disagreement among themselves ... we are not without our private Cabals here, indeed My Lord it would be an impossibility to be otherwise where almost the whole of the people is composed of Scotch, and a very bad addition of the Yankee Race, each Party would be happy to have a Governor of their own Country, the one being as National as the other.[19]

Among the other officials who worked for and with the loyalists, there was little recognition of a positive loyalist image. They were in fact rarely referred to as loyalists, but rather most commonly as "refugees," while consideration of their past sacrifices and present sufferings was overshadowed by their constant demands, unfair criticisms, and fraudulent behaviour to both officials and fellow loyalists. Henry Newton of the Customs found Shelburne merchants using forged registers to import American goods. Benjamin Marston called them, among other things, both mutinous and republican. General Campbell, although often touched by the unfortunate situation of many, was equally disgusted by the abuses of the king's bounty.[20]

It was Charles Morris, as surveyor general, who was particularly involved with the unattractive side of the loyalist image, and there were times when he was driven almost to despair. His opinion of them was rarely flattering. He had succeeded his father in 1781, and soon found himself caught in the loyalist deluge. During the first three years of settlement he was to refer to his calling as "next to Egyptian Slavery." In his official capacity he was to become intimately acquainted with the vice and the greed of man. He witnessed the fraudulent claims and the lands "Surreptitiously obtain'd." He grew angry at the arrogant autonomy of the local boards and their casual ignoring of Halifax and his office. The demands of such a man as Amos Botsford provoked blunt replies concerning Botsford's dictatorial manner. He was aware of the presence of pretenders in this multitude, those who had come seeking land and provisions although entitled to neither.[21] A word he often used was "ungrateful." One Captain Murray of Shelburne "was beging every favor of me at the time he was making his complaints." In the same letter he called the captains of Shelburne "a Set of Ungreatful Rascals."[22] The refugees hindered the pace of settlement by refusing to help with the surveying of their own lands unless well paid. Their greed in hogging land threatened the welfare of other loyalists. He had written to Burbidge that, with 30,000 applying for land, "it is impossible for me to put them off by saying this or that Tract is reserved for any particular Set of People." The early loyalists wanted the township grants to themselves, but Morris insisted on the governor's right to continue making grants to other refugees until townships were filled, without "interfering with land actually Surveyed and laid out for the first grantees." There was, moreover, nothing one could do to satisfy them. Speaking of the efforts of surveyors and boards, he wrote, "I am fully convinced it is not their fault or that of the Surveyors, But the People at Large, whom no Mortal can please." To Morris, these complaints were coming chiefly from transients seeking a quick profit, for "we are well assured the People in every District are disposing of their land for much less than it has cost Govt for laying out and never mean to settle in the colony but to make the most of us."[23]

Unlike Parr and Morris, the executive and legislative branches of government, little involved in settling the refugees, indicated remarkably little concern. Carleton had envisaged an early entry of the loyalists into the power structure, pointing out to Lord North the importance of having both executive and legislative bodies filled "by men of discretion and abilities, and *whose loyalty* is well ascertained: numbers of this character may doubtless be found among the Refugees and other new Settlers, who have suffered much for their zealous attachment to the British Constitution." But the government in Nova Scotia was in no hurry whatsoever to welcome loyalist talent. Following the death of Michael Franklyn, Parr ignored the loyalists, recommending Thomas Cochran to take his place on the council and choosing Charles Morris to fill the other vacancy. On the death of Chief Justice Finucane, the loyalist attornies seemed not to have been considered. "For Gods sake," wrote Parr, "send me out one equal to fill his Seat, in point of honor, justice, and professional knowledge, a Man of abilities, such a Character being much wanted in the Province at large."[24]

There was a dearth of legislative comment on the loyalist flood, remarkable in view of the fact that the population had been more than doubled and Nova Scotia's future radically altered. Parr, in his address to both houses in 1783, made reference to "the Accession of many Inhabitants of different Parts of the Province," and the consequent advantages to be obtained. Council and assembly in their reply did little more than agree with him, both repeating his phrase that their accession "cannot fail to make us a Rich and flourishing People." However, the council did use the "great and sundry Encrease of the number of Inhabitants" to veto the assembly's motion concerning taxes for that year.[25]

If they showed little concern for the loyalist plight, the legislative bodies did show great concern for the plight of Governor Parr caused by the refugees' presence. Parr had already sought an extra allowance from Britain because of his expenses in entertaining the refugees. If Britain hesitated, the assembly did not. One of their few positive actions concerning the loyalist immigration was, after taking note of "the great and unusual number of Strangers, who daily resort to this Province," to praise Parr for his "upright Integrity" and to vote £500 to help cover his expenses, especially "towards the Support of your Table." Perhaps the vote was in some way connected with Parr's assent on December 2, 1783, to an act of oblivion and general pardon for treasons committed in the province during the war. Perhaps it resulted from the desire in a changing situation to keep the governor's good will. Perhaps it simply showed consideration for the problem of Parr's table. But it was one of the few instances in which the "Strangers" flooding the province were officially noticed by the legislature. The civil list went from £5,021 in 1782 to £5,943 in 1783, and down again to £5,559 in 1784, with only an increase in poor relief to indicate the refugees' arrival.[26] The loyalists were regarded as basically a British problem, to be left to the British government. They were not to upset or overthrow the status quo in Halifax. "I am convinced," Jacob Bailey had written about the plight of the earlier loyalists, "that it is a prevailing principle in this province to prevent if possible all refugees, on the one hand from rising into any degree of power or affluence, and on the other not to let them suffer for the bare necessities of life."[27]

The legislative bodies were not prepared to welcome the loyalists warmly into the circle of power. There was little room in the circle, and that vast horde must have looked much like a threat. Yet they could not see the loyalist as an enemy either, for they were not united. Council and assembly, the appointed officials and the elected house, had been squabbling over the wielding of power for decades. They were each other's adversary, and looked upon the loyalist not as part of a new game but as a new element in a very old game. The appointed officials and the Halifax establishment would have difficulty in successfully representing a native Nova Scotian spirit against the threat posed by these "Strangers," for those in authority at Halifax had been basically against the voice of the outports in the halls of power. There was, moreover, a tendency, however slight, for the assembly, especially that part of it representing the outports, to look to the loyalists, outcasts also from power, if not as allies, at least as people sharing a common hostility towards the entrenched regime. The assembly, for example, had voted unanimously for the appointment of Brook Watson to replace Richard Cumberland as provincial agent, whereas the council voted against it. The slight legislative action taken on behalf of the loyalists seemed guided by the initiative of R.J. Uniacke, the Cumberland rebel. When the House approved the setting up of a separate county for the communities around Shelburne, the council opposed it, whereupon Uniacke moved that the governor use his prerogative to create it. A year later, Uniacke brought in, and the assembly passed, a bill for supporting transient poor, disabled troops, "and other distressed People."[28] Since few were more distressed than the refugees, the bill seemed designed to help alleviate the more extreme cases of hardship among them.

The struggle between council and assembly, appointed and elected, resulted from Halifax's assertion of predominance over the rest of the province. Halifax held sway over the council. In 1781 five of its members were from the capital, one from Windsor, one from Lunenburg, and one, Joseph Goreham, listed as being from New York. Parr actually used the need of residence in Halifax to appoint Charles Morris and Thomas Cochran to the council. When a Mr Bruce of Shelburne brought a letter from Lord Sydney directing that he be appointed to the council, Parr "hesitated, Said that my Local Situation was a Bar and for that time declined giving any farther Answers."[29] If the council was not deliberately aiming to be non-loyalist, it was definitely to be Haligonian.

The assembly, however, was seeking to increase the representation and influence of the outports by voting for payment of ten shillings a day for members outside Halifax, an action opposed by the council.[30]

The loyalists shared this fear of Halifax's dominance. Their concern is apparent in the assurance Bulkeley needed to give the Shelburne officials, by insisting that the area had been made a new county which would have due representation, and that the governor wanted them to understand that the assembly "is Composed of Representatives from every part of the Province which has hitherto sent any and not of the Representatives of the County of Halifax."[31] The representatives of the outports and the bulk of the loyalists would at least have this common bond, an intense antagonism to Halifax dominance.

For the average Nova Scotian the impact of the arrival of this huge army of refugees, and of the changes portended, appears to have been somewhat underwhelming. The *Gazette* commented on the arrival and progress of the loyalists in their settlements, but infrequently. The letters of Margaret Hutchinson, a loyalist already living in Halifax, rich in insights into her own problems and adjustments, comment hardly at all on the impact, adjustment, and fate of the refugees. The diary of Simeon Perkins refers very briefly to their coming: "a Great Number of Settlers are arrived at Roseway Lately, I understand thirteen ships, Two Ships are expected at Port Mutton with 700 of the Commissary General's department ... it is expected New York will be finally Evacuated the first week in December next."[32] Much concerned with the religion, commerce, and society of the south shore, the diarist often comments upon his ties with Shelburne but little upon the loyalist phenomenon itself. The loyalists are mentioned, but in a very matter of fact tone. They were accepted, as a winter storm or a remarkably high tide would be, and taken in stride, almost laconically.

Evidence of hostility between loyalist and pre-loyalist is found throughout the province during the early years of settlement. Halifax felt the weight and irritation of their numbers, for many of the loyalists spent their first winter there. The city had done very well during the war, and the merchant and ruling class in particular feared the impact that the refugees would have on their controlled and profitable little world. They also feared that the rapid rise of Shelburne might oust Halifax as the first port and capital.[33]

In Annapolis, where old and new rubbed together too closely, antagonism was to be expected. Jacob Bailey makes it sound endemic. He claimed that the loyalists who had come before 1783 had been treated "not only as runaways, strolers and vagabonds ... but as the most abhorred and despicable miscreants in God, Almighty's creation." In the spring of 1783, Bailey claimed that the natives, anticipating that Nova Scotia would join Congress, were overjoyed. "It is certain that the contention between Loyalists and rebels was never so violent in this country as at present." As late as 1785, the generosity of the loyalists to him, according to Bailey, enraged the pre-loyalists and increased the existing split in the congregation "beyond the power of reconciliation."[34] Charles Morris revealed friction between old Annapolis settlers and new Digby ones in a letter to Botsford, expressing doubt that the Annapolis claimants owned any part of the township of Clements, especially any that would inconvenience the loyalists. "You have no reason to say that I am partial in their favor," he wrote, "as few Public Officers have done more than I have for the Loyalist and you know it and I sincerely wish they and the old Inhabitants may go heart in hand that this affair may not be carried on with rancour and Ill will."[35] The Presbyterians in Cornwallis did not appear to like their new minister, "because he wont be governed by them and is a zealous Loyalist."[36]

There was also friction in Pictou. Patterson mentions that during the revolution Pictou County was divided, men of the *Hope* and their friends for the Americans, men of the *Hector* for Britain. After the war, according to Patterson, an American loyalist from Wallace came to Pictou, and was put up by Mathew Harris, who was particularly pro-patriot. When the loyalist, not knowing of this, bitterly cursed the Americans, Harris told him, "If I had known you were such a Character I would not have Slept under the same roof with you. It is too late to turn you out tonight, but I warn you to be off as soon as it is light enough in the morning."[37] James McCabe had lived on John Fisher's land in Pictou for eighteen years and had built a house on it, but "last mowing time when a party of armed men of the late 82nd Regiment came there claiming a right to said Land, that from these men or some or one of them they have received frequent outrage."[38]

There was also the strange case of violence against Moses Deles-dernier, an act of violence that Bailey felt was deserved because the man had insulted the king. Bailey used the incident to show the disloyalty of Nova Scotians. According to Delesdernier's deposition, however, in July 1783 two strangers, one a Captain Kipp, came to him and demanded that he give up his lodging to Kipp. Upon his refusal, Kipp jumped from his horse, pushed Delesdernier, "& Claspd his other hand on the hilt of his Cullask and repeated you damd rebble I will Seperate your head from your body, with much more Ill Language." Delesdernier refused both a duel and an eviction, since his crops were on the land and his family had no other lodging. On returning to the house the next day, however, he found the captain's baggage already ensconced, and consequently sought legal aid.

Quite as strange as the loyalist's behaviour was that of the three justices of the peace, who refused to act on the grounds that the man had just arrived, that there was no jail, and that he was evidently a friend of the fort's colonel. Delaying any firm action on Delesdernier's complaint, they accepted Kipp's defiance of their requests for his presence until finally Captain Kipp found a boat bound for New York and was gone. To excuse their ignoring of his complaints, they accused Delesdernier of prejudice against the refugees, "a Dangerous Faulshood which might Involv me in every sort of Difficulties and dangers," particularly since Delesdernier had looked upon their coming as very advantageous to the province.[39] Governor Parr, on hearing of the outrage, was so angry that he had Bulkeley send a blistering letter to the justices stating "that on the Proof of any such misbehavior you will Each of you be Struck out of the Commission of the Peace."[40]

Throughout the province, what the old Nova Scotian commonly feared and resented was the loyalist exclusiveness and their attempt to get a stranglehold on the virtue of loyalty. There had been a pro-American uprising in Cumberland and the far south shore had been remarkably friendly with the rebels during the war. And yet the province outside Halifax had been in a peculiar position, attacked and threatened by American privateers without being defended by Britain. The province was, however, in its own way far from being neutral.[41] Perkins, the Liverpool merchant, wrote of Minorca being "captured from us," complained of the American privateers as "them people" and of their "contemptible employment," and rejoiced at Rodney's victory.[42]

The pre-loyalists feared an excess of favouritism towards the new arrivals, and a denigration of their own position as old settlers and, in many cases, war casualties. There is a sense of this in the petitions by pre-loyalists for land. The escheating proceedings, it was argued, made land available not only for loyalists but for Nova Scotians as well. Samuel Poole and other settlers in Yarmouth contended that various lands held but unimproved in that district should be escheated and given to them because, although they had been in the province from nine to twenty years, "they have never had any Lands Granted them by Government but have made improvements on Lands purchased by them in this Province." Similarly a group from Londonderry sought the escheatment of lands in their district. Several Yorkshire men sought free land also, claiming that they had been in the province for ten years, yet, since they could not get land, had been forced to become tenants. The memorial of George Smith sought compensation for the sacrifices he had made, albeit in Nova Scotia. He had been loyal, responsible for saving many shipwrecked off Canso, and hurt badly by American privateers, and he consequently sought compensation.[43]

The loyalists intended to use their position and past to emphasize the contrast between the two communities, to the definite disadvantage of the Nova Scotian. Joseph Gray gives some indication of the extent to which they were exploiting the contrast, and of the arguments with which the pre-Loyalists were countering it. In a letter concerning the danger of having his lands escheated, Gray wrote of "the Endeavors of Envious People who are trying to get every improved Spot of Land escheated and Obtain the Grant of it themselves." He went on to declare:

Surely it is the view and Desire of His Majesty that this province of Nova Scotia and New Brunswick should People Increase and Multiply, it also must Surely be allowed that the old Inhabitants of a Country Naturally Stand as Pillars, though it has lately been Suggested *by a new People* that their movements are Slow, yet must be allowed to be sure foundations of Increase whereas a medley of new Emigrantations are long in a State of fluctuation & generally Dwindle to a Small proportion of their boasted numbers.

In another letter Gray described the war years and their effect upon tenants and farmers, many lost to the militia, many hit by privateers, most seeming to live in a true war zone, with the consequent losses and depredations.

The Old Inhabitants nevertheless I am informed are represented as Rebles and very artful Insinuations are made use of to prejudice and mislead the minds of His Most Gracious Majestys Ministers for the Unjust purpose of Obtaining our Fisheries and the Fruit of all the Toil & our Life and robbing our families of their reasonable and just Expectations. Surely it will not be thought good Policy to permit any measures tending to Occasion divisions and animosities which must Eventually Create Setts of People Hostile to Each Other in the Provinces ...

I am confident Should the real Case be known to Government the Proceedings at the Court of Escheats would not be Allowed to go on with that Degree of Severity which many of the Loyalists think they have a right to Claim.[44]

Gray, of course, would put forth the best arguments possible to save his land. But his reaction represented the feelings of many Nova

Scotians, who also considered themselves as survivors of a war and yet who were now deliberately being type-cast as rebels and slackers.

The antagonism towards the loyalists found expression in a letter-to-the-editor war which flared in the columns of the *Journal* and the *Gazette*. Early in 1784 several letters appeared in the *Journal*, signed "A Loyalist, and well-wisher to Nova Scotia," complaining that since the lands had not yet been properly granted, many loyalists were unable to start improvements. He was answered in the *Gazette* by "a true friend to NOVA SCOTIA" who declared that, since the legislature had done everything in its power to hasten the grants and ease loyalist fears, such people should not complain of matters about which they were ignorant, "least it should be thought that *Envy* and *Malignity*, rather than *loyalty* and *Friendship* are our prevailing Motives ... Does he suppose, that by endeavouring to foment Feuds and Division between His Majesty's faithful Subjects, he proves himself to be a Loyalist? Or by promoting Jealousies and Suspicions between the *new* settlers and the *antient* Inhabitants of this Province, does he prove his Friendship for either?"

A week later "a true friend" wrote again, explaining that he did not wish to fan the coals of animosity, but in effect daring "Loyalist" to answer him. "Loyalist" answered this challenge by going over his previous publications and claiming that they were meant only to show that the governor's goals, stated in his speech opening the session, had not been complied with, to draw attention to the governor's last proclamation, and to express the wish that the loyalists should have a right to elect members to the assembly. He seems to have taken an almost apologetic stand, describing the letters as modest and not deserving of censure. It was the "true friend" who in his reply demonstrated a remarkable aggressiveness, stating that although "Loyalist's" language was modest, "the *inferrence* was insolent in a high degree." "He in vain endeavours to prove the goodness of his intentions and that he has no inclination to promote animosity and discord, while he represents the Government as partial and interested to the injury of the general welfare – How absurd the ideal – No; he must, while he thus continues his *inflammatory* publications, be Considered as one who wishes to 'fish in troubled waters'."

Apparently "Loyalist" wrote again, for he was again attacked mightily, this time by PHILANTHROP, who, because of the publication of this most recent letter in the *Journal*, felt that the intention of the printers to maintain impartiality were being "subverted by insignificant Scribblers, who not only appear devoid of Sentiment, Truth and Candour, but even of Common Sense." As for "Loyalist,"

That a Person of his confused Ideas, from mere Conjecture, that some Neglect had taken Place in expediting the Settlement of the Refugees, should in the first instance apply himself to writing anonymous, and nonsensical Letters, and arraign Officers of Government before his unknown Tribunal . . . is more than extraordinary.

Would it not have been more eligible for Mr. Well-Wisher, in the first Place, to have discovered whether there was, or was not, any Cause for Censure (save what originated, and existed in his own distracted Brain) and in Case there was any sufficient Grounds for Complaint, to have applied personally, or by Memorial, as the Nature of the Case should require, manfully stepping forth in Behalf of his Fellow Sufferers, wherein he might have manifested the Character of a Loyalist and Well Wisher to *Nova Scotia*.

There seem to have been no more letters on the issue after this, although in August the printer of the *Gazette* was asked to insert a prayer by Voltaire from his treatise on toleration. "It can do no Harm, if it should do no good."[45] This was one of the few letters to the editor published since the outburst, and was an appropriate comment on it. The letter-war was remarkable in that the "Loyalist" letters, as quoted by the other two, do not seem either outrageous or inaccurate. His attackers seem to evade his questions by distorting his intentions in language remarkable, in view of the tenor of "Loyalist's" letters, for its excess. The enormity of "Loyalist's" offence was in daring to write publicly about what he and thousands of other loyalists felt were obvious wrongs. Moreover, he was criticized by his two anonymous attackers for attacking government officials anonymously.

The newspaper assault upon "Loyalist" was significant in that it was a public assault intended to establish the refugees' demands as excessive, their motives as suspect. Sounding very much like the output of official hacks anxious to counter loyalist charges of government inaction, the letters may have successfully nurtured hostility towards the loyalists. Yet to foster hostility is not necessarily to reflect it. One cannot assume that the fierce tone of the letters reflected the attitude of Nova Scotians, or even that of the Halifax public, towards the loyalists.

One source of hostility was the issue of loyalty, particularly the loyalist attempt to monopolize it and its attendant advantages, for in the postwar years loyalty was a marketable commodity. The pre-loyalist, threatened by this exclusiveness, sought to neutralize it by implying as Parr did that although there was nothing more wonderful than the true loyalist, it was a pity that there were so few of them, by stressing the damage wrought and sacrifices made in Nova Scotia during the war, and finally by establishing one's own credentials of loyalty. Thus one sees in the postwar years an emphatic eulogizing of king and crown, a steady celebration of royal birthdays, the frequent remembrance of past glories, all of which amounted to a form of gamesmanship in loyalty, for in a country where all express their loyalty zealously, the commodity itself suffers from depreciation.

There is little indication that the early hostility continued to any great extent. In many areas loyalist and pre-loyalist were well separated from one another, and had the chance of developing the low-key cordiality of distant neighbors. Even in mixed communities where one or the other predominated, relations were normally good. The old and new in Guysborough apparently got on very well together and intermarried. "If there was any faction or discontent, no evidence of it appears in the records. The claims of the old settlers had been recognized and legalized; several of them in someway became the owners of town lots."[46] The common factors found among groups of new and old were often as strong as the loyalist exclusiveness. Class, religion, economic and geographic factors formed bridges between old and new settlers. The prominent resentment of the outports towards Halifax gave the settlers living beyond Bedford a common antagonist, and consequently a common attitude.

An example of the manner in which links developed between old and new settlers was the continuation of old country nationalism, shared by both old and new. Those southerners who remained in the province "disappeared into the wilderness and into the fabric of provincial life. Certainly there were no ethnic obstacles to their adjustment. Germans, Scots, Irish, English, Africans – all could find people of their background."[47] Halifax, for example, had a number of old country societies. The Charitable Irish Society drew Irishmen together, whether loyalist or pre-loyalist. Founded by Uniacke, it had such leading officials as the loyalists Hugh Kelly and Gerald Fitzgerald. The North British Society provided another opportunity for intermingling. Macdonald, in his history of the society, lists nine new members, "all Loyalists who came here from New York, all in good positions in the mercantile world in New York and Rhode Island." There were also the St George's Society and the German Society. In fact the *Nova Scotia Almanac* was published in German as well as English, while the *Gazette* carried advertisements in German.[48] On occasion there was intermingling of the societies, representatives of the others being invited on patron saints' days. The concern of the societies for community problems is shown in the 1789 meeting of the Charitable Irish, at which the other national societies were asked to join in an annual conference for promoting "unanimity and harmony."[49] Other fraternal societies, such as the Masons, which existed in the larger communities, also forged links between loyalist and pre-loyalist. When rain cancelled the 1787 parade the members all fled to the club rooms to celebrate in "that Spirit of *Conviviality* and *Harmony*, which so eminently distinguishes that respectable Fraternity."[50]

Whatever the reasons, there are many indications of loyalist/pre-loyalist cooperation and friendship in various spheres. The Perkins diary records his close friendship with Gideon White of Shelburne. They corresponded, and White visited when possible.[51] Thomas Belcher went so far as to brag of the beauty of Nova Scotian girls. Charles Inglis mentioned a church above Annapolis built chiefly through the cooperation of four people, two old settlers and two loyalists from New York. The *Nova Scotia Magazine* carried a warm letter from a loyalist in Barrington on cattle, for the particular benefit of the old settlers in the western parts of Nova Scotia. The author declared that if his advice was successfully followed, "I shall feel sufficiently pleased in having been of service to my fellow-farmers in contributing to their wealth."[52]

Jacob Bailey, in an interesting letter of 1788 to Bishop Inglis, discussed the difficulty of working with such a mixture of people, differing in country, character, religion, manners, and language. He found, moreover, that each sought to retain his heritage, not as loyalist or pre-loyalist, but rather through old provincial loyalties, those from New York sticking together, those from Philadelphia and Boston equally clannish, "without making proper allowance for the same partiality in others – but I find this difficulty lessens in proportion to my continuance among them. And as the young people whose confidence and esteem I endeavour to Secure grow up and form new family connexions, these distinctions in time will be abolished." There is little to quarrel with in Beamish Murdoch's summation of the period, which stresses the settling down of the heterogeneous elements into harmony."Old grievances and hostilities had died out, and the only fancy line of division was owing to fretfulness of lawyers who were unsuccessful in some of their litigated suits."[53]

The non-English in the province, however, were more seriously threatened by the loyalist arrival. Bailey mentioned the irony in the relationship of the Acadians and loyalists, for "Some of those very persons who in their younger years were employed to transport them from Nova Scotia to New England are now compelled to take refuge here and to receive the offices of hospitality and neighborhood from those people they had formerly so injured and ruined."[54] The Acadians saw it less as a reversal than as a second and renewed threat, for as a result of the arrival of so large a body of settlers, and their need for large vacant land areas, refugee communities often bordered on the small, scattered Acadian settlements. Loyalist aggressiveness concerning their rights and the Acadians' lack thereof compounded the new threat. Although Charles Morris tried to ensure that loyalist land grants did "not interfere, with those Acadians who have also a Warrant for land,"[55] infringements upon Acadian claims did occur. According to Dr. William Philan's letter of 1787, approximately twelve Acadian families who had previously cleared land at Chezzetcook were dislodged by loyalists.[56] Rohl's men of the Anspach and Hessian regiments, although granted land in the Shelburne area, were, according to Parr, too lazy to clear it, and wanted the cleared Acadian land around Argyle. Despite warnings from the surveyor general's office, they moved onto it anyway.[57] When Michael Doucet and other Acadians on the Tusket River asked Parr "to prevent the Threatened Encroachments of Certain persons from Shelburne," Bulkeley wrote that the loyalists could take the land only at their own risk, for it was private property and the attorney general "has great doubts in respect of their being liable to forfeiture."[58] However, he did not order them not to take it. Morris worried over the independent action of the board at Shelburne in issuing warrants of survey, fearing that it was giving away land the government had already granted to Acadians and others, "which is the present case – I see no remedy but to prevail on those Acadians to give up part to these poor Soldiers & give them other Land in Lieu."[59]

The Indian population was even more threatened than the Acadian, for they had no claim to land whatsoever, except the unclaimed wilderness. With the coming of the loyalists, huge encroachments were made upon the Indians' hunting and fishing areas. These incursions and the consequent Indian unrest led to a series of incidents between Indians and whites during the first years of the loyalist settlement. In Pictou, Isaiah Horton, a pre-loyalist, had his house burned and young cattle killed in 1783 by Micmac, who "by their depredations threw all the Settlers there into great dread for their own Safety." The Indians claimed that particular land, the Fisher grant, as their own because of a cemetery there, "and have prevented many persons from occupying or improving the said land who were to the Knowledge of the Deponent Desirous to settle thereon."[60] The same fear of losing their land was shown by Indians in the Antigonish area, where the governor ordered G.H. Monk, superintendent of Indian Affairs, to "proceed thither in Order to expel their fears and to Quiet their Minds."[61] Apparently Monk, taking troops with him, was well received by the Indians, who declared "themselves perfectly satisfied with the reservations that are made of their little Settlements on the River, their place of Worship, and their Burying place." In his covering letter to Bulkeley, Monk added that the Indians were "perfectly satisfied & well disposed towards the people settling here."[62] He did not say whether it was owing to the reserves made or to the presence of the soldiers.

This mood of uncertainty and fear is also revealed in the number of applications by Indians for occupation, fishing and hunting rights in particular areas. There appear to be many more of these applications in 1783 and 1784 than in preceding and later years. A licence was granted, for example, to Anthony Eurys to occupy the land on the west side of the Ramsheg "and to Hunt & Fish in Harbours and Rivers of that District."[63] He was also given an exclusive right to hunt and fish on several islands in the area. Many of these licences were sought to prevent potential loyalist encroachment and to ensure that some land would remain in their own possession. Other such licences were to redress encroachments which had already taken place. Philip Bernard, a chief, and Solomon Taumaugh sent a memorial to Parr explaining that they had been promised 500 acres at St Mary's Bay, had obtained a licence to occupy, but then found the land given to Brook Watson, who sold it, "in consequence of which they were dispossessed of it." They were now seeking a similar grant at the head of th bay.[64] Anthony Chury complained to Parr that a Captain Knap "and other Gentlemen of the Loyalists, have prevented himself and others of His Tribe from Enjoying the Privaledges of Hunting & fishing Granted him by His Excellency's Licence." Bulkeley wrote to the whites involved, demanding to know on what grounds the governor's authority was being challenged.[65]

At this stage the government was at least trying to avoid flagrant violations by the loyalists, and to lay the ground rules to avoid future conflict between the new settlers and the colony's oldest. And yet there appears to have been a change in attitude among those in Indian Affairs after the war. Michael Francklin, who had handled the Indians well, treating them as autonomous allies, died in 1782 and, as we have seen, at the time of the loyalist immigration G.H. Monk was supervising Indian Affairs. John Young wrote to Monk in the fall of 1783, listing what he thought were desirable regulations to be laid down for Indian and settler, such as one which would prohibit Indians from taking their dogs with them when going to the settlements, for "it has been the cause of many Disputes and will be more so as people are coming to settle every Day: the country will be full of people makes me think Sir that Good Regulations will be proper and it will be a pleasure on booth Sides to have them."[66]

The great increase in the population and the promise of a further one meant that Indian and white could no longer share the land as they once had, when the extent of wild country allowed both to follow their own ways without disturbing the other. The country was becoming "full of people," a situation which shifted policy, seemingly without conscious effort or decision, from one of courting and consulting the Indian to one of controlling him. This was aided by the Indian's attempt to adjust to the loyalist influx and the shrinking wilderness by seeking and accepting "reservations," an action which assured him of a claim to some land, but which also brought him more and more under the influence and control of the white man's government.

By stressing the elements of fear and antagonism, the attitude of the pre-loyalists can be distorted, for although they worried about being supplanted by the newcomers this did not blind them to the advantages of the loyalist presence. The loyalists represented a greatly increased population, increased capital, experience, and skills. The provisions and pensions they received meant an increase in the wealth and hard currency of Nova Scotia. Their numbers meant that vacant lands held for speculation could now be sold, and that merchants and producers had a new and increased market. The loyalist presence was in many cases an opportunity to be exploited.

The old settlers, especially outside Halifax, had had a very difficult time during the war, and with the coming of the loyalists sought to recoup to some extent, supplying lumber, provisions, and, as in the case of Halifax and Annapolis, shelter. Governor Parr claimed in 1783 that the cost of provisions had increased threefold in Halifax. Edmund Fanning felt that he was worth less as lieutenant governor than in his previous position as surveyor general, owing to "the High Price of Provisions and Home Rent, vastly exceeding from the rapid and amazing increase of the Inhabitants." In the opinion of Jacob Bailey the old inhabitants in the Annapolis valley had "enriched themselves" at the expense of the helpless refugees. Other areas that could supply the loyalists took advantage of the opportunity. Simeon Perkins regarded them primarily as a market to be exploited, particularly when boards were selling at Halifax for £4 to £4.10.[67]

This desire to exploit loyalist needs was the chief factor, although shrouded in a heavy fog of professed loyalty and anti-Americanism, behind the effort to prevent the importation of American produce. Because the influx of people had led to a rapid escalation of food prices which threatened loyalist security and well-being, Parr and the council allowed the import of various foods from the United States. The producers petitioned against this, claiming that Nova

Scotia had been able to support both the early refugees and the armed forces during the revolution, that in relation to the rise in the price of goods from Britain and the West Indies the increase for Nova Scotian produce was moderate, and that if American beef continued to be imported they would be ruined and must leave the country. They expressed their belief that the governor was being "Deceived in this Instance by a few individuals, who know not the situation [in] this Province, & who are in no way connected or attached [to] its Interest."[68] Parr, on the other hand, argued that prices in beef and other produce were prohibitively high, that some merchants in Halifax were keeping the price of flour up to £3.10 per hundredweight, that Nova Scotia needed at this time more than it could produce, and that dependence on local beef would not only drive the prices up but would also lessen the number of cattle, for at such prices the loyalists could not afford to buy stock.[69] Parr lost this particular round, the assembly passing an act prohibiting the entry of American ships. It was feared that as a result "the Farmers in the interior part of the Country (who are Opulent Men), taking advantage of the said Prohibition, will not send their Cattle to Market but in small numbers, and those at an exorbitant price, Beef and Mutton, now selling at ten pence pr pound, and by the best information I can procure, the price will increase as the Winter Season approaches."[70]

The reaction of officials to the coming of the loyalists was even more marked. The image of the official despondent as a result of overwork and ingratitude is deceptive. To most of those holding government appointments, the loyalists were so much fresh carrion. Governor Parr set the tone and revealed the attitude of officials to the expenditure of such large sums of British money. It was characteristic of Parr and the age that his position was one of both service and exploitation. He tried to be a competent governor, but he was also aware of the potential advantages of his position, particularly as a result of the coming of the loyalists.

With the disbanding of the Nova Scotia Volunteers, Parr, as colonel of the regiment, wrote to Evan Nepean, seeking to be put on half-pay with the rest of the officers, arguing that although his emolument as governor was only £1,400, his expenses had greatly increased with the arrival of the loyalists and the consequent need to entertain them. "A decrease of income of between 4 and £500 a Year at this present time, would therefore be too sencibly felt." He wrote to Nepean again in December, seeking to have the British government put aside the "obsolete Instruction" which prevented him from taking money from the assembly, specifically the £500 it had voted him.[71]

He was also aware of the new value of land, taking for himself 500 acres in Shelburne. It was worth little, according to Parr, since it was a mile and a half outside town, and was small in comparison to grants taken by past governors and military figures. Yet had Shelburne fulfilled its promise, it would have been a very valuable piece of real estate. Nor was he selfish with Nova Scotia's land. "If I can be of service to you," he wrote to Nepean, "or to any of your Friends in the Navy who mean to settle in this Province, I beg you will command." Earlier he had made a similar offer, pointing out that Nepean "must be a judge how valuable Land may be hereafter in this Province." In 1787 Morris requested the survey of "a Tract of most excellent land" in the vicinity of Antigonish, "for some particular Persons whom the Govr would be glad to accomodate in the best manner." Jason Dole of Shelburne claimed that Parr had "reserved Two miles length of the best ground along the side of our Town," marked for reserves large sections of land already improved and surveyed by the association, and was laying aside land for every type of outsider except "Halifax Butchers." And, of course, every position created to meet the initial needs of the loyalists, every recommendation for extra or better land, became a source of patronage. Morris, in recommending a man to Major Studholme, revealingly stated that he was "the only man I have as yet recommended to your particular attention without being ordered to do it."[72]

The fees attached to any position were a factor of extreme importance to every official, and the loyalist land grants represented a cornucopia of possibilities. John Breynton, rector of St Paul's, Halifax, underlined this in a letter to Samuel Peters concerning a possible vacancy in the government service. "I should have mentioned above the great fees attending numerous Grants of land lately made." Governor Parr submitted an account of his fees to March 31, 1784, which came to £524.9.6. He protested vehemently against being limited to half-fees, a sum "very far short of any that were upon the Continent of America." The half-fees for the six-month period ending on September 30, 1784, despite all his trials and labour, came to a paltry £1,771.15.6. He assured Nepean that the Treasury would give him full fees if they were only aware of all that he had done for the loyalists. Apparently Parr later had the council establish a new, and higher, schedule of fees for himself and the leading officials, a move which Lord Sydney felt unjustified and disallowed.[73] What rankled with Parr almost as much as the half-fees was the fact that according to the schedule he actually made less than the surveyor general and, even more galling, the provincial secretary. If only Lord Sydney could see "the great *Disproportion*, between the Governor and subordinate Officers, he will think my request not unreasonable, that is, to be put at least upon as good a footing as the Secretary."[74]

In another letter Parr argued for more money from the fee schedule to allow him to continue to live in the style to which he was accustomed in the capital, a style dictated not necessarily by his tastes but by the dignity of his office. "I live well, so as not to disgrace the recommendation of our friend the Marquiss." In a letter to Lord Sydney he stressed another point:

... untill the making of Grants of Land to the Refugees, the Yearly Amount of Fees at the Publick Office was insufficient to pay the Expence of Clerks; and, that after this Business shall be over, and it has, now nearly ceased, there is no prospect of any greater income or Emolument from Fees than before – And I submit to your Lordship's Consideration the consequence which may follow from the Officers of Government being in any Considerable degree, dependant either on the People or their Representatives.[75]

Perhaps the most rapacious of the government officials was Richard Gibbons, appointed attorney general in 1782.[76] Gibbons held himself exempt from the half-fee limitation. Moreover, when the circumstances of such large numbers and such limited time dictated a system of multiple grants, he insisted upon a fee, not for each grant requiring his seal, but for each person named in the grant.[77] In order to relieve this bottleneck of greed, Parr simply passed grants without the attorney general's fiat. The Colonial Office records are heavy with the details of this affair and of Gibbons's appeals to get what he insisted was rightly his, until Whitehall, almost in disgust, banished him to Cape Breton as chief justice, and this only at the intercession of Cape Breton's governor, desBarres.[78]

An odd situation exploited by the higher officials was the difference between sterling and "currency" in the distribution of timber to the loyalists. Although the distribution was well intended on Britain's part, and of extreme necessity, an anonymous writer charged that "these benevolences and bounties have been prostituted to private venality and corruption." Governor Parr drew bills of exchange for the timber upon the treasury. The bills, however, did not express the currency in which they were drawn, although persons receiving them in Halifax were obliged to look on them as drawn in sterling, and to pay into the secretary's office the difference of exchange between sterling and currency. This practice plus an additional premium made for a total profit to the secretary's office of 14 per cent. "This has been uniformly practiced," the writer alleged. To make the scheme plausible, those people having demands on the government were forced to submit to the secretary's office an account of the lumber supplied, and the other necessary details, "without being allowed (as is usually practiced in the Province) to write Currency against the Amo then attested before a Justice, by which means the account and bills exactly conform."[79] Much of the money seems to have gone into the pockets of Governor Parr, for in discussing it he wrote, "This, together with my half fees will not overpay me for the constant trouble, distress and anxiety of mind, I have experienced since the first arrival of the Refugees."[80]

The surveyor general's department also fed upon the loyalists and took what limited advantage they could of this flow of British largesse. From New York Carleton early had pointed out abuse by surveyors. Some refugees, having explored the province on their own and chosen tracts they believed suitable found they were refused such land for no other reason "but because it was imagined they were good judges of land and the tracts they had chosen were therefore thought worth reserving for greater favourites." Carleton also pointed out that the surveyors were demanding presents, without which applications were being ignored.[81] Morris stated that except for three or four cases, "I can declare I have not received a Fee from a Loyal Emmegrant or Disbanded Troops." There is, however, the petition of two loyalists who claimed that Morris charged them £18 as fees for granting them their land. There is also a letter to Colonel Glasior, informing him of the grant of an extra thousand acres and thanking him for the saddle he had sent Morris. Morris, deeply involved in the process of escheating land, did not hesitate to save those of friends and associates. When escheats hit too close to home he demanded that "my Son in Law Captain Solomons Land, will not be applyed for by Soldier or Loyalist, Jew or Turk."[82] Worse, since many of the deputies were loyalists, the refugees were being exploited by their own people. Benjamin Marston, for example, was not at all above taking a "handsome gratuity" after laying out a lot. Captain Booth was later to comment that "none but those who tipp'd Mr. M_____ were allowed to the [choice] of Ground."[83] Charles Inglis explained it well when he wrote in 1790, "that hitherto in this province, public money was considered as a kind of plunder, of which people wished to take as much as possible, & do as little for it as possible."[84]

The comments made and attitudes struck by the governor, the officials, and by other Nova Scotians, were inevitably less the result of a detached contemplation of the loyalists than of an emotional reaction to them. The views of such people were shaped by the impact of the loyalist upon their world and were therefore highly subjective. Few had the impartiality to reflect upon the character and situation

of the loyalists. But there were a few, and their reflections were far
from flattering. Many graphic comments in the preceding pages come
from the pens of two loyalists, Benjamin Marston and Jacob Bailey,
both of whom were very critical of the refugees, finding many of
them both shiftless and shifty, lazy and dishonest. Colonel Dundas,
one of the claims commissioners, found the new settlements "in a
thriving way, although rum and idle habits contracted during the
war are much against them." William Dyott, on his tour of the province
with Prince William Henry, visited Shelburne in 1787 and was
impressed by neither the town nor its inhabitants. "There was a Mr.
Bruce and Mr. Skinner, American Loyalists, dined; they are the only
people tolerably decent at Shelburne."[85]

In his manuscript history, Andrew Brown, although with many
friends and ties in Shelburne, was not much kinder. What struck
him about the early years of the community was the amount of
gaiety and frivolity. He had admiration for the effort expended in
clearing and laying out the town but criticism for the haste, waste,
and vanity shown in building. Moreover, the community was soon
rent by conflict.

Favourite lots were drawn by persons who possessed no other title to
distinction then what a corrupt leaning on the part of the agents employed
by Government had given them; valuable stations had been granted apart
in Halifax which are of course witheld from the decision of the lot. The
Spirit of Nationality was stirred up.
. . . men from the same country had worked their way to undue influence.
By their acts and representations the bounty of the Crown was said to be
intercepted or abused.[86]

Captain Booth was another visitor to Shelburne, one whose stay,
because he could not get transferred from the military establishment
there, was much longer than he wished. Although objective, he saw
the Shelburnian through the eyes of the British gentry. He identified
these people less as loyalists than as Americans. "The *Commonality*
of the Americans seem to possess something of the French nation
– *much Artfulness*, and consequently *Little Sincerity*." He was struck
by their airs and pretentions, all styling themselves gentlemen, and
wrote of having his servants announce a gentleman, only to find
on entering the room "that the Poor fellow was either a Carpenter,
Smith or Mason begging for employment." "The Spirit of equallitty
and consequence seems to reign throughout the Country," he
remarked, "being the fashion in ye States where they last had their
abode."[87]

Perhaps the most critical treatment of the loyalists was the description entitled "Shelburnian Manners" written in 1787.[88] The author saw them as dancing beggars. "The Inhabitants of Shelburne from the highest to the lowest have a pitiable passion for finery, revelling & dancing & every Species of Instant gratification. They vie with one another in making an external appearance in the public eye, as being persuaded that the world will jud[g]e of them much more by this." The snobbery among them had not only made the ladies slaves to fashion but, more seriously, acted as a major divisive force within the community.

It is a matter of regret, that the Assembly for the Season, tho' designed for promoting social & friendly Intercourse among neighbors, should yet become the occasion of Censoriousness, affronts & ill will, thro' the imprudence of Some forward, pert & Gay young People who assume consequential airs by shewing themselves reserved, haughty & distant towards those whom they deem their Inferiors ... If you except their dress, diet & a few articles of furniture, everything else belonging to them indicate that they are of the Dregs of mankind.

What also bothered the author a great deal was the extent to which many would indulge in dishonest and corrupt behaviour in order to sustain their frivolous way of life. The half-pay officers, for example, in order to continue their extravagances "monopolize (if I may use the expression) almost every public office which is in the gift of Government." Some refugees, ruined by war or early extravagance in Shelburne, were forced to live frugally and temperately, a fact that the author considered a fortunate circumstance for their moral character. Others, in their vanity and greed, came to worship easy money. "Hence it is, that they have no Scruple to get gain by illicit trade, to import & to circulate base Coppers, to make use of these gross methods of dishonest Gain; the false balance, deceitful weights, & illegal measure, to adulterate Spirituous liquids, & to make an artificial want of Several articles brought to market." There seemed little concern for the public good. Many of those holding public office treated it as opportunity and sinecure, and thus "betray their trust & embezzle the public money."

The author was struck by the idleness in the settlement. For one thing, after the initial frenzy of settling and building was over, there was not enough business in the community to keep all active. For another, many were simply incapable of sustained labour. "The Bulk of the Inhabitants having been accustomed to a trading & rambling way of life during the late war, contracted an aversion to all kinds of work which are laborious." This idleness led to an excess of "tippling," of games of chance, of gossip, and of "Knavish fraudulent tricks." The idleness, in combination with "the disengenuous turn of mind," led also to an excess of litigation, with much of the property tied up in mortgages and attachments, or "often taken away by [subtlety] of law." The community shaped by all of these factors was a very factious one, the atmosphere one of discord, dissatisfaction, and restlessness.

"Shelburnian Manners" is a harsh portrayal of life in Shelburne and, by inference, in the other loyalist communities. To a certain extent it conveys an unfair and distorted view of the loyalist presence in Nova Scotia. There were such types in the refugee communities, drunks and idlers, the pretentious and the dishonest, as was to be expected under these unusual circumstances. With such a mixed bag of people thrown together into raw, unformed communities, after the dislocation of the war and the exodus, one might expect excesses of behaviour among strangers scrambling to establish and if possible enhance their positions in this fluid society before it hardened. Not all loyalists, however, were of these types. One of the distortions associated with the loyalist presence in Nova Scotia is the image created by the extremes of behaviour. A sizeable portion of the abuses for which the loyalists were blamed could be laid at the feet not of those who would remain in the province and contribute to its development, but of the transients, the opportunists, and the shiftless, who had come for the chance posed by the promised British expenditures, for the provisions, and for the free land, which would be sold at the first opportunity. These, although touching upon the province's development for only a brief moment before departing, did much to tarnish the image of the loyalist in Nova Scotia and were responsible for much of the contumely directed at him.

However, the issue is not simply whether such impressions of the loyalists were accurate but whether they were commonly accepted. Many of the characteristics dwelt on in "Shelburnian Manners" were also commented upon by other observers. It is remarkable how often epithets used and actions described are repeated from writer to writer. For the non-loyalist in the province the term "loyalist" did not have that aura of tragic and noble sacrifice fostered by the loyalists themselves. They were simply Americans, with all that the term implied, many of them lower-class, some of them the "dregs of America," quarrelling among themselves over past provincial loyalties and present prizes, often lazy and dishonest, fractious and quarrelsome, endlessly demanding and "ungrateful." The basic attitude towards the refugee was simply that he was unworthy of the "loyalist" image being foisted upon the province and the government. The image was not accepted; the superiority connoted by the term fiercely resented.

Reaction to the loyalists, however, was moulded by one's own position, problems, and proximity to them. If the image was never really accepted, the resentment, unevenly distributed to begin with, did not retain the intensity of the early years and in time dissipated. Much of it was a reaction to the threat posed by the loyalist's claims and peculiar position. As the threat was confronted and found to be less dangerous than expected, as the loyalist demands and expectations lessened, as the troublesome and vociferous left the province, as those remaining adjusted to their new roles as Nova Scotians, in short, as the unknown became known, the attitude towards the loyalists shifted from resentment to acceptance and, in many cases, cooperation.

The Loyalist in the Sixth Assembly

The politics of the loyalist was not necessarily that of the establishment. He had once been an American colonial seeking greater autonomy in reaction to a growing centralization on the part of Britain, until reform had turned to rebellion, and rebellion had polarized the combatants. Yet once freed from the choice between loyality and rebellion, it is unlikely that he would have completely abandoned what was a natural American reflex, the desire for self-government. Benjamin Marston indirectly explains much of this attitude in speaking of an incident in Shelburne: "the settlers were all called upon to take the oath of allegiance to the King and subscribe a decalaration acknowledging the supremacy of the British Parliament over the whole Empire, but this was explained as not to extend to taxation."[1] The fact that the explanation was needed indicates that the loyalists in Nova Scotia were not so much Tories as Americans who had remained loyal in a polarizing situation. The organization of the refugee associations to handle the exodus was very democratic, as in the case of the New York agencies, where the refugees "chuse their Captains & they appoint two Lieutenants for every class."[2] Nor did the democratic element end with the choosing of their officers, for Marston was continually frustrated by it. In May 1783, after the captains had chosen the site for Shelburne, the multitude objected to the site and decided to choose three men from each company to do it all over again. Marston complained, "This cursed republican, town-meeting spirit has been the ruin of us already, and unless checked by some stricter form of government will overset the prospect which now presents itself of retrieving our affairs."[3] Whether they were voting to seize the boards of a private saw mill and convert them to public use,[4] or were drawing for lots and "indulging their cursed republican principles,"[5] to Marston they were indistinguishable from the rebels they had fled.

Governor Parr shared similar sentiments, for the loyalists' manner of treating governors was one that he found neither customary nor congenial. Sometime in the summer of 1783 he received a rather harsh note from Amos Botsford, in whose correspondence there are two letters referring to the matter. One is from Parr stating that he was doing all in his power for the loyalists, had an immense amount of sympathy for them, but was not to be dictated to by Botsford. He suggested that Botsford should write less and work more.[6] The second letter, from Charles Morris, regretted Botsford's "dictatorial Style" and pointed out that Parr was "the King's Representative, and that there was a difference between him and a Governor of Connecticut – of the Peoples own making whom they may reject and chuse another when they please."[7]

The loyalists' knowledge of the system of government in Nova Scotia was often scanty and based on hearsay, for some believed that the Legislative Assembly was appointed for life.[8] They were consequently apprehensive. Moreover, they brought with them a tradition of self-government, and both caution and tradition dictated that they oppose any form of taxation by a body upon which they were not represented.[9] Such an attitude would lead them in the first years of settlement into a movement with the dual aim of gaining representation in the provincial assembly and as great a measure of autonomy as possible for their local governments. "As to the internal Police of the Settlement," Joseph Pynchon noted, "we must expect to be under the laws of the province – I am in hopes a Corporation may be obtained – I think it will unless the Jealousies of other parts of the province, make it necessary for the Peace and Quiet of the Governor, to be otherwise.[10]

There was a fear among the Shelburne people of seeing what money they had make its way to Halifax. It could take the form of a memorial from the magistrates of Shelburne asking that impost and licence duties remain within the town.[11] It could also be found in the protests of a man brought to court for defying the magistrates and serving liquor without a licence. He believed that "the licence money went to support a set of people who walked the streets with their hands in their pockets, & therefore it was wrong to pay any licence money."[12] Government and the existing assembly were seen as the enemy, distrusted and feared. Joseph Aplin expressed these attitudes in his criticism of an assembly whose only positive action on the loyalist question had been to reward the governor with a gift of £500 on receiving his promise of veiling the treasonable practices of many of the pre-loyalists.[13] At the least the assembly should have held an inquiry into the slow and inept land granting system. "But nothing like this was done, and the neglect of it, has lost to the Assembly all that confidence of the new Settlers which is most immediately connected with the Health and Prosperity of the Province."[14] Their memorials on government often combined the demand for a new assembly with loyalist representation and the appeal for substantial autonomy in local administration, justice, and education.[15]

The announcement in 1784 that the Fifth Assembly was to be dissolved after fourteen years made the loyalists fear that the election was designed to allow the formation of a new assembly before they could qualify as electors.[16] Their fears were not justified, for the decision to dissolve the assembly had been made by the British government before their coming, and Parr was insistent upon their representation in the new House.[17] Even the existing assembly expressed its desire "to see as soon as possible Representatives from the several new Settlements, Joining us in such our Endeavors."[18] In December 1784 an act was passed creating six new seats for the loyalist areas.[19]

The assembly elected in 1770 was dissolved on October 20, 1785, and the polls in Halifax opened on November 8.[20] It was a heated affair with nine elections contested before the House, and in certain ridings it appears to have led to the crystallizing of the loyalist identity in the conflict with the pre-loyalist Nova Scotian. This was definitely the case in the fight for Annapolis County between a loyalist, David Seabury, and a native Nova Scotian, Capt. Alexander Howe. In an election "conducted with unexampled temper and decency, considering the struggle between the former inhabitants and the new adventurers,"[21] David Seabury won. Howe challenged the result on the ground that the sheriff had been extremely partial in allowing non-freeholders and Catholics to vote for Seabury and not for himself. On December 6 the assembly declared the election null and void.[22] A new election was called, and the ensuing contest created an atmosphere in which "such a bitterness rancour and virulence prevails as exceeds all description."[23] Thomas Barclay, an elected loyalist from Annapolis, appealed to leading loyalists in the valley to give their all "to support our Interests, and we shall deserve our fate if we permit Capt. Howe to carry his Election."[24] The appeal must have been effective, for once again Seabury won; but again the House annulled the results, and Howe sat as one of the MLAs for Annapolis. Moreover, when the House took up the matter of Barclay's letter, on a charge of partiality, a straight loyalist/pre-loyalist division occurred on the motion to dismiss.[25] This same appeal to loyalist solidarity occurred in a letter of James Clarke concerning the new House. "Blowers deserves every Attention and Mark of Respect from the real Loyalist," he had written to Gideon White. He insisted that "For political Reasons ... do not be pointed towards Uniacke nor discover any Thing that has the Appearance of Faction or the warmth of Party – Consult Wilkins in every Thing for be assured he ought to be looked up to as the Pole-Star of the Loyalists."[26]

There are factors, however, which alter slightly this portrait of loyalist solidarity. Not all loyalist communities, for example, put up local champions to represent them. Guysborough, recently populated by loyalists, was represented by two Haligonians, James Putnam, Jr, a loyalist barrack master, and J.M. Freke Bulkeley, son of the provincial secretary. To one county historian, the Guysborough inhabitants were simply too busy in resettling "to give any time to any except the most pressing problems."[27] Moreover, there were factors concering the Annapolis election that might call into question the obvious conclusions drawn. Captain Howe was not a representative Nova Scotian, for, although born in Annapolis, prior to 1783 he had been an officer with the 36th and 104th Regiments.[28] Nor would David Seabury automatically have won the support of the loyalist rank and file, for he had been one of the infamous fifty-five.[29] What helped to split the community into loyalist and pre-loyalist camps was the sense of injustice felt by both sides. One party felt that they had been terribly abused by the marked partiality of the House. The other party, and many members of the House, felt that the large pre-loyalist minority should, in justice, have at least one of the four seats for the Annapolis region. And yet Jacob Bailey mentions that some native Nova Scotians who were "formerly great friends to the American Revolution have given their interest very warmly for Mr. Seabury."[30] It is doubtful that those considered by James Clarke to be "real" loyalists and pole-stars would have been accepted as such by the rank and file. Isaac Wilkins was not only another of the fifty-five, but had already earned the wrath of many in Shelburne by his greed for town lots, and the congratulations of his peers for securing a position that placed him beyond the rabble.[31] S.S. Blowers would later gain the distinction of being one of the earliest to sell out his fellow loyalists for the sake of government patronage.[32] And in the pure loyalist soil of Shelburne the long hand of the Halifax clique was felt, for in an earlier letter to Gideon White, Clarke had stated that "Colo. Tongue connected himself with McNeill and Leckie, who availed themselves of that Connexion to serve Largin."[33] Largin had the position of deputy naval officer, which White coveted; M'Neil and Leckie were newly elected members for Shelburne, and Colonel Tonge was a leading pre-loyalist in the assembly.

Only thirteen of the thirty-nine members of the new assembly could be classified as loyalists,[34] yet they wielded an influence out of proportion to their numbers. A loyalist was speaker for the first three sessions. In 1789 the loyalists moved 56 per cent of the successful resolutions and made up 40 per cent of the committee members. In the following year they equalled the old members in both categories.[35] And in 1790 Lawrence and Wilkins, both loyalists, were appointed agents of the province by the assembly.[36]

One marked characteristic of the Sixth Assembly was the cohesiveness of the loyalists. In thirty-two recorded votes, they voted solidly as a bloc on twenty occasions.[37] On at least three other occasions the bloc was abandoned by only one of its members.[38] In almost two-thirds of the recorded votes, then, the loyalists voted as a solid bloc, a marked display of solidarity. There were, moreover, several occasions when the vote in the House was basically a loyalist/pre-loyalist split. On five occasions the loyalist members stood essentially alone against a wall of pre-loyalist members. When the issue of Barclay's letter, in which he urged all loyalists to rally behind Seabury during the 1785 election in Annapolis, was placed before the House, Isaac Wilkins's motion that the House go no further in discussing it was defeated by eight votes. All eighteen opposing it were pre-loyalist. Only one pre-loyalist, J.B. Dight, the member for Cumberland, supported Wilkins's motion.[39] When Belcher, a pre-loyalist, moved that the seats of three members (one of whom was a loyalist) be vacated because they were holding offices under the government, the loyalists alone suppported him.[40] When, in the heat of the impeachment controversy, Wilkins moved that the governor, having been deceived by his council, should remove its members from office until His Majesty's pleasure was known, the motion, defeated twenty-one to eight, was supported by six loyalists and only two pre-loyalists, Belcher and Collins.[41] On votes dealing with the issue of allowing cattle, produce, and timber to be imported from the United States to aid the new communities, the loyalists received limited pre-loyalist support, most of the old settlers fearing the loss of a captive market.[42]

Yet the division between loyalist and pre-loyalist is more remarkable for its infrequency. The most obvious occasion was the Barclay letter, an event occurring very early in the session, when members from both the new and old communities were wary of each other, and resulting from deliberate polarization by Barclay. The issue of imports again arose early in the session, and was more a case of the division of producer from consumer, each intent on protecting his own interests. On those occasions, moreover, there were cross-over votes on both sides. The other two issues on which the loyalists were in a sense abandoned, the proposed exclusion of office-holders from the assembly and Wilkins's motion to dismiss the council, are more instructive if seen not so much as a division between old and new settlers but rather as the abandonment by many of the more cautions pre-loyalist members of the loyalists' aggressive policy of asserting the power of the elected house. Many old Nova Scotians who had gone far in voting with the loyalist bloc hesitated to go as far as these two motions.

Although the loyalists did vote as a bloc in a remarkable number of roll calls, this phenomenon is understandable in members sharing not only the past bond of the revolution and exodus, but also similar problems of the present moment. They were all from new communities facing great difficulties, all temporary consumers dependent upon imports, all distrusting and most detesting the established powers in Halifax, all on the outside of executive power looking in and therefore favouring the assertion of the assembly's power.

What is more important in understanding the character of the Sixth Assembly is the relationship of the pre-loyalist members towards the loyalist bloc. Except for those cited, the votes on which the loyalists were defeated also recorded a sizeable body of pre-loyalist members going down to defeat with them, in numbers which for the most part equalled or outnumbered the loyalist vote. The loyalists were simply part of, and often the smaller part of, the minority.[43] On twelve occasions the loyalists, holding solidly as a bloc, saw their vote carried. In all but two instances the bloc was outnumbered by the pre-loyalists voting with them.[44] The loyalists seemed to have simply joined their voices, as outsiders, to an existing group which often opposed government policy.

Those people who most consistently voted with the loyalist bloc had one common characteristic: they were from the hinterland. Benajah Collins was from Liverpool, S.S. Poole from Yarmouth, Casper Wollenhaupt from Lunenburg, Mathew Archibald from Truro, Benjamin Belcher from Cornwallis, Jonathan Crane from Horton, John Day from Newport.[45] Of those who most consistently opposed the loyalist bloc on votes, Captain Howe was perhaps strongly influenced by the scars of the 1785 election. Freke Bulkeley, Charles Hill, J.G. Pyke, and Charles Morris were Haligonians who were tied, in varying degrees, to the Halifax establishment. John McMonagle, from Windsor, and D.C. Jessen, from Lunenburg, were multiple office-holders. Benjamin Dewolfe, from Windsor, was a very affluent merchant.[46]

The most obvious generalization to be made concerning the divisions in the Sixth Assembly is that they involved Halifax against the hinterland, the establishment against those members outside it, and consequently, those supporting the government and appointed branches against those championing the assembly's powers. There was simply too strong a pre-loyalist contingent cooperating with the loyalists to talk of a loyalist faction in opposition, for the inference is one of isolated opposition.

The first three sessions of the Sixth Assembly had shown a thrust towards economic and social improvements and a quest for reform. As a result of the inquiries into custom duties, collection of revenue, spending of money, and the fee systems, a deputy naval officer was dismissed and new revenue officers appointed in four townships.[47] "The absorption of the House during the first sessions in industrial improvements, educational advance, and above all in internal reform," it has been argued, "was an accurate forecast of the next five years."[48]

Until 1787 the relationship of assembly and council had not been particularly abrasive. The 1787 motion by Colonel Milledge, however, on the dissatisfaction in the province concerning the administration of justice, signalled a change. After that, relations between the two bodies began to deteriorate. The council members, Halifax-dominated, appointed in effect for life and for their support of government policy, tied very closely to one another through marriage and blood, self-interest, and fear of encroachment by the elected House, were consequently stalwart pillars of the prerogative and the status quo.[49] And the growing aggressiveness of the House after 1787 threatened those pillars.

One instance of such aggressiveness was the assault upon the Naval Office. Winckworth Tonge, the naval officer until his death in 1792,[50] had, as early as 1786, complained of the confusion created by the opposition of governor, attorney general, and assembly to his conduct. He countered their criticism by claiming that the fees he collected did not manage to cover the expense of his office.[51] The question of the Naval Office was not really raised again until 1790. By that time complaints had once more arisen about high fees, the naval officer's appointing of deputies in the outports, and alleged inter-ference by the office with fishing and the coastal trade.[52]

A committee of the House moved against all three practices, questioning whether coastal trade fell under the naval officer's jurisdiction, denying his right to appoint deputies where there were no customs officers, and recommending a bill to control his "very high and burdensome fees."[53] It was not an exceptional flexing of the assembly's muscle, but the affair was indicative of a growing assertiveness towards appointed officials. It resulted in greater caution on the part of the Naval Office in exacting fees and the withdrawal of deputy naval officers from the outports.[54]

A major conflict between assembly and council during this period arose over the issue of money bills. In 1786 the assembly had passed an appropriation bill containing council amendments.[55] By 1789, however, declaring "the inherent right of this House to Originate all Money Bills and that they cannot admit of any Amendments to be made therein by the Council," the assembly refused to accept council amendments of a revenue bill,[56] and the unamended bill was passed.[57] In 1790 the contest occurred again, the council amending revenue bills, the House rejecting the amendments, and in a memorial to the governor again asserting its right to be the sole originator of money bills.[58] By 1791 the governor and council, aware of the shaky provincial finances and the assembly's power to refuse them the revenue now necessary to carry on the affairs of government, accepted the assembly's sole right to initiate and amend money bills; the council in 1791 accepted without amendments the bill it had rejected the previous year.[59]

The Sixth Assembly was also determined to gain control of its own membership and proceedings, particularly by asserting its responsibility for deciding who could vote and who could sit in the House. One facet of its assertiveness was the attempt to limit the duration or continuance of Parliament, a bill to which Parr refused assent, "in Obedience to His Majesty's Instructions."[60] Another move was the attempt to divide some of the counties. The House petitioned that several new counties be carved out of the extensive domains of Halifax and Annapolis.[61] The thought of that increase in representation frightened Parr. He argued that, with Halifax County already having seven members, Annapolis five, and the House thirty-nine members, what was needed was a reduction of seats rather than an increase. The assembly's arguments, moreover, "are mere Pretences to gain an Addition of two more Counties in this Province; and thereby to Obtain an Increase of four more Members, I am afraid Factious, to the number of that Denomination already in that Assembly."[62]

Without success the loyalists in the Sixth Assembly fought to restrict membership to the House, seeking to pry loose some representatives of the official establishment.[63] Belcher's motion that the seats of M'Neil, Howe, and Smith be vacated because they were holding offices under the crown was easily deferred by a vote of eighteen to eight. Despite the fact that M'Neil was a loyalist representative of Shelburne, seven of the votes supporting Belcher were those of loyalists. When his motion was again heard, the House agreed with the committee studying it that the precedents were contrary to Belcher's request, and the motion was dismissed.[64] Barclay's later motion to get judges, sheriffs, and customs officials removed from the House met with a similar fate. And once again support was given to his motion by the loyalist representatives.[65]

The assembly did move to gain some control over its own elections. Prior to the Sixth Assembly the council was the sole regulator of elections.[66] There had, however, been several heated, hard-fought campaigns in the election of 1785, and several controverted elections as a result of electoral officials' actions during the voting.[67] Moreover, the Halifax by-election of 1788 between Sterns and Charles Morris was marked by violence and intimidation. The *Gazette* reported that "It was utterly impossible in such Confusion to prevent many persons from being wounded and hurt. Two of whom we are sorry to inform the Public remain in a dangerous State, one having his Skull fractured by some Persons who rushed out of *Laycocks House* on the Beach, and the other having been dangerously wounded by a shot from a window in the same House."[68] Since the orchestration of violence and intimidation was for the benefit of the pro-government candidate, Charles Morris, the results of the by-election, combined with the growing friction between House and government, led to moves by the assembly for electoral reform.

In 1789 the House passed a new elections bill, one which, ironically, was opposed by the reform-minded loyalists. Their opposition stemmed from the fate of an earlier resolution on electoral reform. In March Barclay, a loyalist member, had put forward a two-part resolution. The first gave the House "sole and exclusive Power" over elections. The second, however, did not deal with elections but with the composition of the House, excluding from it judges and government officials. The members, by a margin of eighteen to twelve, voted to accept the first and reject the second. A solid bloc of eight loyalists voted against the recommendation.[69] On the following day a committee headed by Captain Howe brought in a bill "for the better regulating and conducting Elections of Representatives in this Province." The bill contained regulations to reduce fraudulent practices, breaches of the election rules, and disorders during elections. The bill also asserted that the House alone possessed the "sole and exclusive power of examining and determining ... all matters incidental to elections."[70] On the motion, the loyalists again voted as a bloc, this time being joined by eight pre-loyalists, three of whom had voted for the previous motion. Again this group was defeated and the bill passed.[71] The anomaly of many of the reform-minded in the assembly, particularly the loyalists, voting against a bill for better regulating elections must be explained by the weakening of Barclay's original motion and by their doubts of the effectiveness of the bill. They simply felt that it did not go far enough.

The issue which most dramatically heightened the clash between the appointed and the elected, and revealed the loyalists as aggressive supporters, and often leaders, of those championing the elected branch was the affair of the judges. Since the death of Finucane in 1785, Nova Scotia had had no chief justice. Isaac Deschamps, acting chief justice, and James Brenton, the other puisne judge, were in a sense the Court of Nova Scotia, and, since two judges constituted a court, both men had to travel the circuit, making their stay to execute justice in the distant townships brief and insufficient. Deschamps, moreover, although a member of the council, was not a lawyer, having picked up his knowledge of the law through an informal process of osmosis as clerk and judge of the courts.[72] Some felt that, with the new counties, "it is rendered impossible that as the Bench now is, Justice can be administered."[73]

Governor Parr was aware of the weakness in the administration, writing of "the great inconvenience" caused by the lack of an able, impartial man who would nevertheless support "that Order so absolutely necessary." Such a man, however, had to be "an Englishman, of professional knowledge and understanding, to protect him from the abuse and Browbeating of a Tribe of Lawyers from the United States."[74] When Evan Nepean suggested that Colonel Barclay, a loyalist, be appointed as a third assistant judge, Parr rejected the suggestion as emphatically as he dared. Not only could the province not afford the extra salary, but Barclay had been away from the law for at least ten years, and, although he could say nothing against Barclay personally, Parr was "told that he is a violent vindictive Temper, prone to Wrangling and fond of Party Disputes ... This province being composed of People from different Countries is therefore very liable to Parties, and unless a Judge upon the Bench conducts himself with the greatest moderation, he would soon be laid hold on by one Party, and become obnoxious to all the others, and his Decisions be made the Subject of party Animadversion."[75] Ignoring the fact that the present puisne judges were already obnoxious to many, Parr strove to convince Nepean that under no circumstances should Barclay or any of that "Tribe of Lawyers" be allowed on the bench.

Not long after Finucane's death, members of the House began to comment on the purveyance of justice in the province. In the spring of 1786, Colonel Delancey wrote on the state of the judicature, pointing out the difficulties of administering justice under the existing conditions.[76] By the fall of 1787 the issue had shifted from difficulties to "Dissatisfaction having prevailed in the Province relative to the Administration of Justice in the Supreme Court," and Milledge moved that the House investigate the situation, a motion which passed unanimously.[77] The House then addressed the governor, requesting an inquiry into the conduct of the judges "in such a manner that a fair and impartial Investigation may take place, that the public may be fully satisfied of their Innocence or Criminality, and that they themselves may be satisfied in what they have an undoubted right to expect, a trial by their Peers."[78]

The governor, although assuring the assembly that the matter would be studied, expressed his disbelief in the charges.[79] The council was even less impartial, Deschamps being a member, Brenton a brother-in-law of one. Moreover, an attack on the judges was an attack on the appointed administration of the province and consequently a threat to the council members themselves, if only indirectly.

Although the session ended with no counter-move by council, the issue of the judges arose in the 1788 by-election in Halifax to fill the seat of S.S. Blowers who had been appointed to the council. Jonathan Sterns, the loyalist attorney who had been the leading witness against the judges, was opposing Charles Morris Jr, pre-loyalist councillor and office-holder.

Sterns and his group hammered away at the threat of another office-holder and "Sycophant" in the assembly.[80] A Sterns advocate, discussing the necessary qualifications for a member, felt that the man should possess honour, integrity, and spirit in order "to step forth and counteract the dark Designs of public Plunderers, in whatever station they may be; he should be a man of Independent Circumstances, who will despise to be bribed, by either honourable or profitable Appointments, to betray the important Trust reposed in him by his constituents; (a man with these Appointments should by no means have a Seat in that House.)"[81]

At their mildest the Morris group stressed the advantages of having a native son rather than a transient stranger, Morris speaking of his commitment to "the Prosperity of a County I have been endeared to, from my earliest infancy."[82] As the election wore on Sterns was portrayed as a demagogue and rabble-rouser attacking evil and corruption that existed only in his own mind. In a satirical verse published in the *Gazette*, a Sterns victory was depicted as making Nova Scotia a land of milk and honey, of fruition without effort. The verse was a counter-attack on both his claims of extensive evil and corruption and his promises of correction. The writer mocked "The Golden Age this *Patriot* shall restore."[83] A long letter written by an alleged visitor made much of the immense economic progress which had recently taken place in Nova Scotia under a sound, honest, and inexpensive government. The author then expressed his incredulity, under such conditions, on learning of the excessive complaints of oppression and abuse in government being made by Sterns and his camp, pointing out that this same type of rhetoric had brought about the revolution. "O! Nova Scotians beware of Patriots and your *Grievance* Redressers, for they are Wolves in Sheeps Cloathing."[84] The *Gazette* itself, reporting on the election, attacked "the base attempts that have been made to render the Government unpopular by the Scandalous Reflections cast upon it by a Number [of] anonymous Writers in their recent Publications."[85] Sterns's campaign had been based on revealing abuses allegedly committed by placemen and office-holders, and warning of the danger of having such men also dominate the elected body. For his efforts he was portrayed as a transient troublemaker from New York, whose brand of rhetoric and excessive behaviour had wrecked the old empire, and if allowed to continue in Nova Scotia would threaten the new empire. He was an American, and thus imbued with that destructiveness which threatens all sound governments.

Shortly after Morris's victory in the election, the council answered the assembly's charges against the judges in a published attack which stated "that the Alligations made by the Attornies in the House of Assembly against the conduct in office of the Justices of the Supreme Court are groundless and scandalous, and that the Justices of the said Court have by their Answer thereto fully acquitted themselves of all imputation of Malconduct in Office."[86] Such a statement was not only a slap at the House, but a spur to Sterns and William Taylor, the other loyalist attorney involved, to publish the evidence they had given to the House, a move which enabled Deschamps to disbar them.[87]

The establishment reacted to the assault on the judges as if republicanism and anarchy were on the verge of triumph in Nova Scotia. Parr, although relatively conciliatory with the House, wrote in scarlet prose to England. "Whatever Loyalty these Lawyers may have brought with them from the States, is so strong tinctured with a Republican Spirit; that if they meet with any encouragement it may be attended with dangerous consequences to this Province. One of them (Sterns) aims at being the Wilkes of Nova Scotia."[88] In April he was accusing the lawyers of simply wishing to replace the judges with their friends. "They have made a strong Party, chiefly among the new Inhabitants, who have shewn a Seditious factious Spirit upon occation, many of whom I am sorry to say have introduced republican Principles, who came here under the Specious pretence of Loyalty."[89]

When Sterns and Taylor sailed for England to present their case, Parr was quick to warn Lord Sydney that any consideration given to their appeals could eventually threaten the continuance of the British Empire in America.

these Gentlemen have stired up a seditious factious Party against most of the Officers of Government here, and I hope they will be considered as turbulent Spirits on your side the Atlantic, otherwise it is not known how or where the Business may end, for if they succeed in any one point, it may be attended with bad consequence;–I further take the liberty to inform your Lordship, that if the several Officers of Government are not supported, a few Years may put a period to the Brittish Constitution in this Province.[90]

It was fear of the threat to the prerogative that had led Parr to indulge in this rhetorical overkill. He was concerned in particular about the danger of an extension of democracy and the power of the elected house. In a letter to Nepean of May 5 he attributed Sterns's dangerous appeal to the fact that the attorney was "looked upon as the Man of the People." He spoke of being "surrounded with a number of Fanatical, diabolical, unprincipled, expecting, disappointed, deceitfull, lying Scoundrels, who exist upon Party of their own creating. eternally finding fault with, and complaining against their Superiors in Office. My great comfort is that I am not singular, all the World seems to Breathe leveling Principles."[91] Perhaps it was also his opportunity to vent the anger, resentment, and frustration aroused by these arrogant, demanding refugees who had given him so much difficulty in those early years when he had to pay lip-service to their loyalty and sacrifice.

When the assembly met in March 1789, Parr answered their address of the previous session in more conciliatory terms than the council's, stating that he and the council had heard the judges' answers and had unanimously agreed "that the Charges against the Judges were not supported by the proofs which Accompanied your Address."[92] Barclay then moved that Parr be asked to give the House a copy of the council's minutes and other papers relative to their decision. His motion was defeated by a vote of fourteen to thirteen. All the loyalists voted with Barclay, but so did seven pre-loyalists. None of the thirteen was from Halifax.[93] Milledge thereupon asked the House whether it found the governor's message satisfactory. It was found satisfactory, but only by one vote. The members voted the same way, except for M'Neil, absent on the previous vote, who sided against the governor, and Charles Morris, the newly elected member for Halifax, who voted, as expected, with the government.[94]

Two days later Isaac Wilkins moved that, since "His Excellency the Lieutenant Governor has been deceived by the evil and pernicious Advice of his Privy Council and had by their Means been inadvertently induced to give his Sanction to a mode of Trial absurd, unjust and altogether unconstitutional," he should dismiss his councillors until the king's pleasure was known.[95] Captain Howe attacked the motion as tantamount to rebellion. Wilkins argued that the House was within its constitutional rights in requesting the removal and the governor in accepting the request. As to the action of the council towards the judges, it was to Wilkins similar to acquitting a prisoner simply on his own plea of not guilty.[96] Another loyalist, Barclay, attacked the council's imputation of disloyalty even more sharply. The members of the assembly as representatives of the people had the right to study and question not only the council's but also the governor's actions. "True it was, that the King could do no wrong, but it did not follow ... that his representative was equally perfect. By this remark he by no means intended to find fault with the conduct of his Excellency. What he had done was dictated by his Privy Council, and they alone were and ought to be answerable for that advice."[97] Shortly after, he asked, "How could the Council possibly declare the information ... scandalous and groundless? Could the simple answer of the justices justify so harsh a decision? If their answer could legally be admitted as evidence of their innocence, justice was at an end, and every species of villainy might pass unnoticed."[98] The sweep of Wilkins's motion, however, was too much for many who had until then sided with the loyalist bloc. The motion to have the council removed was defeated by a vote of twenty-one to eight, with Tonge, Archibald, Schwartz, Crane, Day, and McMonagle, who had supported the loyalists on the earlier two votes, abandoning them on this more aggressive one.[99]

Although the assault on the prerogative continued on other fronts throughout the session, the defeat of Wilkins's motion ended the assembly's involvement with the judges for that season. Even Parr was moved to comment on how quiet affairs had become, "having had no seditious meetings since the Republican Attornies went to England."[100] The session and season thus closed with the charges against the judges stilled, and dignity, decency, honour, and the empire triumphant in Nova Scotia, along with Parr, the placemen, and the appointed officials.

In the following year, however, the affair of the judges was reopened. "The return of Mr Sterns, and my not receiving any Dispatch in answer to the Proceedings of myself and the Council on the former Complaints against the Justices of the Supreme Court, have induced the House of Assembly to resume that untoward Business, which is now thrown into the shape of a formal Impeachment by the Commons of Nova Scotia as they stile themselves."[101] Before a packed gallery, the House organized its inquiry "with all the Forms of a Court of Judicature," even to the extent of appointing a sergeant at arms. Barclay acted as prosecutor and Sterns as chief witness.[102]

On March 10, 1790, Barclay brought in for the House's consideration thirteen articles of impeachment against the judges, charging them with "high Crimes and Misdemeanors." The motion to consider passed seventeen to ten, with the pre-loyalists outnumbering the loyalists in support of it. Pyke's motion that, since the council had already determined the issue and the matter was now referred to Great Britain, the House should not consider the charges against the judges, was defeated by a vote of twenty-one to eight. Of the twenty-one, eight were loyalists, thirteen pre-loyalists.[103] A resolution allowing the judges to reply was deferred to another day by a vote of eighteen to twelve, the pre-loyalists again outnumbering the loyalist bloc in supporting the deferral.[104] Having gone through Barclay's articles, heard witnesses on them, and debated the strengths and weaknesses of each,[105] the House created a committee to prepare specific impeachment articles,[106] and eventually sustained seven articles of impeachment against the two judges.[107] "Impeached as they the said *Isaac Deschamps* and *James Brenton*, Esquires, now stand by all the Commons of *Nova Scotia* for high Crimes and Misdemeanors, the *House of Assembly*, beg leave to represent to your Excellency the impropriety of suffering those Judges to act in, or execute the said Offices until they shall have been duly tried and acquitted of the Crimes, with which they are so solemnly charged."[108] In rejecting the request, Parr stated that he accepted the advice of council against suspension until the king's pleasure was known.[109]

Blame for the aggressive behaviour of the House, as represented by the affair of the judges, Parr placed squarely upon the loyalists, ignoring the fact that they were outnumbered by pre-loyalists in most of the anti-government votes. He declared that "it intirely proceeds from a cursed factious party spirit, which was never known here before the Emigration of the Loyalists, who brought with them, those levelling republican Principles ... the Prosecutors of this business are composed of those, who actually wish to succeed the Judges upon the Bench. those who have joined them are about six or seven, but they are most violent dissatisfied Spirits."[110]

After the session Parr sent the assembly's charges, with the judges' answers, to the secretary of state.[111] In that year Nova Scotia received a needed addition to its court with the appointment of Chief Justice Strange.[112] The year 1791 was quiet, with little mention of the judges and less marked conflict between assembly and council. The matter was now in the hands of the authorities in Great Britain. In August 1792, the Privy Council, having heard the case, announced that justice had been impartially administered. Yet it also had to admit that justice had sometimes been ignorantly and incompetently administered, a point which was the basis of the assembly's charges to begin with.[113]

The House was not unduly dismayed by the decision. For one thing, the Privy Council, although it had handed down an adverse decision, still had felt impelled, despite the frantic recommendations of governor and council, to hear the assembly's charges and to accept some of its views. Moreover, the appointment of Chief Justice Strange had alleviated some of the grievances against the system of justice. It must also be remembered that the Privy Council's decision was two years in the making, two years in which the House found itself in new crises and conflicts. By 1792, John Parr was dead, and Nova Scotia had a new lieutenant governor, the loyalist John Wentworth.

The assault upon the judges was not the only act of aggressiveness by the Sixth Assembly. It was simply the most heated, dramatic, and prolonged of the conflicts between assembly and governor, assembly and council, elected and appointed. Describing the 1790 session as "one continued dispute," Parr blamed this friction upon "an Assumption of Authority and a degree of Turbulence" on the part of the assembly that threatened the other branches of government.[114] In another letter he stated that if the conduct of council was not approved and supported, "I can not answer for the consequences"[115] With Pavlovian skill he sought the conditioned reflex in Britain by drawing more and more frequently upon a parallel with the revolution, pointing out to Whitehall that "some of the Members of the Assembly tread exactly in the same steps with the leaders of the late Rebellion, their factious, seditious, levelling principles are much the same."[116] It seems a remarkable irony, in a period rich in ironies, that, by threatening the office-holders and championing the powers of the elected body, those who had actively opposed rebellion while Nova Scotia remained neutral were now classified as children of that rebellion.

Yet in a limited and perverted way Parr was right. His recurring use of the words seditious, levelling, and republican to isolate and condemn the loyalists was both inaccurate and unfair. Yet the entry of the loyalists into the assembly of Nova Scotia had coincided with a growing aggressiveness on the part of a "Commons" determined to assert and extend its control over a multitude of matters pertaining to the economy, the appointed officials, the electorate, its own membership, and the finances of the province. These were not isolated skirmishes but all part of an intensifying atmosphere of challenge and conflict between the elected and appointed branches which culminated in the explosive session of 1790.

As Parr pointed out, the loyalists were Americans, moulded by the same land and tradition which had led to a bloody revolution against the mother country. They seemed, moreover, to be everywhere in the House, in the speaker's chair, on committees, introducing, seconding, and supporting motions inimical to the other branches, voting against the government in a markedly consistent bloc, pushing the House on some resolutions farther than it felt ready to go. This seditious tribe had entered the House with the Sixth Assembly. The Sixth Assembly had become an aggressive, defiant, turbulent body. The correlation is difficult to avoid.

Yet this correlation must be treated cautiously. Several factors make it difficult to regard these events as simply the assault of an isolated loyalist faction upon the government and its prerogative. For one thing, the polarity is somewhat disturbed by the fact that by 1790 several loyalists, having embraced the establishment, were particularly fierce in their criticism of their fellow loyalists and the levelling Assembly. S.S. Blowers, who had publicly attacked Sterns and Taylor for their harsh treatment of the judges, was elevated to the council in 1788.[117] John Haliburton, a loyalist who had attacked Sterns and Taylor in long letters to England, was also appointed to the council.[118] Even Brenton, one of the judges impeached, qualified as a loyalist.[119]

Nor did the loyalists dominate in the assembly. On Blowers's appointment to the council, for example, the pre-loyalist Uniacke was elected speaker over the loyalist Barclay. When, in two instances, loyalist motions went farther then the House wished to go, they were defeated. What is remarkable, moreover, is the strength of the pre-loyalist bloc which sided with the loyalists on issue after issue. Where Parr misleads is in his inference that a handful of loyalist levellers were obstructing a popular government. Many of the votes indicate that a handful of assembly members with ties to the government supported it against the wishes of a majority of the elected House. That majority was composed of both loyalists and pre-loyalists.

The easy identification of the loyalist bloc with many of the assaults upon the appointed branches and officials obscures a most important postrevolutionary development: the swelling voice of the hinterland against the entrenched interests in Halifax. Awareness on the part of the outports of Halifax dominance and neglect was not new. It was only with the doubling of the population beyond Halifax, and the entry of its representatives into the assembly, that the hinterland's grievances and ambitions could be expressed and its old enemies challenged. Yet Parr would not recognize this. In a sense he could not, for if it were recognized that a majority in the assembly was opposing the government's actions, intentions, and prerogatives, it might also be recognized that there was just cause. The visible assault upon the government had to be explained, and the explanation that Parr seized upon was the existence of an isolated loyalist faction whose intrusion upon the body politic had created this tumultuous assault upon the government and the British traditions of Nova Scotia. After all, they were Americans, and by 1790 this factious group had apparently become, in the American manner, seditious, levelling, and republican. The inversion of the loyalist image seemed complete. From the position of refugees driven to Nova Scotia because of their undaunted loyalty they had been reduced to that of transients from that dangerous republic, bringing with them the virulent politics of their native land.

The Sixth Assembly was in many ways a reforming assembly, and much of the impetus for that reform came from the loyalist members. Although it was more a matter of their adding greatly to the strength of existing reform sentiment than of creating a loyalist party, they still played a dominant role in the fight for reform. They had men of outstanding ability among them and, despite Parr's attack, they were able to lift reform out of the mud of sedition. Because they were represented in the Legislative Assembly more than within the executive, they sought the supremacy of the legislature. Some among them, once invited into the realm of executive power, quickly jettisoned their crusading zeal and donned the attitudes of the oligarchy. But these were a very small percentage of the refugees, and the desire of the loyalists for the supremacy of the elected branch of the government had roots other than a sense of exclusion, and of as compelling a nature. As Americans they had been nurtured on certain standards of representation, and they found the Nova Scotia government wanting. One of them observed: "This is the misfortune of Great Britain in respect to the colonies – placing in their own minds the landholders in the colonies upon a footing with those they call peasants in Britain, when really that character is scarcely to be found in the colonies."[120]

It is perhaps as Americans that the loyalists and their attitudes are most easily understood, for while the select were usurping the loyalist image and shaping it to their own ends, the great majority were placing increased emphasis upon the democratic principles and instincts that had been their prerevolutionary heritage but had lain dormant for close to a decade.

CHAPTER NINE

The Loyalist in the Economy

More immediately pressing than the political realm was the economic, for the first task of the loyalist was to ensure economic survival, and the period of this struggle was dominated by the dependence on provisions, the confusion surrounding the clamour for land, the rush to put wives and families under some form of roof, and the beginning of land clearing. And yet if one could stand back and weigh the changes wrought along Nova Scotia's coastline since 1783, the clearing, the building, and the growth, they seemed impressive.

This is what Jacob Bailey did in his description of Nova Scotia written about 1786.[1] He found Digby "a very handsome town ... built by the Loyalists, the situation of it is exceedingly well chosen both for the fisheries and every other trade adopted to the Province." People were spread along both sides of the Annapolis River. The town, with the arrival of the loyalists, had grown sixfold to a population of 2,500, "the country about it clearing fast of the woods." The loyalists around St Mary's Bay, with good timber stands, had already begun shipping off cargoes to various ports. In a favourable description of Halifax, its harbour, wharves, and potential growth, the minister mentioned that with the loyalists and others drawn by the revived British largesse, the population of the centre had been doubled. The loyalist settlement at Chedabucto, with good land and timber, was "seemingly well chosen to become a place of some consequence, being equally adapted for carrying on the Cod and Salmon fisheries upon an enlarged scale."

Shelburne, with a harbour "not exceeded by any one in America," contained, according to Bailey, 3,000 houses and 13,000 people. By that time, moreover, the refugees were getting onto their farm lots. "All the country for several miles about is exceedingly populous."

The lands are greatly improved, and have in several places produced fine crops of wheat, barley, and oats, as well as of garden herbs and dwarf fruits, as currents &c. The good effects of their being possessed of a large capital shews itself very plainly in the great number of shipping belonging to the merchants nearly equalling that of Halifax itself, being at least 300 sail of all sorts, several of which are employed in the whale fishery, a still greater number in the West Indies and the rest in the cod fishery upon the banks.

Sawmills were already shipping timber to the West Indies. Besides dealing in timber and fish, Shelburne was apparently becoming a clearing house for other goods for that market. The dominance of the concept of trade was seen early in the rush to build warehouses and ships. According to Bailey,

Many large wharfs and convenient store houses are erected for landing and securing goods; their trade particularly to the West Indies having increased very rapidly within the last eighteen months. Below the town and upon the same side of the harbour, the lands quite down so that a vast number of vessels have been built by the proprietors, chiefly for the fishing business, and some of them as large as to 250 tons burthen; 70 sail were upon the stocks in October last and it is conjectured that near 400 sail will have been finished by this time, since the evacuation of New York by this one settlement alone.

Shelburne's aggressive thrust into trade was owing to the potential development of its harbour and the firm conviction of its populace that it would be a major commercial centre. It was hurried along, according to Andrew Brown, by the fact that a lot of investment capital salvaged from the war was brought to the port by the loyalists. "In the first embarkation £100,000 was put on board in the shape of public bills or of the various denominations of American Silver. Every vessel that entered the harbour during the summer, more or less augmented this first investment ... it was computed that eight or nine hundred persons at the least had a free money stock of five hundred pounds."[2] This helps to explain the swift establishment of merchants in Shelburne before the merchandise, or the markets for it, had been acquired.

By 1788 the loyalists of Nova Scotia were "not as yet so well sheltered from the inclemency of the Weather, as they will be hereafter."[3] Long before this, however, they had begun to move away from the position of being wards of the state, and to enter into and expand the Nova Scotian economy within the new parameters of the postrevolutionary period. If most were miserable in the present, they seemed to envisage a more promising future. Marston had nothing but praise for the province's many "natural advantages," from fishing to timber, including its "rich mines of coal, likewise copper and iron."[4] Parr, after a second tour of the interior in 1785, was almost ecstatic over the land's potential, describing intervales and rich land, praising loyalist industry in fishing, farming, and clearing the lands "with great chearfullness." Two years later he was still praising the progress being made, although "the Poor suffer exceedingly for want of Cloathing, as well as Provisions."[5] The agents of Nova Scotia in Britain were laying particular stress on the sea and trade, emphasizing the future development of whale fishing and the West Indies trade.[6]

In a letter of 1785 concerning Edinburgh, near Sissiboo, Samuel Goldbury indicated a similar direction and emphasis for the developing economy: agriculture, fishing, timber, and the building of ships for the export of these primary products. He implied, moreover, that a typical loyalist community, avoiding specialization, might be involved in all of these activities. Goldbury described the good land around Sissiboo, fine tracts of timber, and the streams necessary for the sawmills. Four mills had already gone up and more were being built. There were also 1,000 head of black cattle, as well as horses and sheep.

There was taken and exported from this place the Last Year 1200 quintals of Cod fish, besides a considerable quantity consumed by the Settlers, most of which Fish were taken in Log canoes and small Boats. There undoubtedly will be four times that quantity taken this year, as the Settlers will not be necessarily employed in Building. We have at present but few Vessels, and those Small, except a Brigg of 120 Tons and a Sloop of 80 Tons, which are now employed in the West India Trade.

... The Settlers are generally Poor but industrious, their exertions cramped for want of Provisions, but should Government continue their Bounty a little longer, I am persuaded the fertility of the soil, and the advantages derived from fish and Lumber would soon restore them to those agreeable Circumstances they Sacrificed in consequence of the Late War.[7]

In order to fulfil the ambitions of the loyalists and exploit the province's slim natural resources, aid would have to come from the government. The two major forms of provincial aid were road development grants and economic bounties. In 1783 there were only two roads in Nova Scotia, branching out from Sackville to Truro and Windsor. The coming of the loyalists forced the province to provide new and extended roads to permit trade and communication between the new communities and between them and the older communities. In 1785 the assembly made its first major appropriation, £1,500, for "opening roads from Halifax to Shelburne and from thence to Yarmouth." In 1786, £1,450 was granted, in 1787, £1,800, and in 1788 £1,060, "amounts which were, by comparison with the sums expended on roads in the years prior to the Revolution, enormous."

Despite the increased expenditure, however, success was very limited. The road through the Annapolis valley varied in the decade after the loyalists' arrival from the barely tolerable to the excessively bad, "and no road at all from Annapolis to Digby." Despite petitions, nothing was done in the Ramsheg region to provide the settlers with a road to Amherst.[8] Settlements such as Rawdon had neither roads nor water routes to link them with the rest of the province.[9] In 1786 £200 was granted to start a road "from Country Harbour in the County of Sydney, towards Pictou by way of Manchester and Antigonish," although little is known of this undertaking and no further efforts appear to have been made in the region during the eighteenth century. There was, as late as 1790, no real road to link the well-populated area of Pictou with the provincial capital.[10]

With the growth of Shelburne and its great dependence upon developing a hinterland that it could tap, roads leading from the loyalist centre became essential. Sums were granted to build roads from Shelburne to Halifax, Barrington, Yarmouth, and Liverpool.[11] There was also an attempt to connect Shelburne with the granary of the Annapolis region.

The Enterprise and exertions of the inhabitants of Shelburne exhibits the strongest proofs that perseverence and industry when judiciously applied will rise superior to every difficulty and discouragement and perhaps in no part of America is there an instance of cutting a road through an almost impassable forest nearly the distance of 80 miles in so short a time and at so small a cost as Captain Pell and his party have effected the Road to Annapolis and rendered it passable for Cattle.[12]

Although grants were still being made in 1790 to finish the road, the lack of settlement along it and the decline of Shelburne itself permitted the road to go back to wilderness.[13]

Roads were obviously essential to the loyalist communities, the lack of and need for them a grim reminder of their situation and the long road they themselves had to travel before achieving security and success. To the *American Gazette* in Shelburne, "it is of the utmost consequence to the prosperity of this settlement, that immediate and extensive communications should be opened as speedily as possible to the other cultivated parts of the province, and to

Annapolis in particular." And they worked hard on their roads in the attempt to get grants from the assembly. Yet, despite the importance of the roads, the efforts of the settlers, and the amounts granted by the House, little was really achieved. A report of 1794 indicated that, owing to the thinly scattered population throughout a country "covered with woods, much intersected by waters," the roads were still in a desperate condition, "in the new settlements more especially."[14]

Government aid to the fledgling communities through a system of economic bounties seemed more successful. A committee appointed to consider what premiums and bounties were most expedient to the growth of agriculture and commerce in the colony recommended that Britain continue her bounty on American hemp, that 2/6 a bushel should be granted for flax, and £5 a ton for potash, so "that the new settlers may have employment & become attached to their lands & possessions." In order to encourage the timber trade the owner of each sawmill erected was to get £20; to encourage shipbuilding an amount of 10 shillings a ton was to be granted for each provincially built vessel over forty tons. By October 1787 the government had granted bounties of £449.3.9 for shipbuilding, £282.12.0 for sawmills, and other amounts for flax seed and other items. There was also a recommendation in 1787 for bounties on the manufacture of iron, and within a short time a forge was erected and bounty awarded at Nictaux, Annapolis County.[15]

Most of the settlements along the broken Atlantic coast quickly entered the fisheries, at first to augment their provisions but soon after to try to supply the domestic and West Indies market. With so much poor land at Country Harbour, for example, the settlers were soon forced to combine subsistence farming with lumbering and fishing.[16] Marston found in the first four months at least fifty sails in Shelburne. "About half the number are employed in the cod fishery." Of the remainder some were engaged in the whale fishery or the West Indian trade, but a larger number in voyages to and smuggling from New York. In a long, very detailed letter Marston had little but praise for the economic potential of the fisheries. He felt that the entry of the refugees into the cod fishery would prove difficult because catching cod demanded a great deal of skill and experience, qualities which few loyalists possessed. Yet because of the prevailing winds and the location of Nova Scotia the province had the advantage of New England, where passages of three weeks to a month were common, "which often spoils their fish entirely ... With the same wind vessels may come directly from the Banks to these coasts; and add to that the distance is shorter by 100 leagues, or more as it may be." Marston expected more immediate returns from the whale fishery, in which "there is a considerable sum subscribed to fit out vessels for that business. Whaling is a more simple business than the cod fishery – in one 'tis only requisite to get people dextrous in killing the whale, in the other all depends on proper dressing and curing."[17] An example of the whaling ventures of Shelburne was the operation of the Richard Townsends, who had taken their remaining capital and spent it on erecting stores and wharves in Shelburne, "and in laying the foundation of a General and Extensive Trade; which [in] its Consequences promised to be promotive of the growing Wealth, and Commercial Dignity of this Infant Settlement." Part of this trade was the fitting out of a schooner, the *Rosetta and Polly*, about eighty-five tons, on a whaling voyage to the coast of Africa at a cost of $4,800.[18] In 1787 mainland Nova Scotia exported 44,723 quintals of dried fish and 13,363 barrels of green fish.[19] In 1788 Shelburne alone exported 13,151 quintals of dry cod, 4,193 casks of pickled fish, sixty-one casks of smoked salmon, 149 barrels of fish oil, and 14,793 gallons of sperm oil.[20] This wealth of exports does not indicate wealth among the fishermen, but simply that the fish were there and the loyalists moved into the fisheries quickly for a cash crop. In 1786, for example, prices in Halifax were low and those in Jamaica worse.[21]

The province's timber stands were quickly exploited, at first to cover the new settlers, and later in pursuit of markets and barter. Within a short time three sawmills were set up on the Jordan River near Shelburne, and "kept going night and day for the merchants of Port Roseway who are constantly shipping off lumber to the West Indies from these mills and two other[s] lately erected above Shelburne."[22] In June 1785 the *Prince William Henry* took in a cargo of squared timber for London. "Captain Meader, who is owner as well as commander of said ship, has the honor of being the first gentleman who carries a cargo to England of the produce of this province."[23] Shelburne was also reshipping timber from the Penobscot.[24]

The export of timber was important enough to warrant the General Sessions of that centre ordering that the "Surveyors of Lumber be particularly Ordered to pass no Lumber what is not altogether Merchantable" and laying down regulations to control and make uniform the lumber business. Throughout Nova Scotia thirteen saw mills had been erected in 1786, with a bounty of £20 each. Some of the settlers, finding the white pine set aside by Wentworth for the king's ships too tempting to resist, were raiding the preserves and "shipping the same for Europe, either as masts or Ton Timber."

The House of Assembly declared that "We have used the utmost endeavours to encourage the lumber trade of this province which is one of its greatest exports to the West Indies and we are happy to inform Your excellency that our endeavours have been crowned with success, the number of saw mills have increased beyond our most sanguine expectations and the quantities of lumber now ready for market far exceed the shipping we have to transport the same."[25]

Before the revolution, Nova Scotia had been largely dependent upon New England for carrying her goods. After the exclusion of the Americans from the Nova Scotian and West Indian markets, many in Nova Scotia, particularly the government and the loyalists, saw the opportunity to expand both markets and carrying capacity. The shortage of bottoms created by the losses during the war and the increased demands thereafter resulted in a mini-boom in shipbuilding throughout the 1780s. The bounty of 1785 further stimulated the development of the industry. The bounties were to run until the end of 1787, and were to be granted only to "such as are built Staunch and Strong, with a sufficient quantity of Iron in proportion to their Tonnage." About sixteen ships were being built in 1786, calling for a bounty of £613. The *Gazette* reported an auspicious launching:

Shelburne, Dec. 28 – On Friday last was launched from this ship-yard above King Street, the beautiful ship Roseway, about two hundred and fifty tons burthen, and built for Messrs M'Lean and Bogle of this town, Merchants. This is the *First Ship* that has been launched in this province since its first settlement, and if good stuff, excellence of workmanship, strength, and a handsome model, are recommendations in a vessel, she will do no little credit to the Builder and the settlement of Shelburne.[26]

Halifax also built a brig, "the first vessel of her size ever built in this town," and was planning more. At Sissiboo, Captain Moody built a ship of 250 tons. "The vessels which have been built in this Province in the last year, afford the greatest reason to suppose, that this valuable branch of business will, 'ere long, be well established in this Province."[27]

Loyalists and others in Nova Scotia pinned much of their hope for economic expansion upon replacing the Americans within the British trading empire. After the peace, as we have seen, the Navigation Acts continued to exclude the Americans from the West Indies. Although the orders in council of 1783 allowed the importation of a wide range of American produce including timber, livestock, and "live provisions," if carried in British ships, they excluded fish and salted meats.[28] This omission gave Nova Scotians, along with other British colonies, a basic monopoly in the supply of fish.

The loyalists, however, did not take this market for granted. The pressure of American demands for entry upon a conciliatory England, the pressure from the West India planters for entry of American goods, and the efforts of Lord Shelburne in 1782 and Pitt in 1783 to restore trade to its prewar status, with America included, created an air of uncertainty concerning the future of Nova Scotian trade; there was also a fear of powerful forces moving to rob the colonists of their prize. Although aware of American exclusion by the fall of 1783, the Nova Scotian press in general, and the Shelburne newspapers in particular, gave extensive coverage to discussions and rumours in Britain concerning American trade. Disturbing letters from London were published describing the strength of pro-American feeling; one writer warned "that there is danger of that interest prevailing, if it be not properly counter-balanced, and this should be by addresses to the King and Parliament, from the Loyal Colonies, praying that they will not take the bread out of the mouth of their own faithful subjects and give it to the revolted rivals."[29] This fear was lessened in 1785 when American vessels were rigidly excluded from the West Indies.[30] Although some uncertainty remained, Nova Scotia's agent in London felt that the threat was over. "I hope the West India trade is opening fast upon you: In fish and lumber you can supply them to a great extent; I wish I coud say as much for flour, and that your Traders woud take off their Rum: It is this last Article which still stands out as such an obstacle to all my Efforts, and upon which the West India Proprietors ground all those complaints."[31]

Rum was a problem. Although only one of the two distilleries in Nova Scotia was in production, it was turning out from 15,000 to 20,000 gallons a year. "This Rum is generally preferred by the Indians, and lowest Class of People, and a Gallon of it is sold Sixpence cheaper than British West Indian Rum." Since, moreover, Americans were distilling rum from the cheaper molasses of the French West Indies, some American rum had been smuggled into the province, especially "into that part of this Province which lies on the Bay of Fundy." To encourage the drinking of rum from the British West Indies, Parr suggested that a bounty be granted on timber and fish exported in British vessels to the West Indies, "provided that the Vessel returning should come hither directly with the produce of some of those Islands."[32] By 1787, despite the lower price of the smugglers' and local distillers' rum, Henry Newton, one of the customs officials, found that smuggled rum was used only by the poorest fishermen in the more distant harbours, "and but few of them are not supplied from Halifax, Shelburne and other Trading places in the Province from whence a West India Trade is carried on." According to Newton's figures the amount of rum imported from the British West Indies in 1786 was 86,600 gallons. In 1787 it had almost doubled to 162,613 gallons. "By which it appears our West India Trade has increased very rapidly owing in some measure to the Bounty on Vessels Built in this Province."[33]

In their exploitation of the captive southern market Nova Scotians were limited by what they could produce, and their exports were small in comparison with the West Indian market and need. In the beginning they were also limited by the lack of shipping. In 1786, for example, the province had cut far more lumber than available transport could carry.[34] Loyalist partners in England were quick to conceive of a triangular trade on ships chartered by them. In 1784 a man named Parker had chartered a ship for the West Indies and was sending her to Shelburne as quickly as possible. "It is my present wish to send you Ships frequently Consigned with Salt and other bulky Goods that will pay a freight to the Ship if their Cargoes can be readily sold and Remitted for, That I would greatly prefer to a lingering Sale on any terms." Within two months he planned to send a large ship from Portugal to take lumber and cured fish to the West Indies.[35]

The loyalists continued to be dependent on England for dry goods, and Shelburne merchants continued their involvement with Lisbon and southern Europe.[36] But the boom in their own shipbuilding led the loyalists to concentrate upon the West Indies trade, and gave the trade a slightly different character marked by more flexibility and local control. Many of the ships they were building were relatively small, often built on shares and carrying the owner's cargo as well as other freight. Harold Innis noted that "The divisibility of both vessels and cargoes and the relatively small size of the ships made it easy for merchants and others along the coast to take a very extensive part in trade."[37] And the ships clearing were going chiefly to the West Indies. In 1795 Munro described the Shelburne involvement in this fashion:

Their exports are chiefly if not altogether fish and lumber. The latter gets scarce; but the former increases, no doubt from more hands being employed in it and also their knowing better the places where to find them and no doubt being more expert in their Business by long practice. These two articles they export to the West Indies are Rum; Mollasses sugar and Salt; and dry goods from Britain and sometimes from Hallifax; they import corn and sometimes flour from the States, and sometimes flour from Canada; as to meat whether beef or small meat they supply themselves. Square rigged vessels belonging to the Town are 6 or 8. fishing and coasting vessels are about. There were two excellent vessels launched here this Summer 95, the one 280 Tons burden the other near as much.

Other loyalist centres were also involved heavily in the southern trade. Digby, for example, was shipping timber, fish, spruce beer, and even some dairy and farm produce.[38] But the outstanding development was Shelburne's attempt to become the economic metropolis of the province. The growth of such a metropolis was encouraged by the dependence of the province on the manufactured items and other goods shipped from England on big ships. Prior to the war, the centre for the Nova Scotia region had been Boston. By the nineteenth century it was Halifax. "Previous to the American Revolution, Boston was to [Barrington] what Halifax now is to the present generation, there they got their supplies – and that was the home market for their fish." But in the flux of the postwar period Shelburne was for a time a potent candidate for the role of metropolis. In 1789 the province exported a total of 20,000 quintals of cod.[39] In the previous year, Shelburne alone exported 13,000 quintals, a figure which indicates that much of the province's export of fish was being cleared through the loyalist centre. Shelburne was by that date "the centre of a large custom House Trade." The *Packet* noted that "The Convenience and Safety of making this port and harbour must surely be sufficiently evinced, by the number of vessels that constantly take the advantage of it, particularly at this season of the year."[40]

Hollingsworth's *State of Nova Scotia*, published in 1786, marked the climax of the image of a bright Nova Scotian future in the British trading empire. "Americans! You have lost much: where are your gains?"[41] With her fisheries, lumber, potential share in the West India trade, and her new population, Nova Scotia was to the author the best colony in all of America for Britain to own. The book was a glowing portrait of promise that could not really be fulfilled.

By the time of the book's publication, however, it was obvious that one major segment of the refugees would not share in that prosperity. By that time few black loyalists had received the promised provisions, and far fewer any land. With no real assurance of provisions and no land to work, most had no option but to try to sell their labour. The involvement of many white loyalists in clearing the land they had recently received, combined with the greatly increased demand for services created by these operations, put a tremendous strain on the existing labour market. This demand could be met cheaply by the black loyalists, to such an extent that in several parts of Nova Scotia they became "the Principal Sources for Labour and Improvement."[42]

Some blacks became day labourers and servants in such centres as Halifax and Shelburne. Those close to the sea often supplemented their income by inshore fishing; others joined ships' crews; still others employed the skills they had learned on their old plantations to work as carpenters, masons, blacksmiths, bakers, weavers, and at a wide range of other occupations, although not at the wages received by whites. Hundreds of others, however, were "obliged to live upon white-men's property which the Govt has been liberal in distributing – and for cultivating it they receive half the produce so that they are in short in a state of Slavery."[43] Many others, desperate for any income, became indentured servants, a status that differed little from slavery. The hope that the province had offered these people in 1783 was fading rapidly. Nova Scotia was not to be their promised land.

Nor was the promise all that secure for the white loyalist. One of the major threats was the changing policy concerning trade with the West Indies. Although enumerated items were not allowed into the islands from any foreign port, the governor in council could admit them in British ships from such ports in case of distress or emergency. "This discretionary power seems to have been exercised after 1788 to the chagrin of the Nova Scotia merchant." From this date, moreover, fish were being admitted into the West Indies in American bottoms, a fact which threatened not only Nova Scotian fisheries but also her shipbuilding and carrying trade.[44] Munro, in his report on Nova Scotia in 1795, found the fisheries in great decline "not only in the Rivers but along the coasts."[45]

The fisheries, although a natural staple for the province's export trade, were not necessarily a source of affluence or even comfort for the average fishing community. The loyalists at Sheet Harbour were to discover this to their dismay. "They at first unfortunately got connected in the fishery and building vessels and neglected their farms – for some years past they have found out their error and, ever since, have stuck solely to farming."[46] William Paine, writing to Wentworth on the economy of New Brunswick, made a telling point concerning the fisheries and the fishermen: "The people, as a Body, will ever be *poor* and *miserable* – From my own observation at Passamaquoddy, I am persuaded that a coast calculated for fishing, is so far from being a benefit, that it really is a *curse* to the Inhabitants. Who ever knew a Fisherman Thrive? – At Salem, Marblehead and Cape Ann, they are the most wretched of the community."[47]

By 1789 timber, the other staple depended upon, was also in a declining condition. The timber trade in Nova Scotia and New Brunswick suffered from the zeal of the surveyor general of the woods and his deputies who were reserving not only white pine of over two feet in diameter but also pines of any size, thus locking away many convenient tracts. Moreover, the first loyalist mills had been erected as close as possible to the navigable rivers, and often tied closely to the new settlements. Consequently, as Carleton observed, "the proper sort of timber being soon cut up in the vicinity of each Mill seat, the labor and expence of collecting it from a distance were found to increase far beyond the present ability of the adventurers in this branch of business – hence several of them have been obliged to abandon the undertaking."[48] Munro mentioned the same phenomenon of good timber located farther and farther from the mills. "And this is the case all over the province where I have been."[49]

The one area of the economy which was rarely represented among Nova Scotia's exports was the one in which the largest percentage of loyalists were involved, agriculture. The loyalist attempt at farming was not very successful. As they cleared their lands, their emphasis was less on an instant cash crop than on the necessity to feed themselves. Unfortunately, few went beyond this initial stage, and many failed to reach it. Moreover, had the land been excellent and the loyalists skilled farmers, there would still have been the major problem of lack of roads to transport their surpluses to markets. But little of the land upon which the loyalists were placed was excellent, and many of them were not skilled farmers.

So much had been stacked against them. By the time they arrived in Nova Scotia the greater part of the intervale land was already taken and most were faced with a much more disconcerting forest growth than they were used to. Perhaps as important, for too long a period of time many received no land at all. In a province where the interval between clearing and cultivation was several years, to delay in getting land was often fatal. Once trees were cut, it took several years for stumps to rot sufficiently to be removed. The land in this state could be used for pasture or hay but wheat or winter ryes were most often the first crops, unless one needed food for the winter, in which case turnips, potatoes, and Indian corn were grown.[50] Provisions could have supported the refugees as they passed through those bad years between clearing and cultivating, had they been on their land and assured of their provisions. The inability to get them all quickly on their land was critical, for the delay meant that many were consuming these supplies while they sat idle in temporary settlements, unable to put an axe to trees on any land they could be assured was theirs.

Even on good land there was little hope of early affluence. Jack Wiswall, having spent a winter with a friend and two helpers clearing thirteen acres around Wilmot, managed to plant thirteen acres of winter grain, four of summer, five of clover and timothy, all on plain or intervale, two acres of potatoes and one of oats on the mountain. The land was good and their accomplishment solid in comparison with that of other loyalists, but this immense effort assured only that "this year they will have bread enough & potatoes of their own raising & Hay sufficient to winter their small stock which consists of a breeding Mair, Yoked Oxen & Milch cow."[51] Alexander Howe, in the fertile Annapolis valley, was less sanguine in his invitation to a correspondent "to come and see How a Nova Scotian farmer exists (for I cannot call it living when I have a retrospect to better days) who has to maintain A wife & five Children and all their appurtenances, by the Sweat of his Brow."[52]

Many were simply cursed with bad land and left soon after either seeing it or attempting to clear it. A large number of the disbanded soldiers lacked the diligence and commitment to clear the land no matter what its quality. Many were so destitute that they had little chance of starting or succeeding.[53] Moreover, a large percentage of the loyalists, those from urban centres, warmer climates, or more bountiful lands, were simply poor farming material for this sparse province. Mrs Hutchinson often mentions her son-in-law's bad luck in farming, and his frequent changing of farms in search of a change of fortune.[54] Rev. George Gillmore spoke over and over again of his hardships and trials in eking out "a Scanty Subsistence [cul]tivating the land on Ardoise Hill; but I find myself very [mu]ch disappointed."[55] He lacked the experience, knowledge, strength, stamina, and desire to be a farmer. Gillmore, like so many others, was an incongruous pioneer.

The attempts to improve agriculture in the late 1780s indicated that many believed it badly needed improvement, that the dream of prosperous loyalist agricultural communities would remain just that, a dream. The atmosphere surrounding these attempts was less that of boosterism than of fear, more an attempt to avert failure than an optimistic pursuit of progress. This was the attitude pervading the Society for Promoting Agriculture in Nova Scotia, organized in Halifax in 1789. Established by members of the official and professional classes, it had Governor Parr as its patron, Richard Bulkeley, the provincial secretary, and William Cochran, publisher of the *Nova Scotia Magazine* and later head of the academy at Windsor, as moving founders. The society published articles on agriculture in the local papers and the magazine, and worked to establish local societies throughout the province. Although the officials and directors were a mixture of loyalist and pre-loyalist, the leading loyalists were strongly represented among them.[56]

The articles, and any improvements stemming from them, did not come soon enough to prevent many of the loyalists abandoning their attempts at farming. The effort required to clear the thickly wooded areas, the quality of the land once cleared, the frustration of subsistence farming, the difficulty of finding markets if one had surpluses, and the unsuitability of many for the task of farming, all were factors in defeating great numbers of those who tried the land. Another factor was the peculiar loyalist mentality. As Alexander Howe had indicated, the settlers were always aware of the contrast between the struggle for subsistence in this wooded, rock-strewn land and the way they had formerly lived, and there was much futile impatience in their attempt to regain that former existence too quickly.

In all facets of the economy with which the loyalists were involved, timber, shipbuilding, fishing, the carrying trade, and farming, little of the anticipated progress was achieved, and during the late 1780s an actual decline was evident. Times were hard and getting harder. In 1788 a law had to be passed allowing the import of essential foods from the United States, because the province was still unable to feed itself, and this measure would have to be kept in effect until 1792. James Walker notes that "By 1789 Nova Scotia, and indeed all of British North America, was in the grip of a serious famine ... Special relief measures had to be passed to provide assistance both for Loyalists and for pre-Loyalist settlers whose farms though longer established, could not produce the necessary amount of food even for their own inhabitants."[57] Bishop Charles Inglis found the loyalists at Digby "very poor, & I fear will continue so unless they disperse & settle on farms." In 1789 the loyalists at Digby petitioned the assembly for medical aid. "More than three Quarters of these are on circumstances extremely indigent and cannot without much difficulty procure the mere necessaries of life." Before the revolution most had lived in comfort, some in affluence, but now they were exposed to a great deal of sickness through "hard labor, incommodious Lodging, open Huts, Long Fastings and Unwholesome provisions."[58] The Hessians and Waldeckers remaining on the Bear and Moose rivers described themselves as "real objects of Charity" in their "excessive distress."[59]

William Dyott, on visiting Annapolis in 1791, found the trade there "very trifling." He did not mention the high cost of living that drove William Clark to Digby, where costs were "one third cheaper." In 1786 the loyalists at Annapolis, on hearing that provisions had ceased, implored the governor to grant them another year's supply. "The little Fruits of their last Year's Labour is consumed (with the one third Allowance of Provisions granted by Government) and they are now driven to make use of that part of their Crops which they intended for the next years seed to satisfy the Cravings of real Hunger." The request was refused by Lord Sydney.[60]

In order to get a minister, the people of Guysborough had promised Peter Delaroche to pay his removal expenses from Lunenburg, and provide him with a house and fuel. He never did get his moving expenses and by 1789, in order to obtain the £70 due to him from the parish, he was forced to abandon his claim to be provided with a dwelling and fuel. He blamed this not on meanness but on poverty.[61]

In 1791 Wiswall described the disbanded soldiers around Aylesford and Wilmot thus:

This part of the Province is very thinly settled by persons of all discriptions in general extremely poor & scattered over the country in all directions, they chiefly live in Hutts little if anything superior to the Cabins in Ireland – and can scarcely be said to have even the bare necessarys of life. They have been for so long a time habituated to what may be called a savage life, that it is extreme difficult to bring them off from it to a civilized state.[62]

Shelburne exemplified the bankruptcy of the loyalist hopes. A letter from Halifax as early as 1784 focused on Shelburne's precarious position and forecast her imminent failure.

The inhabitants vie with each other in making fine appearances, which in the present state of things they cannot long support. All commerce is at a stand, and the very large sums of money they brought from New York are nearly exhausted, without having fixed upon any staple commodity, or attempted to settle back into the country, whence they might supply their market with vegetables, and in time with stock. When the King's bounty to the Loyalists shall cease, it is a mystery, to what hand they can turn themselves for the means of subsistence.[63]

The most glaring fault, repeatedly mentioned by observers of Shelburne, was the lavish expenditure of the limited wealth of the loyalists upon the appurtenances of wealth, great houses and stores, before it could be judged whether an economy would rise to support them. In 1784 Dr Walter had described this lavishness as the reason why the inhabitants had not entered the fisheries or made progress in agriculture. William Chew, comparing his settlement on the St John with that of Shelburne, commented, "Your Town Exceeds ours I belive but whats a fine house without something to put in it." Even Colonel Bluck, the talented mulatto leader of Birchtown, "like many others in Shelburne Settlements, – set off on the great Scale" and built "a spacious house." Nathaniel Whitworth, advising his brother on establishing a business in Shelburne, told him to purchase a store already built, "as many people have reduc'd themselves to the last shilling in building, and have not at present wherewithal to support themselves." Boston King, in describing the distress around Shelburne in 1791, likewise concentrated on the vanity of the big houses. Only when the money was spent did the townspeople turn to the sea's wealth and begin to build small fishing vessels, "but alas, it was too late to repair their error. Had they been wise enough at first to have turned their attention to the fishery, instead of fine houses, the place would soon have been in a flourishing condition; whereas it was reduced in a short time to a heap of ruins, and its inhabitants were compelled to flee to other parts of the continent for sustinence."[64]

The investment of so much capital in life-style rather than livelihood was a grievous blow to Shelburne's chances of survival. Yet it was not the only source of weakness. Even if the inhabitants had invested their money more wisely, Shelburne would still have failed to live up to their expectations. Their attitude toward the fisheries indicated the extent of their ambition. They had not settled in Nova Scotia to be humble fishermen. They hoped that the town would become a clearing house for the catches of other fishermen along the south shore, but a lot of Shelburne's money and energy went into something more grandiose, the whale fishery. A company established in 1784 failed in 1789, after having lost one-third of its initial capital of £8,350.[65] The antithesis of such a venture, the inshore fishery, could be little more successful. The very length of the harbour, the great distance from the town to open water, combined with the uncertainty of the runs off Shelburne, left it with no advantage over many other harbours along the coast. The notion of the inshore fishery being the staple of the largest centre in British North America seems somewhat ludicrous. The inshore fishery was for fishing villages, not for a centre of 8,000 people. Shipowners involved in fishing off the Grand Banks or other grounds, and carrying the catch of others to the West Indies, were badly hurt by the growing British tolerance of American trade with the West Indies. In 1791 a memorial from Shelburne claimed that the superior experience of the Americans, combined with the "liberal indulgencies" of the peace treaty in the matter of fishing, "hath hitherto precluded us from becoming their Rivals in this valuable branch of Commerce."[66]

The timber industry looked promising until the easy timber was stripped from Jordan Bay. The memorial of 1791 asked the governor to take steps to help the collapsing industry, pointing out that "the scarcity of proper Timber on the shores in the Vicinage of the Port, the want of Inland Navigation, and of Roads of Communication with the Interior Parts of this New Country (where only any Quantity of Lumber can be cut) so greatly enhances the price of this Article to the Shippers as to put it out of their power to continue that trade without considerable Loss."[67] An attempt was made to reship timber from the Penobscot to the West Indies and Britain, but this reexport trade never developed.[68]

One of the most glaring weaknesses of Shelburne as a commercial centre was the fact that it had no immediate hinterland, no real population surrounding it to feed it the produce it could use for export, and to feed upon its imports. Andrew Brown and many others blamed this upon the failure of the people to leave the town and go into the country to clear their farm lots. But even if most of the population had done so, it is difficult to imagine a strong or viable hinterland developing, for much of the land was poor and unfit for farming. "I am told," wrote Thomas Milledge, "that the Land is most Intolerably bad and Totally unfit for Cultivation."[69] Moreover, the lack of roads prevented the centre from tapping the harvests of Annapolis or other productive areas.

The Shelburne settlers sought to create a metropolis in a small province where one already existed, entrenched in purse and power, and wary of the fledgling down the coast. Yet Shelburne fulfilled no function that Halifax did not already fulfil. There were too many merchants, traders, and service people, and far too little hinterland supplying the markets and produce to support and cushion the trading centre. Charles Whitworth could not sell his hardware and dry goods "because of the large quantities on sale."[70] It was apparently assumed that the very presence of 8,000 people was enough to create a powerful metropolitan centre. It was not, and Shelburne as a commercial centre collapsed almost as rapidly as it had risen.

The decay set in surprisingly early, the storm signals fluttering soon after the town's founding. In 1785 a friend of S.S. Blowers was "shocked to hear just before he embarked, that the house of Finch, Taylor & Co. had failed in Shelburne." In the following year Blowers wrote, "They are all there as poor as Rats in an empty house."[71] In time there was a rash of sales through the Court of Chancery, many like that of the property of the merchant John Miller, "together with a large elegant Dwelling House thereon." In one issue of the *Packet* in 1786 two companies were reported to have been dissolved.[72] In 1787 there was a marked increase in executions for debts over £100, many leading to the public sale of property and buildings at a time of no buyers, others, where property did not cover debts, leading to jail.[73] The decline of the town can be seen in the number of ships clearing and the amount of duties collected. By 1787 the vessels entering and clearing Shelburne numbered little more than half those entering and clearing Halifax. By 1790 they numbered approximately one-fifth.[74] In impost and excise duties for the first three quarters of 1789, Shelburne paid to the treasury approximately £430, while Halifax paid £5,302, over ten times as much.[75]

Of Mathews's Scots, in *The Mark of Honour*, all failed in their attempts to put roots down in the harsh soil around Shelburne. George Chisholm, one of the last to leave, had done his best "almost for Seven Years to support himself and Family but was at last obliged to abandon his land." In April 1793 he sold his land and made ready to leave Jordan Bay.[76] A visitor commented on the dying town:

The spell which lasted longer than it ought to have done was at last dissolved. At the end of the third year when Government allowances stopped silver and every substitute of silver disappeared ... Attachments were laid on all property whether real or personal. Store after store was sealed up. The Newspapers of the province contained whole pages of the Sheriffs sales that were to take place at Shelburne. But purchases had long since ceased. Every thing brought to the hammer was literally given away. In the seat of this universal wreck, energy and resources perished together. No one thought of retiring into the country which had lost the market that would have given the products a value. A few public spirited individuals united their credit and made a trial of the fishery. For the first two years there exertions were crowned with success; and there seemed to be a probability that Shelburne might prolong its existence as a fishing village. In the failure of more splendid hopes such a destiny could not satisfy those who had been ruined.[77]

Nature played an important role in the crushing of loyalist hopes. Having shown her benevolence in the crucial first year of settlement, she spurned the loyalists, and Nova Scotia, in many of the following years. The summer of 1784 had been so dry that the new mills for timber established at Shelburne could not run. The summer of 1786 was even worse with severe drought and fires. "The winter following was the Severest known among the early Settlers for many years." Wiswall described his parishioners as "poor & hardly put to it to support their families thro the severitys of a winter the hardest that ever I experienced & in a wilderness country." There was a smallpox epidemic in 1787, and, according to George Gillmore, one long drought with mills closed, pastures scorched, "less hay by two thirds this season than last," and then in late September heavy rains which played further havoc with the crops. "In fine leaness of Teeth, Paleness of Faces and want of the outward Bread of this world are upon us poor creatures." The following winter offered no relief for Gillmore, killing all of his winter grain and chances of a crop in 1789, "and my poor neighbors have shared the same." T.W. Smith blamed the winter for forcing many in Shelburne to sell their property in order to avoid starving.[78]

Shelburne in particular was badly hit by fires. The town had been surrounded in 1790 by fires which swept through Jordan River destroying close to fifty homes.[79] It was again hit severely in the summer of 1791. In that year the town also experienced a smallpox epidemic which was not only a crisis of health but also of the economy, for it prevented the people of the outports from coming to Shelburne for supplies and trade, "to the manifest detriment of this Town and Port."[80]

The departure of many black loyalists for Sierra Leone added to the problems of Shelburne, for they were not only a sizeable market but also a cheap source of labour. The beaten mood of the town, following the fires, smallpox, and the departure of the blacks, is evident in a letter from Gideon White.

The town is saved – but the Inhabitants being constantly fatigued in fire and smoak for fifteen Days – the Men Women + Children from the Country – with their Cattle – refugees from their destroyed farms – all dependant on the Hospitality and Charity of the fiew who could assist them, it is impossible for me to give you an adequate Idea of this Truly Tradgical Scene – When you are informed that fifty Dwelling Houses besides Mills Barns and other Outhouse are destroyed – which belonged to the Loyal Industrious Husbandmen who have for Nine Years been contending with this unfriendly Soil – to gain a subsistance – to have all these Labour and Prospects blasted in One Year – I say knowing this to be fact – you may form some faint Idea of Shelburne ... Such is my situation that it is impossible for me ever to replace my Loss. This last stroke has completely knock'd down this Settlement, the 800 Negros who were carried to Serea Leone was a serious loss but more so to me than any One – but the most serious matter is my Grist Mill.[81]

A wheat blight and more crop failure struck much of the province in 1791.[82] Boston King wrote a striking description of that year.

About this time, the country was visited with a dreadful famine which not only prevailed at Burch town but likewise at Chebucto, Annapolis, Digby, and other places. Many of the poor people were compelled to sell their best gowns for five pounds of flour, in order to support life, When they had parted with all their clothes, even to their blankets, several of them fell down dead in the streets, thro' hunger. Some killed and eat their dogs and cats; and poverty and distress prevailed on every side.[83]

The economic hopes of the loyalists in Nova Scotia fell drastically short of fulfilment. There were success stories. Sissiboo and the township of Clare were "in the most flourishing State of population of any Settlement in the Province."[84] There were other fortunate areas and many individuals who did well. Some had come with money or connections, and for them success was measured primarily by the extent to which they had been able to maintain their former status. Others, who had come from New York with little but the promise of land and provisions, had been lucky in the draw or subsequent purchase, and had carved out farms and a modest livelihood in fertile areas. The majority, however, found that their lives in Nova Scotia fell far short of their expectations.

One factor which contributed to the economic disappointment was the colony's inability to contend with such large numbers quickly. Almost overnight the population was doubled and the colony forced to absorb the immigrants into its rudimentary economic and commercial patterns. The result could be nothing less than economic indigestion. The province's resources were simply not that abundant or easily exploitable. The timber industry, the fisheries, and the carrying trade soon crested and declined, and farming never really gave grounds for optimism. On top of it all was a series of bad breaks over which the loyalist had no control. There was little he could do concerning changing policy and overwhelming competition in the West Indies trade. And over the ravages of nature that took place he could do little more than curse or weep.

Strangely, the granting of provisions, the key to the loyalists' early survival, was also a factor in their later decline. Provisions ceased before many were well enough established to believe that they could survive without them. Facing the immediate future without the sustaining crutch of provisions was too much for these people, and soon after the cessation they gave up. Provisions became Mr

Micawber's twelvepence difference between happiness and misery, success and failure.[85]

The loyalist himself was also partly responsible for the widespread failure among the refugee communities. Nova Scotia, although no economic miracle, was not collapsing. The loyalists were not a great deal worse off than other pioneers breaking new land. But most loyalists were neither pioneers nor suited for pioneering, a role demanding much sweat and offering little expectation over a prolonged period of time. Disbanded soldiers rarely make good settlers, and many of those who came to Nova Scotia, finding it difficult work, were content to sell and leave. Other refugees were neither trained for nor desirous of lives of scratch farming or inshore fishing. The merchants of Shelburne were too ambitious to recognize the limitations of their new home, for Shelburne was not simply a settlement but an act of proud defiance, and such an act in such a place was folly breeding failure. The loyalist experience in Nova Scotia was as much a failure of expectations as of economics. The refugees did not have the expectations of pioneers but of loyalists seeking restitution and a final triumph for their cause. With its limited resources the colony could offer them neither.

CHAPTER TEN

Adjustments and Departures

So much had turned out not at all as they had hoped or expected. The loyalists knew within a few years that there was little assurance of an easy economic future in Nova Scotia. Within those few years other perspectives were also shifting. New attitudes were being shaped while old attitudes were being altered. One such evolving attitude was that of the refugees towards the United States.

All great passions are difficult to sustain, and even more so when one is removed from the object of that passion. The loyalists came to Nova Scotia at the very flood-tide of their anger. Although they had sometimes been generous and conciliatory towards the American people during the revolution, the year of the peace and the expulsion traumatized them, and they lashed out, like a grievously hurt child, with an intensity more fierce than during the war. It was in this state that they came to Nova Scotia, bringing with them what seemed to be a strong and enduring hatred of those who had expelled them, an emotion which permeated the settlements during their first years in Nova Scotia. But there are few constants. In Nova Scotia the refugees could not reserve for the Americans that obsessive concentration upon which hatred can thrive. With time, new circumstances, and new enemies, the memory of the revolution receded, the loyalist attitude mellowed, and the American as enemy was relegated to a far corner of the loyalist mind.

Although they had lost much in the revolution, the early loyalist attitude was based on more than loss. They had not only been beaten; they had been dismissed. They had had forced upon them the role of contemptible foil for the virtuous and triumphant revolution, and, unable to accept this, they were driven to make of their fate a positive thing. As revolution polarized America, the loyalists, denied the centre, found themselves where they did not necessarily wish to be, on the right. In a world with no centre, they accepted the polarity into which they were thrust by enemy and events, adopting and exaggerating the postures of their position. Losers of a civil war, they became unbowed defenders of a noble cause. Unable to remain, they made of their leaving a virtue, being "Voluntary exiles to this place, Chusing rather than to live under the Tyrannic power of a republican Government to quit the lands of our Nativity." Treated with contempt, they reacted with utter disdain for all that the new nation symbolized. It was this need to put the best face on their situation which gave their anti-Americanism in the first years much of its aggressive quality. They spoke bravely about quitting "this damned country with pleasure." It was now an accursed place, "a land of banditti," and a special resentment was often reserved for those loyalists who chose to remain in such a land, under the domination of petty tyrants. To one loyalist, the country had become "Satan's Kingdom," the collapse of which he anticipated with certainty and pleasure. "Was I once clear of them, I should not Care, how soon they went to the devil."[1] The humiliation of their expulsion was alleviated by the assertion that they had been about to leave anyway.

The impact of the lost war is seen in the dreams and the expectations they held concerning their place of exile. Nova Scotia was not only a refuge, but a place in which the loyalists would still triumph. "By heaven," said Edward Winslow, "we shall be the envy of the American States." Brook Watson saw Nova Scotia as growing affluent and populous within the British Empire, while "Their neighbours, like vinegar fretting on their lees will soon curse the day which made them independent." To many, the Nova Scotian venture was to be an extension of the war, in which loyalists and their principles would triumph, while the independent states would slide inevitably into decline and anarchy. In an exile's verse the province was hailed as that happy land where peace, love, and harmony would reign, and where liberty would be extended.

> Under a Sov'reign whose mild sway
> We shall flourish and be free
> While the land from which we fled,
> Shall be oppress'd with Tyranny.[2]

As early as 1779 Jacob Bailey was describing his escape from the regions of tyranny and rebellion to a land of freedom, tranquillity, and affluence. Within a few years he was hedging sharply on Nova Scotian affluence, but still preferred "the gloomy retreats of the wilderness" to the land of mobs and committees.³ This note was struck again by another loyalist who described the new settlers as breathing "a much greater share of *Free Air* than those renowned Sons of Freedom."⁴

Despite their own difficulties, the Nova Scotian loyalists clung tenaciously to the belief that the troubles in the new states were worse, and their future bleak. They still talked of the promise of their situation and the comparative collapse of their enemy. One Nova Scotia refugee, in 1785, described the Americans – poor, tax-ridden, and oppressed – as regretting their achievement of independence. "They now look back with regret to those happy times when under the wings of Great Britain, they enjoyed peace, plenty and real freedom." Similarly, a friend wrote to Gideon White describing the imminent collapse of the United States. With exorbitant taxes, cramped trade, political and social uncertainty, the country was on the brink of total dissolution and inevitable revolution. White, visiting New Hampshire in 1787, felt that, in comparison, Shelburne was a veritable paradise, and an object of great envy by the unfortunate people of that state. Benjamin Marston in the same year was permitting himself the luxury of sympathy for the revolted states. Although they richly deserved what had already befallen them, Marston expressed some pity for them in the calamities yet to come.⁵

The extent of this early obsession with the United States is seen in a New Year's verse found in the Shelburne *Packet*. The occasion appears to have been a traditional attempt by the printer's man to sum up the year's events and to wish the customers a happy new year, in light but laboured verse. This particular example began with references to local places and events, but the lightheartedness was abruptly dropped as the writer moved swiftly into a paean to the king and his province of Nova Scotia. The bulk of the verse was then concentrated upon the new nation, the many conflicts within it, and the ugly fighting over the spoils of victory.

> Our trade protected shall each year increase
> And in its train bring freedom, plenty, peace;
> Whilst independence sons shall curse the hour
> That first gave birth to Independence pow'r.

Even in doggerel, intended for local amusement, this theme of Nova Scotia's rise and the United States' decline was dominant. While the American experiment faced imminent collapse, the loyalists were "laying the foundations of a New Empire," and establishing "a *place* chosen by the Lords elect."⁶

The loyalist newspapers played an important role in reflecting and extending this attitude, offering the refugees a steady flow of stories from and about the United States. In the summer and fall of 1786, the *Packet* was very busy with stories of discord and discontent in that country, and particularly with the troubles in New Hampshire where, according to the *Packet*, a Cromwell had lately arisen. It also ran detailed stories on uprisings in Massachusetts, Rhode Island, and Philadelphia, noting that with the continuing anarchy and confusion throughout the states, "many of the better thinking among them, are totally quitting them, and mean to seek an asylum from such distractions in this settlement."[7]

While the American difficulties were reported with satisfaction, the American position vis-à-vis the commercial empire of Britain was discussed with concern and fear, comments on the subject appearing repeatedly in the refugee newspapers. Its prominence prodded the memories of revolution and provoked renewed comments on the past sins and possible future treachery of the independent states, on the folly of further rewarding rebellion, and on British credulity regarding the deceptions and designs of a desperate people. *The Royal American Gazette* even reprinted fierce diatribes from American newspapers.[8] The Shelburne newspapers were very sensitive to any American slighting of the loyalist communities, and answered in kind any derogatory comments they found. One column of a 1786 *Packet* contained a biting verse on affairs in the United States, and below it an attack on American distortion of loyalist affairs in Nova Scotia. Commenting on the progress of shipbuilding in the province, the *Packet* stated that American newspapers deliberately exaggerated the difficulties of the refugees in order to stop the constant emigration of their citizens to Shelburne. The shipbuilding controversy was continued by the *Packet* with the launching of the brig *Governor Parr* at Shelburne. "Be hush'd ye inhabitants of Shelburne nor with your skyrending acclamations on these occasions, *disturb* the *quiet* tranquillity of the peaceable people of Massachusetts."[9]

By their constant attention to the United States, by their comparisons and contumely, the Shelburne newspapers helped to sustain the intensity of loyalist hostility. With three newspapers dragging the past with all its rancour before them, the inhabitants were given little respite from the war. The Shelburne papers, however, like their community, were short-lived, their demise coinciding with a shift in the loyalist attitude towards the United States.[10] By the time of their passing, loyalist antipathy was receding, the response to their former home becoming less automatic and less harsh. Other comments on the Unites States can be found, but after 1787 the references, both in newspapers and private correspondence, were less frequent and less bitter.

The *Nova Scotia Magazine*, for example, published in the last years of the decade to encourage both economic and cultural improvement within the province, contrasts sharply with the Shelburne newspapers in its attitude towards the United States. Originally published by William Cochran, an Anglican minister who had come from New York after the revolution, and later by John Howe, a Sandemanian loyalist, it was dependent upon the support of loyalist readers throughout the province, yet showed none of the blatant anti-Americanism of the Shelburne papers. It shamelessly borrowed many of its articles from American journals and sources, most of them on agricultural methods, but others on topics ranging from school systems to the fate of the free negro. There was one fierce loyalist reaction in the magazine to a biased history of the revolution, and a plan for education in Nova Scotia made much of the weakness of the American system of education and the threat of American democratic institutions.[11] But these were isolated incidents in a journal otherwise devoid of derogatory comments on the Americans.

After 1786 there appeared an increase in and easing of communications between Americans and loyalists. Cooperation between the ethnic and fraternal societies on both sides of the border was more marked. The North British Society of Halifax, although studded with loyalist members, thought it fitting to have representatives of the New York and Philadelphia societies in attendance for its celebration in 1787.[12] Ties with relatives and friends, although frayed by division, emotion, and the wayward post, had not been sundered. In time, letters to and from the United States became more frequent and the circle of acquaintances broadened. As these ties were renewed and strengthened, visits to and from Americans increased.

One result of these visits, and perhaps also a cause, was the growing number of marriages between Americans and loyalists. "I hear by accounts from Boston," wrote Mrs Hutchinson, "that one of your youths has thought fit to detain one of our pretty girls by marrying her." Andrew Belcher, another loyalist, expressed delight at the engagement of his sister to a doctor from Cambridge. The only derogatory comments were humorous ones by a friend who reminded Miss Belcher of her former opinion of doctors, and threatened to visit Boston to tease the prospective groom.[13] Those who had not long before severed their ties forever with Satan's Kingdom, now seemed happy to witness and encourage marriages with Americans. The scarcity of suitable matches in Nova Scotia would have overcome most obstacles, but what one notices is the lack of any comment on nationality as an obstacle.

Comments made by loyalists visiting the United States after 1787 lacked the antagonism and bitterness found earlier. Although Gideon White painted a doleful picture of the state of New Hampshire upon his visit, he also emphasized how impressed he had been by the kindness he had received, and by the number of people who had called on him, all "very polite, friendly and social." Frederick Geyer, writing of his visit to Boston in 1787, omitted any comment on public matters, "having long since determined to leave those matters to whom they are interested." Gregory Townsend of Halifax had very much wanted to visit his friends in Boston. Arriving at last in the spring of 1788, he had a delightful, if too brief, stay among "all our Boston Friends." Circumstances at home forcing him to cut short his visit, he "reluctantly left that best of Countries."[14] The family of Mather Byles, the Anglican clergyman, was also visiting the United States. An uncle had sailed in 1787, and in the following year Mather Byles III planned to visit relatives and childhood haunts. In 1790 the elder Mather Byles journeyed to Boston to settle his father's estate. It was a sentimental journey which gave Byles the opportunity of embracing sisters not seen for a decade, of praying at the family tomb, of visiting relatives, of entertaining and being entertained by a host of friends and acquaintances. He preached at Trinity Church, and was astonished to receive an invitation to preach to his father's congregation at the new meetinghouse. It was a very happy trip, and the journal kept by this acerbic gentleman is noteworthy for the expressions of warmth, gratitude, and generosity towards his American hosts. From the moment of his arrival, when he remarked upon the politeness and courtesy of the customs official, until his return, there were no unkind comments on the Americans, no stirring of the revolution's residue.[15]

Nor did it take a visit to express the altered views. One reads of the gradual softening in the letters of Margaret Hutchinson, from sharp hostility towards the new order to a casual acceptance. At the war's conclusion she would not entertain the idea of returning to the new Massachusetts. "The ideas I have of what it once was, and what it is now, has sufficiently wean'd me from it." As the years passed she still did not return, but the altered American was no longer a factor. The reasons she later stressed were the difficulties of age and of leaving husband and family for any period of time.[16]

Even Jacob Bailey was softening. Few in Nova Scotia had written as much on the loyalist fate in the revolution, nor as violently against Britain and the rebels alike, as this Anglican minister in the Annapolis

Valley. Towards the revolting states, the ambitious leaders, and their foolish supporters, he had been merciless in his ridicule.[17] In time, however, he came to identify Britain as the chief cause of loyalist woes, and the United States as villain receded somewhat into the background. In December 1787 he wrote to Rev. John Gardiner on his appointment to Bailey's former church at Pawnalborough, wishing the new minister well, and expressing his own continued affection for the parishioners. He had hoped to return after the war, he explained in most diplomatic terms, but the spirit of revolution had prevailed and gallic perfidy had led to a separation from Britain. "My long absence has not in the least diminished my tender regard for the happiness of those dear friends, which stubborn faction had compelled me to forsake."[18]

William Clark, an Anglican minister in Digby, by the end of the decade also expressed new views on the revolted states, finding the Americans much changed from earlier years. Having travelled to Boston in 1789, he commented on the immense difference he found in the people since the revolution. "In times of Rebellion or public Commotion, the Body politic resembles a man under the Dilirium of a Fever, who when he gets well and returns to his natural Temper, is quite a different man."[19] Clark, far from condemning, now appeared to be rationalizing earlier American actions, and drawing a sharp distinction between revolutionary America and the moderation of the postrevolutionary period.

The altered attitudes of such individuals as Clark and Bailey, White, Mrs Hutchinson, and the others, reflected the changing attitude of the loyalists in general. The rank and file left few letters, but they did express themselves graphically by their actions, for many of them were now leaving Nova Scotia and returning to the United States. This movement testified to the altered feelings of the refugees toward their birthplace, as a result of which the old rhetoric, the old cries of loyalty and treason, no longer necessarily reflected the attitudes of the rank and file. It is difficult to return to a people you profess to hate. Since so many were returning with so little remorse, it may be assumed that the professions of hatred were no longer very extensive or very intense.

As we have seen, the first years of settlement had been too close to the revolution to allow the abatement of harsh memories. The scars were still raw. Moreover, reality had not yet caught up with the loyalists, and it was still imaginable that they might create in Nova Scotia what had been lost in the former colonies. The strength of this hope, spurring the many comparisons with the Americans, helped to keep alive the hostility. But the intensity of their reaction was too much to sustain. The passage of time and the reality of life in Nova Scotia were bound to have a mellowing effect upon their views, and to elicit a more generous and friendly attitude to the United States. The revolutionary experience was, in effect, being supplanted by the Nova Scotian, the immediacy and the predominance of which overwhelmed the memory of the earlier, traumatic occasion. If the hostility towards the United States was to be sustained, that country had to remain the principal focus of envy and hatred. In Nova Scotia, however, these hostile emotions were increasingly loosed upon Britain, local officials, Nova Scotians, and fellow loyalists.[20]

Twenty thousand loyalists had descended upon Nova Scotia seeking restitution and opportunity from a province too poor to support them. The natural result was a fierce scramble for the prizes. Moreover, the refugees were often placed in large, uncultivated areas, somewhat isolated from the rest of Nova Scotia. Much of the discord and conflict inevitable in such a large movement of population was between and among loyalists. The pent-up hostility and resentment created by their grievances, instead of being channelled to the outside world, frequently turned inward, loyalist bickering with loyalist over fundamental questions of property and place. Noting this on a tour of Shelburne, Andrew Brown wrote that "all the bitterness seemed now to be shed between the different knots of Loyalists in Shelburne which they had lately directed undivided against the members of Congress and the independence of the United States."[21]

An even deeper resentment was soon expressed towards the officials of the Nova Scotia government. From the very beginning there had been harsh complaints about Governor Parr, about the treatment received and the obstacles placed in the way of settlement, and accusations of corruption, incompetence, and favouritism. To Charles Morris there were "unmeritted ungenerous complaints which have been made against all the officers of Government without exceptions." These complaints and hostile attitudes did not ease with time, for the loyalists had come to a province ruled tightly by a small circle in Halifax, and their attempts to share in and to limit this power exacerbated feelings on both sides, deflecting much of the loyalist venom onto the ruling body. Jacob Bailey declared that many of the respectable people returning to the United States had been in effect driven out by affairs in the province, where only the wicked prospered. A returning loyalist expressed his sympathy for those remaining, "who are obliged to live under the arbitrary, cruel & unjust Government as at present administere'd in Nova Scotia." The comments of the returning loyalists represented a common attitude among the refugees towards official Nova Scotia. "This is an ungrateful place," said one who had seen his son return in 1788.[22] They spoke as if they had fled a land under mob rule only to find themselves under a rule which seemed almost as arbitrary. The bitterness once felt towards the revolted states was being shouldered aside by the growing anger and resentment felt towards the establishment in Nova Scotia.

Britain also shared in the deflecting of loyalist anger. Their early attitude towards the mother country was somewhat tempered by the situation in which they found themselves. Because of the circumstances of their defeat their expressed enmity was focused upon the revolting states. The corollary of this attitude was the rite of loyalty in which they indulged so zealously. As antagonists of the rebel forces, they sought both to glorify and to embody the antithesis of rebellion, the quality of loyalty.

This combination of circumstances, however, obscured a festering resentment towards Britain. They had not accepted a peace which they felt betrayed them in order to appease the rebels.[23] To a degree judgment on Britain was withheld until it was seen how far she would go in compensating the loyalists for their losses. By 1788 they knew, for by this date Britain had met her basic obligations. The land had been distributed, half-pay and pensions granted, provisions ended, and, for many refugees, too much given to too few. With their destiny in Nova Scotia crystallizing, the loyalists tended to weigh less generously Britain's part in their fortunes, and to place at her doorstep much of the blame once monopolized by the independent states. In 1790 William Clark wrote that "The People of New England never treated me with that Barbarity the Government of Old England has, all things considered."[24]

In contrast to the chill from Britain and Nova Scotia was the increasing warmth of the American response to the loyalists. With the passage of time American anger had subsided, and the returning loyalists found a cordial welcome. Settling in New York in 1790, a Dr Huggeford wrote of how pleased he was with his reception, and only wished he had gone sooner. Another found that the most friendly treatment was being given to all the loyalists returning to America. Dr Walter's return from Shelburne was well reported in an American newspaper of 1791: "He has been invited to officiate in several of our Meeting-Houses, and met with universal approbation – the places of Worship have been crowded with the most respectable audiences on those occasions."[25] Such examples of American generosity and cordiality would have done much to modify the loyalist attitude, for the ebbing of American hostility weakened the foundations upon which mutual antipathy had rested. No longer treated as an enemy, the loyalist found it increasingly difficult to act as one.

It would have been impossible in any case to sustain the intensity of the earlier attitude. Even hostility must have priorities, and, as we have seen, the attention once focused in splendid concentration upon the revolted states had been diverted in Nova Scotia to other, more immediate, and more dominant objects of anger. As a result of the loyalist difficulties in the new land, the ugly conflicts with pre-loyalists and fellow loyalists, and the growing resentment toward both the British and Nova Scotian governments, the American as enemy was relegated to a minor, somewhat distant role.

Republican institutions would remain alien to the loyalists, for they had not shared that desperate American experience which had given birth to their political system. The influence of the French Revolution and its excesses would harden their attitude towards republicanism. Such events of the 1790s as Jay's Treaty and the American flirtation with the French, combined with the conservative regime of Governor John Wentworth, with its emphasis upon the virtue of loyalty to the status quo, would rekindle some of the old rhetoric.[26] But it is easy to exaggerate the anti-Americanism of this later period in Nova Scotia and misleading to see the period, shaped by its own events, as a simple continuation of the 1780s. Between the bitterness of the exodus and the conservatism of the Wentworth years there was a distinct pause in which the attitude of the Loyalists towards the American people, those detested rebels of the past, had mellowed remarkably.

Both paralleling and strengthening this changing relationship with the United States was the settling of the loyalist claims, an occurrence that would have a major impact on the lives of many of the Nova Scotian refugees. In July 1783 Parliament appointed a commission to classify the services and losses of those loyal to the crown during the American Revolution.[27] Soon after, the commission began examining the claims, those seeking redress having to present written and sworn statements of their losses, and submit to a rigorous interview in defence of their claims.[28]

When the appointment of the commissioners was announced, letters appeared in the local press from friends in London advising on the documents and forms needed for submitting claims.[29] But the fact that the hearings were in England put redress beyond the reach of most loyalists, since no claim was to be considered "without the personal Presence of the Claimant." There were a few, presumably with sizeable claims, who went first to England to settle them before coming to Nova Scotia. Most in America appeared with their witnesses before justices to present their affidavits, which were then sent to agents in London for presentation.[30] For the loyalist in Nova Scotia it was a very awkward and often futile procedure. One of them described their predicament in these terms:

The Commissioners appointed to examine the Claims of the American Loyalists may be of advantage to you who are upon the Spot: but can be of none to us who remain in America, as it is impossible for us to produce our Claims, and support them with proper Vouchers, within the Time to which we are limited. I am perfectly at a loss how to act; nor can any one here instruct me. It is very obvious that the conditions required from us, are absolutely impracticable.[31]

Led by one of their chief agents, ex-Governor William Franklyn, the loyalists pushed hard to get the commission transferred to America. By the spring of 1785 they appeared to have succeeded. "We are encouraged to think that the reports of the Commissioners will be brought before Parliament this session, and the act renewed and amended, for the relief of absentees."[32] Claims and compensation were dominant issues in the loyalist communities during that spring. On May 30 the *Royal American* published "Summary Case of the American Loyalists," a detailed precedent-studded case for more generous compensation of loyalist losses. Two weeks later there appeared in the same newspaper "A Brief State of the Case of the American Loyalists," a thirteen-point summary of their brief for compensation which, while stressing both the sacrifices they had made in responding to the king's appeal for their loyalty and their present suffering owing to procrastination and the stringent demands for proof, attacked the concept that the nation could not afford the compensation. "Where is that inability or that poverty to be seen? ... Upon what principles then can public justice be denied by the Great Councils of the State, to men who have risqued their lives, and whose fortunes have been sacrificed by the State itself to the public peace and safety?"[33]

On November 15, 1785, Col. Thomas Dundas and Jeremy Pemberton, the commissioners of enquiry into the losses of the loyalists, opened an office in Halifax and advertised for claims, affidavits, and other necessary materials. By June 1786 Dundas was in Shelburne clearing claims, and while the parliamentary debate continued in London the commissioners pursued their difficult task of reading, listening to, and assessing loyalist stories of losses.[34]

The British desire to have the claims processed and done with as quickly as possible conflicted with the peculiar circumstances and difficulties which prevented the loyalists from getting their claims in on time, resulting in the extension of the time-limit and renewal of the pertinent acts. In February 1787 a notice in the *Gazette* stated that new claimants must explain why they had not taken advantage of the earlier act. Parr wrote seeking to have the claims of seventeen East Florida loyalists excused for missing the deadline of March 1, 1787, because "the several persons who lodged those Claims were at considerable expence, and lay under several difficulties in being obliged to come to Halifax from distant parts of the Province." As late as 1790 a memorial of the House of Assembly, pointing out that many loyalists, owing to their remoteness, their poverty, and their uncertainty as to the procedure required, were unable to file their claims under the first parliamentary act, asked that the king "take into consideration their deplorable case; and to grant them such relief as in your Royal wisdom may be deemed expedient."[35]

According to the commissioners' statement of 1789, the loyalists had received compensation by acts passed in 1785, 1786, 1787, and 1788. Of 2,211 claims examined, 939, examined in England, amounted to £893,710 and the claimants were allowed £977,397. Those examined in Nova Scotia and Canada, numbering 1,272, amounted to £975,310 and the claimants were allowed only £336,753.[36] Timothy Hierlihy had originally claimed £9,000 in losses, reducing that later to £7,500. In the "final decision" of 1790, he was granted only £276. The claims of Mathews's Scots, McKenzie and Chisholm, were both disallowed.[37] Yet the claims represented only a fraction of the losses incurred during the war, the claimants being those who had the necessary witnesses, affidavits, and opportunity to make submissions.

The awarding of the claims came as a second and desperately needed wind to those receiving them. Captain Booth noted in his diary that a Mr Neil had received £3,200, while a Mr Banton, since receiving £70, "had got fat ... and dresses better." He now "wears a fashionable Green Coat with Buttons on his waistcoat as broad as my hand." But for each receiving compensation, there were others resentful at not receiving similar assistance. Roger Viets in Digby wrote of the unfairness of many who had lost all being neglected, while others losing little were receiving much. Rev. George Gillmore also referred to this disparity. "Its finally settled it seems that Loyalists shall have no more compensation allotted them. Some have got enough, some have got none, others have got a little."[38]

The settlement of claims was one other factor in bringing to a close a particular period in the loyalist experience – that period in which, dependent on British largesse, the refugees sought to carve out homes, homesteads, and new lives in Nova Scotia. Many, of course, remained in the province only for as long as they could maintain their dependence upon Britain. As British aid ended so would, for many, the loyalist experience in Nova Scotia. The cohesion of the settlements was greatly weakened as many departed, and the great departure coincided with the ending of British aid.

By the late 1780s the claims had been settled, and by 1787 provisions had ceased. The impact of the latter development was compounded by the granting of portable pensions. Since the end of the war the provincial troops had worried whether they would be given the status of regular battalions, and the ensuing half-pay. "Until the End of this month we cannot know the fate of your Battalion," wrote a friend to Gideon White, "but I have hopes your officers will be put upon the List of half Pay." Eventually the officers of more than twenty loyalist corps were placed on the half-pay list.[39] In the beginning they had to sign affidavits before magistrates within the colony before receiving their pension money. "This was Done to prevent Gentn that formerly lived in America from returning there to reside & spending That Poor Pittance out of his Majestys Dominions." By the fall of 1787, however, this policy ceased and the half-pay officers were allowed to receive their pensions without residing in the empire, a concession which in Jacob Bailey's opinion was having a momentous impact on Nova Scotia. "And if this permission is not discontinued it will ruin if not unpeople these provinces." It was not simply the loss of the pensioners that was so frightening. It was the fact that others in the community were dependent upon these clusters of army veterans for employment. A service trade had developed, and when the recipients of the pensions left so must many of those who had become dependent upon them. The ramifications of the new policy were graphically described by Roger Viets.

... the measure will ruin the loyalist settlements – tis these Men's Pay we depend upon to keep our poor alive by finding Employment for labouring men ... if they go the poor must follow them or starve. It has had the most disheartening, the most pernicious Influence already. As soon as all the Monied men are gone the Labourers for Want of Employment must perish or emigrate to the Country of Traitors to be Fugitives & Vagabonds to be Hewers of Wood & Drawers of Water to those who were once their Tenants & Servants.[40]

The loyalists had received their claims and portable pensions. They no longer received provisions. There was little to keep them in Nova Scotia now but the desire to remain. Since many lacked this desire there was, from 1787 to 1791, a re-exodus from what Joseph Peters had often called the province of Tenebra.[41]

Margaret Ells estimated the number of loyalists leaving by measuring the number of escheats, and found that very few left. The total number of grantees was 6,220, the number of escheats was 724, and therefore the number of permanent grantees was 5,496, of whom 5,088 were white. A total of 3,059 or 62 per cent were civilians, 2,029 or 38 per cent soldiers. "These grantees, when subjected to the various checks as indicated above, yielded a total of 18,424 permanent white settlers, of whom 14,271 were civilians, 111 squatters, and 4,042 soldiers. Counting the 938 negro settlers, the grand total of permanent Loyalist settlers in Nova Scotia proper was 19,362."[42] This method of subtracting escheats from grants gives a very low estimate of the number leaving, one not in harmony with the many contemporary references to departing loyalists. It does not take into account the many who had come, stayed a few years, and left before grants were finally issued. George Patterson, for example, comments on the casual abandonment and occupation of land, the transferring of title "for sums of four and five pounds. A number never sold, and their land has since been unoccupied or occupied without title." This phenomenon would not appear in a simple tallying of grants and escheats.[43] Nor does it take into account the many who sold their tickets or titles for a pittance or a bottle of rum to the few buying and building up large holdings cheaply, and the later transfer of land to the incoming Scots both in Digby and northeastern Nova Scotia. It also assumes that the government was very diligent in escheating land left by the loyalists. Whatever the reason for the discrepancy, the number who actually left the province was much greater than the number cited by Ells.

It was soon evident to the officials that many had no intention of going on their land, even when surveyed.[44] Many of the soldiers in Antigonish, without experience of farming, sold their land for a few pounds and moved on. Similarly in Pictou County some of the disbanded soldiers took one look at their land and reenlisted at Halifax, while others sold out for as little as £4. A large number left Clements early. Almost all of the 38th and 40th regiments left before even drawing for their lots, and many others, drawing bad land, left soon after. The land was simply not worth working. The situation was similar in Guysborough, as indicated in a letter from John Wentworth to Parr on the fate of the Cumberland Regiment. "There are not thirty of the privates living within one hundred miles of Chedabucto, five or six officers only are in this country, the rest are abroad: many of the Privates Sold their lotts for a dollar, or a pair of Shoes, or a few pounds of Tobacco – but most for a Gallon of New England rum, and quit the Country without taking any residence."[45]

Most of these early drop-outs were those who had come to take what advantage they could of the offer of free land and provisions. There were others who attempted various enterprises, especially at Shelburne, were early losers, decided it was unwise to throw good money after bad, and cut their losses. Such was Archibald Morten who in the spring of 1785 was "intending to leave this place, as soon as the affairs of A. Morten and Co. can profitably be settled." A memorial of Shelburne's Church of England in 1785 stated that "multitudes have removed and from various causes of discontent are still daily leaving us, that the Settlement has diminished to one half of the original Number," and the remaining through their expenditures in clearing land and building houses were "reduced to Poverty and Distress." By 1786 the general sessions of Shelburne had to prohibit the issuing of passes to any persons seeking to leave the province before their taxes were paid.[46]

With the ending of provisions in 1787, and the allowing of portable pensions, Shelburne began to empty quickly. William Dyott, who visited it in 1788, noted that the town "has as poor an appearance as anything I ever saw." He estimated that there were fewer than 3,000 inhabitants, whites and blacks, and as of the past winter, 360 empty houses, "which clearly proves the rapid decline of the settlement." In 1789 Captain Booth wrote of the loss of one of Shelburne's schoolteachers. "The People quitting the Place so fast has reduced her now to 18 [students] – She is going to keep School at Halifax ... As the Vessels begin to prepare for their voyages the Families begin to think of quitting – many are talking of leaving some went off Yesterday in the Schooners for New York." In a memorial to Sir Richard Hughes the leading citizens of Shelburne wrote of "the present reduced state of this once populous and flourishing settlement."[47]

In 1791 Charles Inglis moved to correct an abstract sent to Dr Morice, stating that there were only 600 souls in Shelburne. Inglis claimed that the children alone numbered that many, "and the members of the Church of England to greatly more than double; yet the Dissenters of all denominations are nearly equal to the Church people." In his diary he noted the figures given him by the wardens of the combined Anglican churches, who, after studying the poll tax and other sources, estimated that there were 605 taxable persons in Shelburne and the surrounding township. Inglis listed them as families, added 100 who would be too poor to be taxed, and concluded that there were 3,525 still residing in the township of Shelburne.[48]

This figure, which includes the population of both the town and the surrounding countryside, indicates a marked decline in the area's population since the period following the arrival of the loyalists. Yet the estimate is probably somewhat high, for Inglis ignored the number of bachelors, perhaps a sixth of the taxable people,[49] and perhaps overestimated those not paying and not listed. Another source believed that by 1792 only 2,000 remained.[50] By 1796 only 125 of the 710 rate payers of 1786 appeared on the assessment roles. According to Rev. Andrew Brown, "Every vessel that touched at the harbour carried out openly or by stealth whole swarms of the inhabitants. Houses were gutted and abandoned and streets left without occupant or claimant." Brown visited the settlement in the August of its sixth year. "Something like langour mixed up with a heavy depression pervaded all orders of the inhabitants. The sound of the axe was no longer heard. Almost the whole of the two uppermost ranges of streets was deserted." Captain Booth also commented on the departures: "a Mr Narvey who is quitting this Place, and going to Philadelphia, sold his Goods, House &c. yesterday – The house was put up at £100 and nobody would bid for it. – Two years ago 500 £ was refused for it. – What can be the Views of the Merchants here? not to continue in the Place one would think!"[51]

The decline of other loyalist settlements was not as spectacular as at Shelburne, but it was marked. Two loyalist seats were declared vacant in 1789, that of Stephen Delancey in Annapolis, who had obtained an office in the Bahamas, and Joseph Aplin in Barrington, who had been absent from the province for two years.[52] According to Charles Inglis, Annapolis and Granville had declined little, a view not held by the local Anglican minister, Jacob Bailey, who commented several times on the exodus.[53] In all of Sydney County there were 555 men from sixteen to sixty years in 1787. Country Harbour had but thirty families in 1790. In Wilmot "some principal familys on whom we depended for assistance have removed from this part of the Province since the Frame of the Church was raised, & there are but few left who are able to contribute anything towards finishing it." In Clements the early drain simply continued after 1787.[54] Digby suffered much from emigration. As early as 1786 Roger Viets spoke of the town as "yearly decreasing and in Danger of a Total Dissolution." By 1789 he claimed that most of the half-pay officers, pensioners, salaried men, and successful claimants had left Digby with expressions of "Contempt, Insult, Reproach & Ridicule." In a letter to Inglis of 1791 the wardens and vestry of Digby claimed that only half of the original families remained. Viets as early as 1786 estimated that only a third were still in the settlement.[55]

Another disturbing development was the departure of almost a third of the black loyalists to Sierra Leone. By the end of the eighties the black experience in Nova Scotia was one of disillusionment. Many who had been denied provisions and land, and had been condemned to a life of share-cropping or the status of indentured servants, feared that it was their destiny in Nova Scotia to become second-class citizens. As the reality of their situation crystallized, many longed for another "promised land" where they might obtain not only property but also greater security and independence.

It was in this state of mind that the black loyalist encountered the plans and ambitions of "a philanthropic and commercial organization that had recently been invested with a colony in West Africa."[56] In May 1790 the Sierra Leone Company was incorporated with power to establish a government, hold land and carry on trade in the area of Sierra Leone.[57] Needing settlers, the company became very interested in the plight of the black loyalists in the Maritimes and sent one of the directors, John Clarkson, to Halifax. Clarkson's recruiting visits to black settlements in the fall of 1791 were extremely successful. Promised free passage, free land, and racial equality, most who met the company's criteria and who were sufficiently solvent to be allowed to leave the province accepted the offer to go to Sierra Leone. On January 15, 1792, 1,196 black refugees sailed from Nova Scotia for their new home in Africa.[58]

Such was the exodus throughout Nova Scotia that in 1789 the assembly passed an act preventing people leaving the colony without a pass. It was necessary for would-be emigrants to put up their names publicly at the provincial secretary's office for seven days before receiving the pass. Fines were to be levied upon vessels carrying persons without passes. The provincial secretary requested the sheriff's office of each county to organize a census to find out how many people remained.[59]

To observers at the time, the most remarkable thing about the loyalists was not so much their abrupt arrival as it was the extent of their exodus. Munro, in his tour of southern Nova Scotia in 1795, estimated that there were only 150 families in the town of Shelburne, and fewer than 2,000 in the vicinity. He found only sixty-eight families in the town of Digby. He knew little of the loyalist communities of Wilmot and Aylesford, "Only that they are thinly settled." In 1804 William Black, a Methodist minister, described Shelburne as "A small town about ten leagues to the west of Liverpool," whose population was one-tenth of its former size. In describing the province's principal centres in 1815, Joshua Marsden, the Methodist preacher, omitted the former loyalist hopes, Shelburne and Manchester. "Shelburne and

Manchester, once so flourishing and populous, are now almost deserted; the former in 1783 contained 600 families, now in 1815 it has not as many individuals; in Manchester the same year there were 200 houses (rather huts) now there are five houses and three barns." The historian Judge Savary was very wary of some estimates of the number of loyalists who stayed in the township of Annapolis. He believed that "no one whom I have read on the subject has taken sufficient account of the large number who in a few years returned to the United States. They build up a City of 12,000 inhabitants in Shelburne, and soon deserted it. I look over page after page of the Loyalist muster rolls of [Annapolis] and Digby County and find many with but two or three names now among us."[60]

They left their communities throughout the province to go to other, more hopeful, parts of Nova Scotia, or to try their luck in other parts of British North America, but the greatest number returned to the United States. There was substantial shifting about within the province. As the land was granted, the movement out to the farm lots reduced the size of the town centres. Many loyalists, unsuccessful in their original sites, drifted to other areas of the province. Some of the Anspach and Hessian veterans became servants to the old Germans in the Annapolis valley. With Shelburne's decline some loyalists drifted west, settling at Argyle, Tusket, and Yarmouth. Others went to Barrington, although they did not remain long. At least one doctor and some skilled labour drifted into Liverpool. With the decline of Clements some moved to Annapolis, Digby, and Halifax. The refugees at Horton left to found a settlement at Parr Town "across the Bay" from Horton, while Rev. George Gillmore was moving from Ardois Hill "further into the country of Nova Scotia" to Horton. The amount of shifting about is indicated in a note on the poll tax records for Cumberland: "The above list of the Refugees is taken from the Survey and grant of their lands, but as many of them are shifting from place to place, Several of those marked in the Settlement at Remsheg & on the Road to Londonderry may now be in the other different districts within the province but are not returned at any other district."[61]

A few returned to the British Isles, but these were limited to officers and prominent individuals whose chances were better in England than in Nova Scotia, and others whose emigration from Britain was so recent that they regarded that country rather than America as "home." In 1788 the North British Society in Halifax "was called upon to aid several refugees in returning to Scotland; amongst the number was the Rev. Andrew Mitchell, who played a conspicuous part as a Loyalist in Boston during the rebellion."[62]

With the encouragement of Governor Paterson, some of the loyalists after a brief stay in Shelburne made their way to St John's Island, where it was reported in November 1784 that "Numbers of people came from that sitty here this Fawl – and likes the place very well." More went to join old friends on the more purely loyalist soil of the St John River. Benjamin Marston, Edward Winslow, and most of the latter's friends made their way to the river. Mather Byles found an easy living there. His son went from Halifax to New Brunswick and finally to Grenada upon getting an appointment there. Captain Brownrigg, forced out of Chedabucto to Halifax, by 1785 had opened shop on the Miramichi as a merchant. Amos Botsford, after the discord in Digby, ended up in the New Brunswick House of Assembly. And the mother of Eliza Cottnam, finding Halifax "a very expensive & not a very pleasing place," moved to New Brunswick and opened a boarding-school for girls in Saint John.[63]

Some, regarding New Brunswick as no more promising than Nova Scotia, made their way to Jamaica and the West Indies. Captain Booth mentioned aiding a refugee seeking a new start in New Providence. Philip Jarvis wrote that he was only one of several persons who had left Shelburne to find work in Jamaica without letters to people of influence there.[64]

It is difficult to find material on the extent of loyalist migration from Nova Scotia to Canada. Some individuals are mentioned. William Campbell, who had been a young loyalist quartermaster, went from Port Mouton to Guysborough, moved to Cape Breton and then to Upper Canada where he eventually became chief justice. James Stuart, leader of the attempt to impeach Chief Justice Sewell and Judge Monk in Lower Canada, had been a Nova Scotia loyalist. Mathews's Scots, on the collapse of Shelburne, made their way to Canada, being drawn there by the presence of friends and family.[65] There is little evidence that any large number of Nova Scotia loyalists went to Canada.

There is a great deal of evidence, however, that many returned to the United States. Parr noted as early as 1784 that "its' a common thing at the several Settlements, for people to sell their Land as soon as they obtain grants, and then sett out for New England." He referred to this trend again in the following year: "The Quarrels among themselves begin to subside as the idle and dissipated disperse through the Province, or return to the States, which many do when they have got all they are to get, I wish some more of their Gentry would follow them whose Loyalty might be comprehended in a Nutt-shell."[66]

The return accelerated with the ending of provisions. As provisions were cut back, Roger Viets estimated that Digby lost two-thirds of its population, half of those leaving "gone back to Egypt after living so long in Idleness on the King's Provisions." Rev. William Walter returned to Boston from Shelburne, Rev. William Clark from Digby. Dunbar Sloan, a member of the North British Society, was a loyalist from New York who had come to Halifax via Barbados to open an iron business and now returned to New York. When Colonel Barton, one of the richest loyalists in Digby, was killed in an accident, his wife gravitated back to the United States. William Shipman, who had sailed to New York from Shelburne, reported that he had had no difficulty in finding work.[67] Many took advantage of the portable pensions to go back, "not indeed after the leeks and onions (which are here very fine) but the peaches and water melons of the land of bondage." According to Jacob Bailey, most of those leaving Annapolis were returning to the United States, although, "as they were chiefly indolent people of a restless and roving disposition, or notorious for their criminal conduct," they were no loss, at least to the Anglican church. Yet they were having a dire effect upon the community for they were encouraging others to desert Nova Scotia. Bailey warned that "These have exerted such a spirit of discontent among people of all characters, farmers, mechanicks, labourers, and traders as threaten a total depopulation and though several have returned with a confirmation that the deserters are miserable beyond expression – yet it has no effect, nothing is able to resist the torrent, except the wisdom and vigorous exertions of government."[68]

Digby was hard hit by this exodus. "This Place," William Clark wrote in 1790, "is nearly desolated by emigrations or more properly re-emigrations." It was also found that "many of the People [have] Quitted the Township of Clements & gone to the States." Roger Viets had described the chain reaction of the labouring class leaving because the gentry had left, and the gentry leaving because of the portable pensions. What annoyed him as much as the effect of their departure upon the community was their attitude on returning to the United States. He contended that "many, if not the greater Part of these Stipend Gentry to conciliate their new Masters, insult, ridicule & vilify the British Government & Constitution beyond any other People in the states ... To hear of the Taunts and Reproaches of a pensioned Loyalist who has now become an American is more mortifying than either the Persecutions we suffer'd from the Insurgents or the neglect of our own Rulers."[69]

Most of those leaving Shelburne made their way to the republic. Colonel Dundas mentioned that on the cessation of provisions many, unable to exist, left the town for the United States. Parr described the "Dregs and Banditti" of Shelburne who returned as soon as provisions ended, joined later by those who were caught in the town's rapid decline and who had to dispose of their fine houses for a pittance. "And latterly some have gone off, after receiving Compensation for their losses." In 1793 the magistrates and Grand Jury wrote to Charles Inglis of their concern over "the emigration of a number of industrious poor, to those parts of the States of America ... and a dread that many more will follow their example." A list of Shelburne residents intending to leave the province in 1786 and 1787 showed that 74 per cent of them were returning to the United States, of whom 68 per cent were going to New York. Munro had written "that there was scarce a vessel that went out of the Harbor to the States for awhile, but carried some of them away that the Town in a short time was deprived of its Inhabitants in a great measure."[70]

The epidemic return to the new nation was province-wide. The evidence of other destinations is sparse. There were repeated references to the prodigal's return, in such a fashion that other destinations seemed exceptions. Even Inglis was forced to state, in 1790, that "many of the Emigrants who came here in 1783, have since returned to the Revolted Colonies." Roger Viets seemed utterly aghast at the extent of the return.

Thus with the utmost Grief and Indignation that I mention to you, the great Emigration from this Province to the States ... Ever since the King's Allowance ceased they have been running back to the States and more now than ever. Some Hundreds of Families have left this Province within 18 Months last past & some Hundreds more seem to be preparing for Removal. This greatly gratifies the Vanity & Ill-Nature of the American Whigs, especially as these Emigrants were those who were in the best Way of living comfortably *here*, and now they have gone to the States, in a most necessitous and almost starving Condition.[71]

As many of the loyalists departed, the government was already turning to welcome another group of immigrants. The coming of the Scots, in contrast to the abrupt arrival of the loyalists, would be spread over decades, but they were already coming, and in sufficient numbers that, in the rush and concern to settle them, the loyalist as needy settler was being slightly upstaged. Charles Morris expressed his delight in their coming by claiming that "there is no Duty that can be more pleasing and grateful for us to Discharge than the accommodation of the Valuable People in whose fate you are so deeply & warmly interested."[72]

By 1791 Inglis was commenting on "the new Scotch settlements" in Digby. There were said to be 400 families in Pictou. Their petition to be granted the land they were on was supported by the surveyor general, Charles Morris, and as far as he could by John Parr, who sought Britain's advice on "how far I may encourage these people so as to prevent their going to the American States; of which I am very apprehensive ... I have certain information that between Four & Five hundred Souls were actually Embarked at Greenoch for this Province." In September 1791, 650 people from Glasgow were landed at Pictou "in wretched condition." Unable as yet to obtain funds for them, and fearing they might emigrate to South Carolina, Parr arranged for the new arrivals to spread into the country while he sought permission to grant them land and took what action he could to get them settled and housed before the approaching winter. As if in reaction to the more demanding and less accommodating loyalists, the Scots were lauded by Morris as "the only People who are calculated for well directed and laborious Husbandry."[73]

There were many loyalists still in the province, but the loyalist wave had peaked and was ebbing, while the swell of a new wave of immigrants had begun to break along the shores of Nova Scotia. As the province turned to meet the Scottish settlers, it seemed the end of a distinct period, that time when the loyalist as settler could command the whole attention of government and people.

Epilogue

Not all of the loyalists experienced failure. Many of the refugees had come simply to get what they could in free land and provisions and then, having received and disposed of those, they drifted away. They had achieved their goal in Nova Scotia. Others attempted to put down roots in the colony and succeeded. The fisheries, with loyalist fishermen involved, continued off the coast. As the loyalist centres declined many of the tradesmen drifted out of the colony, but some remained in the shrunken centres where, despite the decreased population, they found sufficient demand for their labour. Others moved to those parts of the colony where their skills were marketable. Some of the merchants remained in the original settlements and managed to survive the bad times. Others left their holdings and made their way to Halifax where determination and talent, capital and connections enabled them to profit from the complacency of the established merchant class. Many farmers had put too much of their sweat into the land to leave easily, and by the 1790s the land was beginning to repay their efforts. In general, those who accepted Nova Scotia on its terms managed to survive and to prosper.

Moreover, despite the lessened numbers, the loyalist presence seemed a more potent factor after 1792. A loyalist, John Wentworth, was now governor and under him many of the refugees moved into positions of power and influence in the altered establishment. Jonathan Sterns, the Wilkes of Parr's correspondence, who was struck off the roll of attornies for his part in the affair of the judges, was solicitor general of Nova Scotia by 1797.

There is, however, a watershed between the two eras. In the earlier period the refugees were attempting to settle; in the later period they were settled. In the former period they were loyalists confronting an alien land and people; in the latter they were becoming Nova

Scotians or they had gone. The period of transition was not at all uniform, varying from individual to individual. One milestone in the transition is the period in the late 1780s when thousands, having failed in their attempt to settle, gave up and returned to the United States. The death of John Parr in 1791 was another such milestone marking the end of one era and the beginning of another.

The object of this study has been the examination of the earlier period, the formative years of settlement and adjustment. In many respects the refugees were like other immigrant groups. In common with almost all immigrants they suffered the trauma of uprooting. Others had likewise faced a new land with mingled hope and frightened uncertainty. The loyalists, like others before and after them, went through the difficult task of settlement, of clearing sufficient land to assure them subsistence and survival. And, as with other settlers, preconceived notions and concepts were altered to meet the challenge of the new surroundings. There is in fact a danger in seeing these immigrants only as loyalists rather than as people who happened to be loyalists. The danger lies in looking for a "loyalist" reaction to all of the facets of their new life. If the people are seen as one-dimensional, then one anticipates a response that encompasses them all. Such an emphasis would be misleading in the light of the varied reactions that did occur.

There is an equally grave danger in treating the refugees as simply another group of immigrants without delving into how their stay was shaped by their background. To understand their early years in Nova Scotia it is necessary to take into account the emotional and ideational baggage that the loyalists brought with them and how it affected and was affected by the Nova Scotian experience.

For some Nova Scotia appeared to be the final defeat of the late civil war. It was to have been both asylum and vindication. They had left New York in humiliation, envisaging with a child-like hope their inevitable triumph in Nova Scotia. The illusion continued for some time, nurtured by several factors. One was the flux and uncertainty of the postwar world where anything seemed possible. Another was Britain's promise to have the loyal colonies supplant the thirteen in the new empire and to establish the loyalists firmly in those colonies. These factors, combined with the great numbers swarming over the colony and the changes to be wrought by their presence and energy, created a deceptive atmosphere of imminent economic revolution. Ignorance of the colony, and of possibilities and limitations, allowed one to exaggerate what might be achieved.

Yet for many time could only shatter such illusions. Hope began to crumble in the first year with the failure to get the loyalists on their lands quickly enough to enable them to establish themselves while they possessed the cushion of provisions. Hope inevitably collapsed as the refugees awakened to the fact that the little colony of Nova Scotia was too limited in resources and potential to absorb such a large influx, much less to assure them of affluence. Those clearing farms soon became aware of how little good land was available, of how distant were markets, and of what a brutal task was entailed in raising sufficient surplus for market. The coastal waters were no panacea. The inshore fisheries could offer subsistence but not wealth. The refugees lacked the knowledge and skills to compete successfully in the Grand Bank fisheries, and most of the grandiose plans for the whale fisheries collapsed. As the prime timber belts receded farther and farther from the rivers the refugees found themselves priced out of competition in this field. Shelburne, founded on a remarkable wave of optimism, possessed no marked advantage that would ensure metropolitan status, secured no hinterland to service, and collapsed rapidly, dragging down with it the hopes and ambitions of thousands of refugees. Nova Scotia was an unsuitable colony in which to pursue greatness. Many refugees, lacking the skills, endurance, or desire to be pioneers, were inadequate to the task of settling such a colony. In short, neither the colony nor the refugees had the necessary resources to ensure easy or inevitable success. As loyalists they demanded too much too quickly of the land, and the departure of thousands by the end of the decade indicated that among those hoping for triumphant vindication, Nova Scotia had proved to be simply an extension of their defeat.

A characteristic of the period was the progressive weakening of the loyalist identity. In the alien setting of Nova Scotia a fraternity of loyalism was inevitable. It survived at first because the remembrance of the war and its results was still vivid. It also survived because in Nova Scotia there existed for a while a protagonist/antagonist situation, in which the loyalists were pitted against the unknown people and government of the colony. A product of this sense of identity was the image that the loyalists attempted to project to the world at large: they were the tested keepers of the virtue of loyalty.

This exclusiveness was challenged quickly by the Nova Scotian, who was not at all willing to grant the loyalists a monopoly on loyalty. He had little respect for the mass of refugees and less incentive to recognize in them any select virtue. To the Nova Scotian they were not so much loyalists as they were displaced persons, not so much martyrs as simple casualties of a war, thrown upon his shores by the upheaval of revolution. He was aware, moreover, that in a postrevolutionary period an exclusive claim to loyalty opened the door to power and influence. The loyalist claim to any such position was therefore challenged. The pre-loyalist questioned the motives and sacrifices of many of the newcomers. He pointed to the role played and price paid by his colony during the war. And he sought to outbid the refugees in the oaths and professions of loyalty, in the symbols of crown-worship. Amid the din of such rhetoric the voices of the loyalists were to a great extent neutralized. Where all are loyal, the value of loyalty depreciates, even for the original claimant.

This effort to dilute the impact of loyalist exclusiveness was, however, less important than the weakening of the loyalist identity in the minds of the refugees themselves. Despite the rhetoric their common bond was a fragile thing. In a sense it precluded the cohesion found among other immigrant groups, for a war of such magnitude encompassed many types. They had come to Nova Scotia from almost every region of America. They included the rich and the poor, the learned and the illiterate, the powerful and the weak, the flexible opportunist and the supporter who would remain loyal no matter the cost. The many different types that sheltered under the broad umbrella of the term loyalist lacked the community of background and purpose found among most immigrant bodies. The scale of their diversity was indeed an active factor in fostering schism and division among them. They differed radically in background and motivation, in wartime contribution and sacrifice, and those with strong credentials resented being lumped indiscriminately with all the questionables passing as "loyalist." Their common status was too frail a cord to restrain the force of such differences.

The years in Nova Scotia only served to weaken the bond. Had the Nova Scotian been the principal antagonist the weakening might have been less marked. But the issues arising in the isolated loyalist communities were of concern chiefly to the refugees, and the Nova Scotian was not really involved. The scramble over the spoils of defeat was a loyalist affair and the rancour arising out of it was directed at one's fellow loyalists. Within these rather closed societies the often vicious fight for good land and water lots, for supplies and provisions, for office and influence, created an implosive situation that saw loyalist pitted against loyalist rather than against any outside threat. In a situation where one's most immediate antagonist and greatest threat was a fellow refugee the loyalist sense of a common identity tended to disintegrate.

Moreover, the intensity of this common awareness depended upon the antithesis to be found in the "patriot"; the rebellion had to remain the focal point of a pent-up anger. In Nova Scotia, this anger was dissipated by other, more immediate issues and other, more immediate enemies. It was further dissipated by the passage of time. After nearly a decade the revolution's ashes were grown cold, the central issue of "independence" had become somewhat distant. One's commitment to the crown in a war long past had lost its immediacy, some of its stature, and perhaps some of its relevance.

The weakening of the loyalist sense of identity, like the shattering of their dreams of inevitable success, was part of a final acceptance of the war's outcome. The American Revolution, along with the special claims of its loyalist victims, was now a thing of the past. As much as anything, this story has been a study of the acceptance over time of this reality. On their arrival the rhetoric was that of a morality play, their world seemingly divided into loyalists and rebels, the virtuous and the villains, their fondest ambition to make Nova Scotia the envy of their enemy. During the hard years that ensued such illusions were shed, and with them were discarded much of the rhetoric and the shibboleths that had surrounded them. With tempered realism the loyalists came to accept the results of the revolution, and to set about arranging the rest of their days within the limitations of this reality.

Notes

ABBREVIATIONS

CO   Colonial Office Papers, Public Archives of
                      Canada
Coll. NBHS   *Collections of the New Brunswick Historical
                      Society*
Coll. NSHS   *Collections of the Nova Scotia Historical Society*
JHA   *Journals of the House of Assembly of Nova Scotia*
PAC   Public Archives of Canada, Ottawa
PANS   Public Archives of Nova Scotia, Halifax
SPG   Society for the Propagation of the Gospel
Winslow Papers   *The Winslow Papers, A.D. 1776–1826*, edited by
                      W.O. Raymond (Saint John 1910)

INTRODUCTION

1 Bernard Bailyn, "The Central Themes of the American Revolution," in
  S.G. Kurtz and J.H. Hutson, eds., *Essays on the American Revolution*
  (Chapel Hill 1973), 16.
2 Compare, for example, Bernard Bailyn's *The Ordeal of Thomas Hutchinson* (Cambridge, Mass. 1974) with his *The Ideological Origins of
  the American Revolution* (Cambridge, Mass. 1967) or his introduction
  to *The Pamphlets of the American Revolution* (Cambridge, Mass. 1965)
3 Robert M. Calhoon, *The Loyalists in Revolutionary America, 1760–
  81* (New York 1973).
4 For three examples, see R.O. MacFarlane, "The Loyalist Migration: A
  Social and Economic Movement," in R.C. Lodge, eds., *Manitoba Essays*
  (Toronto 1937); Gerald Craig, *Upper Canada: The Formative Years, 1784–*

1841 (Toronto 1963), 1–19; Esther Clark Wright, *The Loyalists of New Brunswick* (Fredericton 1955).

5 Jo-Ann Fellows, "The Loyalist Myth in Canada," in Canadian Historical Association, *Historical Papers, 1971,* 96.

6 Louis Hartz, *The Founding of New Societies: Studies in the History of the United States, Latin America, South Africa, Canada and Australia* (New York 1964).

7 See, for example, Kenneth McRae, "The Structure of Canadian History," in Louis Hartz, *Founding of New Societies;* Gad Horowitz, "Conservatism, Liberalism, Socialism," *Canadian Journal of Economics and Political Science* (May 1966); David V.J. Bell, "The Loyalist Tradition in Canada," *Journal of Canadian Studies* (May 1970); S.F. Wise, "Liberal Consensus or Ideological Background: Some Reflections on the Hartz Thesis," in Canadian Historical Association, *Historical Papers, 1974.*

8 Mary Beth Norton, *The British Americans: The Loyalist Exiles in England, 1774–89* (Boston 1972).

CHAPTER ONE

1 Ward Chipman to Jonathan Sewell, December 9, 1781, Sewell Papers, MG 23, GII 10, vol. 2, PAC.

2 S.S. Blowers to William Pepperill, March 23, 1782, Shelburne Papers, MG 23, A4, vol. 67, PAC.

3 Ibid.

4 E.L. Jones, "Sir Guy Carleton and the Close of the American War of Independence, 1782–83" (PHD thesis, Duke University 1968), 30.

5 Whitehall to Sir Guy Carleton, April 4, 1782, CO 5, vol. 106.

6 Jones, "Sir Guy Carleton," 75.

7 Hugh and Alex Wallace to Frederick Haldimand, August 25, 1782, Haldimand Papers, MG 21, vol. B74, PAC.

8 Carleton to Secretary of State, Southern Department, September 12, 1782, CO 5, vol. 107.

9 Ibid.

10 Carleton to Hamond, September 22, 1782, CO 5, vol. 107.

11 Esther Clark Wright, *The Loyalists of New Brunswick* (Fredericton 1955), 30.

12 Ibid.

13 J.P. Edwards, "Shelburne That Was and Is Not," *Dalhousie Review* 2, no. 2 (1922): 180; T.C. Haliburton, *An Historical and Statistical Account of Nova Scotia* (Halifax 1829), 192.

14 Port Roseway Association Minute Book, 37, MG 9, B6(1), PAC.

15 Ibid. The committee was composed of Joseph Pynchon, James Dole,

Joseph Durfee, Peter Lynch, Thomas Courtney, William Hill, and Joshua Pell.

16 Ibid. Memorial to Parr, December 21, 1782, 35.

17 Jones, "Sir Guy Carleton," 233.

18 Wright, *Loyalists of New Brunswick*, 39–41.

19 Sarah Winslow to Benjamin Marston, April 10, 1783, quoted in ibid., 40.

20 Nathaniel Whitworth to brother Charles, April 18, 1783, White Collection, PANS.

21 Sarah Winslow to Benjamin Marston, April 10, 1783, quoted in Wright, *Loyalists of New Brunswick*, 40.

22 Ward Chipman to Jonathan Sewell, December 18, 1782, Sewell Papers, MG 23, GII 10, vol. 2, PAC.

23 Clopper to Whitworth, April 18, 1783, White Collection, PANS.

24 *Connecticut Journal*, March 20, 1783, CO 5, vol. 109.

25 ——— to Ward Chipman, July 1, 1784, MG 23 D1(1), vol. 2, PAC.

26 Extract, letter from Halifax, February 25, 1783, *Pennsylvania Packet or General Advertiser*, CO 5, vol. 108.

27 Extract, letter from Halifax, January 28, 1783, ibid.

28 Joshua Upham to Edward Winslow, August 21, 1783, quoted in Wright, *Loyalists of New Brunswick*, 63.

29 Carleton to Lord Townshend, January 13, 1783, CO 5, vol. 108.

30 Digby to Stephens, April 12, 1783, MG 12, Admiralty 1, vol. 490, PAC.

31 Committee of the Associated Loyalists to Hamond, April 15, 1783, CO 5, vol. 103.

32 Port Roseway Association to Carleton, April 21, 1783, MD, vol. 369, PANS.

33 Port Roseway Minute Book, April 8, 1783.

34 Wright, *Loyalists of New Brunswick*, 42–4.

35 Circular letter, New York, 1783, Lawrence Papers, MG 23, D1(1), vol. 71, PAC.

36 Carleton to Washington, May 12, 1783, CO 5, vol. 109.

37 Carleton to Townshend, May 28, 1783, ibid.

38 Carleton to North, June 2, 1783, ibid.

39 Ibid.

40 Ibid.

41 Return of refugees embarked for Nova Scotia June 17, 1783, CO 5, vol. 110. Of these 205 were bound for Annapolis, 122 for Port Roseway, and 491 for Fort Cumberland.

42 Admiralty 49, vol. 9, 35–8, PAC. A return of that day listed 1,335 people embarked for Nova Scotia. Return of July 8, 1783, CO 5, vol. 110.

43 Embarkation Return, August 5, 1783, CO 5, vol. 110.

44 North to Carleton, June 15, 1783, CO 5, vol. 109.

45 North to Digby, June 15, 1793, ibid.

46 Wright, *Loyalists of New Brunswick*, 61.

47 Ward Chipman to Jonathan Sewell, September 6, 1783, Sewell Papers, MG 23, GII 10, vol. 2, PAC.

48 Carleton to North, August 28, 1783, CO 5, vol. 110.

49 Lawrence Papers, MG 23, D1(1), vol. 71, 77; MG 12, Admiralty 49, vol. 9, 35–8, PAC.

50 Carleton to North, November 22, 1783, CO 5, vol. 111.

51 *Nova Scotia Gazette and Weekly Chronicle*, December 16, 1783; Admiralty 1, vol. 491, no. 261, PAC.

52 Digby to Stephens, January 8, 1784, Admiralty 1, vol. 490, PAC.

53 Digby to John Hebetson (?), December 3, 1783, MG 12, Admiralty 1, vol. 490, PAC.

54 See J.B. Brebner, *The Neutral Yankees of Nova Scotia: A Marginal Colony during the Revolutionary Years* (New York 1937), 336.

55 Massey to Germain, October 6, 1776, *Public Archives of Canada Report*, 1894, 354.

56 Unsigned to Peters, October 22, 1782, ibid.

57 Wright, *Loyalists of New Brunswick*, 32; Audet Collection, MG 30, D62, vol. 24, 298, PAC.

58 Memorial of Mrs John Parr, CO 217, vol. 36, 117–18.

59 Audet Collection, MG 30, D62, vol. 24, 298–300. See also memorial of Mrs Parr.

60 See Parr to Grey, October 23, 1782, Shelburne Papers, MG 23, A4, vol. 96, PAC.

61 Ibid.

62 Parr to Shelburne, October 29, 1782, ibid.

63 Parr to Grey, October 23, 1782, ibid.

64 Wright, *Loyalists of New Brunswick*, 33.

65 Parr to Shelburne, October 29, 1782, Shelburne Papers, MG 23, A4, vol. 69.

66 Carleton to Hamond, September 22, 1782, Samuel Peters Papers, 1, vol. 1, PANS.

67 Carleton to Paterson, December 22, 1782, British Headquarters Papers, no. 6469, PAC.

68 Bulkeley to Joseph Durfee, September 28, 1782, MD, vol. 136, PANS.

69 Parr to Townshend, October 26, 1782, CO 217, vol. 56.

70 Ibid.

71 Parr to Townshend, December 7, 1782, ibid.

72 Parr to Carleton, January 17, 1783, MD, vol. 369, PANS.

73 Beamish Murdoch, *A History of Nova Scotia; or Acadie*, 3 vols. (Halifax 1867), 3: 17.

74 Memorandum dated April 23, 1783, *Public Archives of Canada Report,* 1894, 104.
75 Lands Escheated, January 25, 1782, to December 23, 1784, CO 217, vol. 59.
76 Memorial to Charles Morris, May 14, 1783, CO 217, vol. 56.
77 Parr to Townshend, May 13, 1783, MD, vol. 221, PANS.
78 Parr to North, August 23, 1783, CO 217, vol. 56.
79 See unsigned to Lord President, Whitehall, May 12, 1783, NS-A, vol. 103; Order in Council, May 16, 1783, CO 5, vol. 32.
80 North to Parr, June 24, 1783, CO 217, vol. 35.
81 Ibid.
82 Morris to Botsford, October 8, 1783, MD, vol. 394, PANS.

CHAPTER TWO

1 They arrived on October 19. Jacob Bailey's estimate of their numbers varied from 400 to 600. See Bailey to Dr Morice, October 19, 1782, Bailey to Byles, October 19, 1782, and Bailey to Thomas Robie, October 19, 1782, all in MG 23, D1(1), vol. 72, PAC.
2 See the three letters cited above.
3 Parr to Nepean, January 22, 1783, MG 11, NS-A, vol. 103, PAC.
4 John Sayers to New York Agency, May 2, 1783, MG 23, D4-1, vol. 1, PAC. See also W.O. Raymond, "The Founding of Shelburne," *Coll. NBHS,* no. 8 (1909): 205.
5 *London Chronicle,* July 31–August 2, 1783, 115.
6 Parr to Secretary of State, January 15, 1783, *Public Archives of Canada Report,* 1894, 402.
7 See, for example, Bulkeley to John Curry, April 12 and 23, 1783, MD, vol. 136, PANS.
8 Raymond, "Founding of Shelburne," 205.
9 Ibid., 210.
10 Ibid.
11 Ibid., 211.
12 Ibid.
13 Ibid., 65 and 215.
14 Ibid.
15 Parr to Carleton, July 25, 1783, MG 23, D1(1), vol. 71, PAC.
16 *London Chronicle,* August 23–30, 1783, 216.
17 Ibid.
18 T.W. Smith, "The Loyalist at Shelburne," *Coll. NSHS* 6 (1888): 65.
19 H.C. Mathews, *The Mark of Honour* (Toronto 1965), 111.
20 J.P. Edwards, "Shelburne That Was and Is Not," *Dalhousie Review* 2, no. 2 (1922): 189.

21 Ibid., 189–90.
22 Wentworth to the Duke of Portland, October 21, 1783, Wentworth Papers, vol. 49, PANS.
23 Ibid.
24 MG 23, D1(1), vol. 74, no. 28, PAC.
25 Quoted in J.R. Campbell, *A History of the County of Yarmouth, Nova Scotia* (Saint John 1876), 87.
26 E.C. Wright, *The Loyalists of New Brunswick* (Fredericton 1955), 209–10.
27 New York Agents to Botsford, Hauser and Peters, May 25, 1783, MG 23, D4, vol. 1, PAC.
28 James Peters to Botsford and Hauser, May 12, 1783, ibid.
29 New York Agents to Botsford, Hauser and Peters, May 25, 1783, ibid.
30 New York Agents to Botsford, Hauser and Peters, May 31, 1783, ibid.
31 See Wright, *Loyalists of New Brunswick,* chap. 4.
32 Raymond, "Founding of Shelburne," 229.
33 W.S. MacNutt, *The Atlantic Provinces: The Emergence of Colonial Society, 1712–1857* (Toronto 1965), 92.
34 Morris to J. Prescott, August 25, 1783, MD, vol. 394, PANS.
35 Raymond, "Founding of Shelburne," 244.
36 Ibid., 236.
37 Morris to Constant Church, December 22, 1783, MD, vol. 394, PANS.
38 Diary of an unnamed Loyalist, August 18, 1783, White Collection, no. 1539, PANS.
39 R.S. Longley, "The Delancey Brothers, Loyalists of Annapolis County," *Coll. NSHS* 32 (1959): 68–9.
40 Quoted in C.W. Vernon, *Bicentenary Sketches and Early Days of the Church in Nova Scotia* (Halifax 1910), 137.
41 MacNutt, *Atlantic Provinces,* 92; T.H. Raddall, "Tarleton's Legion," *Coll. NSHS* 38 (1965): 29.
42 Parr to _____, October 4, 1783, CO 217, vol. 59, 18.
43 August Fricke to "Noble Lord," January 22, 1784, MG 11, NS-A, vol. 104, PAC.
44 Bulkeley to Edward Barron, December 13, 1783, MD, vol. 136, PANS.
45 Parr to North, January 15, 1784, CO 217, vol. 56.
46 Parr to Lord Shelburne, July 9, 1783, *Public Archives of Canada Report,* 1921, App. E.
47 Morris to Botsford, n.d. (c. July 1783), MD, vol. 394, PANS.
48 Morris to Major Studholme, July 2, 1783, ibid.
49 Morris to Studholme, August 5, 1783, ibid.
50 Ibid.
51 Morris to Rev. Sayer, September 1, 1783, ibid.

52 I.M. Sutherland, "Clements Township: Its History and Its People, 1783–1870" (MA thesis, Acadia University, 1957), 34; I.W. Wilson, *A Geography and History of the County of Digby, Nova Scotia* (Halifax 1900), 76.

53 Morris to Marston, August 8, 1783, MD, vol. 394, PANS.

54 Morris to Marston, August 20, 1783, ibid.

55 Morris to John Harris, August 6, 1783, ibid.

56 Morris to Botsford, July 2, 1783, ibid.

57 Thomas Milledge to Botsford, November 20, 1783, MG 23, D4, vol. 1, PAC.

58 Morris to Studholme, February 11, 1784, MD, vol. 394, PANS.

59 Paterson to Townshend, May 20, 1783, CO 217, vol. 41.

60 A.W.H. Eaton, "The New York Loyalists in Nova Scotia," *The Grafton Magazine*, 167, Vertical file, PANS.

61 Digby to Philip Stephen, April 11, 1783, MG 12, Admiralty 1, vol. 490, PAC.

62 Douglas to Philip Stephen, June 10, 1784, ibid.

63 Standing Orders for those under Commodore Douglas' Command, July 31, 1784, MG 12, Admiralty 1, vol. 491, PAC.

64 Parr to Townshend, June 6, 1783, MD, vol. 221, PANS.

65 Morris to Marston, February 5, 1784, MD, vol. 394, PANS.

66 Parr to North, September 20, 1783, CO 217, vol. 56.

67 Parr to North, September 21, 1783, MG 11, NS-A, vol. 103, PAC.

68 Parr to Shelburne, October 25, 1783, *Public Archives of Canada Report*, 1921, App. E.

69 Parr to Nepean, October 4, 1783, MG 11, NS-A, vol. 103, PAC.

70 Unsigned, Whitehall to Parr, March 12, 1783, CO 217, vol. 56.

71 Parr to North, February 4, 1784, CO 217, vol. 59.

72 Bulkeley to Botsford, August 19, 1784, MD, vol. 136, PANS.

73 Morris to Dugal Campbell, May 20, 1784, MD, vol. 394, PANS; Morris to Daniel Lyman, June 8, 1784, ibid.

74 Marston to Parr, May 1 and 4, 1784, MD, vol. 223, PANS.

75 Morris to D. Campbell, July 13, 1784, MD, vol. 104, PAC.

76 Parr to Sydney, April 16, 1784, MG 11, NS-A, vol. 104, PAC.

77 Col. Morse's Report, *Public Archives of Canada Report*, 1894, note C, xi.

CHAPTER THREE

1 Brook Watson to Major Mackenzie, September 13, 1783, and T. Williams to Brook Watson, August 25, 1783, MD, vol. 368, PANS.

2 G. Robertson to Commissioners of the Navy, MG 12, Admiralty 49, vol. 9, PAC.

3 John Bourke to _____, August 14, 1783, CO 217, vol. 56.

4 Memorial of the Magistrates of Shelburne to North, January 3, 1784, MG 11, NS-A, vol. 104, PAC.

5 Campbell to North, December 18, 1783, ibid.

6 Parr to North, February 2, 1784, CO 217, vol. 56.

7 Campbell to North, February 2, 1784, CO 217, vol. 41.

8 *Gazette*, November 4, 1783.

9 Parr to Shelburne, March 22, 1784, *Public Archives of Canada Report*, 1921, App. E.

10 Campbell, proclamation of March 31, 1784, *Gazette*, April 6, 1784.

11 Campbell to North, April 1, 1784, MG 11, NS-A, vol. 104, PAC.

12 George Rose to Governor Haldimand, March 31, 1784, Haldimand Papers, MG 21, vol. 52, PAC.

13 Sydney to Campbell, June 7, 1784, *Public Archives of Canada Report*, 1894, 177.

14 Parr to Secretary of State, August 10, 1784, in Beamish Murdoch, *History of Nova Scotia*, 3 vols. (Halifax 1865–7), 3: 33.

15 Commodore Douglas to Philip Stephens, December 7, 1784, MG 12, Admiralty 1, vol. 491, PAC.

16 Campbell to Sydney, April 27, 1785, MG 11, NS-A, vol. 107, PAC.

17 Parr to Sydney, June 11, 1785, *Public Archives of Canada Report*, 1894, 433.

18 Parr to Campbell, November 18, 1785, MD, vol. 137, PANS.

19 Campbell to Sydney, April 20, 1784, MG 23, D1(1), vol. 7, PAC.

20 Campbell to Sydney, May 6, 1784, MG 23, D1(1), vol. 24, PAC.

21 C.J. MacGillivray, *Timothy Hierlihy and His Times* (Halifax 1935), 111–12.

22 *Winslow Papers*, 248.

23 Ibid.

24 Report of the Agents of the Associated Loyalists, n.d. (c. 1783), Peters Papers, vol. 1, PANS.

25 General Return, MG 23, D1(1), vol. 24, PAC.

26 Campbell to Sydney, October 30, 1784, MG 11, NS-A, vol. 106, PAC.

27 Campbell to Sydney, June 24, 1785, *Public Archives of Canada Report*, 1894, 433–4.

28 Campbell to Sydney, November 30, 1785, MG 11, NS-A, vol. 107, PAC.

29 Enclosure with letter, ibid.

30 *Gazette*, April 8, 1783.

31 Stewart to Winslow, September 29, 1784, MG 23, D1(1), vol. 24, PAC.

32 Wright, *Loyalists of New Brunswick*, 201–2.

33 Ibid., 210.

34 Ibid., 209.

35 Samuel Seabury to Lord North, July 21, 1783, CO 217, vol. 35.

36 August 10, 1784, CO 217, vol. 56.

37 Unsigned, Whitehall, to Parr, August 25, 1784, ibid.
38 Thomas Miller to Evan Nepean, May 20, 1784, ibid.
39 Campbell to Sydney, September 2, 1784, MG 11, NS-A, vol. 105, PAC.
40 Murdoch, *Nova Scotia* 3: 34–5.
41 Parr to Nepean, Octrober 9, 1784, *Public Archives of Canada Report*, 1894, 427.
42 Extract, letter from Halifax, September 18, 1784, *London Chronicle*, November 27–30, 1784, 525. See also September 30–October 2, 1784, 325.
43 North to Parr, August 12, 1783, CO 218, vol. 25.
44 Bulkeley to John Taylor, November 13, 1784, MD, vol. 137, PANS.
45 H.C. Mathews, *The Mark of Honour* (Toronto 1965), 112.
46 Ibid., 114.
47 Rev. William Walter to Sydney, November 20, 1784, CO 217, vol. 57.
48 Rev. William Walter to Samuel Peters, August 4, 1786, Peters Papers 1, vol. 2, PANS.
49 See *Gazette*, December 23, 1783.
50 *Gazette*, September 7, 1784.
51 Quoted in J.R. Campbell, *A History of the County of Yarmouth, Nova Scotia* (Saint John 1870), 87–8.
52 Memorial of the officers of the North Carolina Regiment, Land Grant Petitions, vol. 4, PANS.
53 I.M. Sutherland, "Clements Township: Its History and Its People, 1783–1870" (MA thesis, Acadia University, 1957), 56.
54 *Gazette*, November 22, 1785.
55 There were 194. Parr to Sydney, April 24, 1785, CO 217, vol. 57.
56 Ibid.
57 *Royal American Gazette*, Shelburne, August 1, 1785.
58 Parr to Sydney, November 15, 1784, CO 217, vol. 56.
59 Charles Morris to Joshua Grant, July 3, 1787, MD, vol. 395, PANS.
60 White Collection, vol. 4, no. 384, PANS.
61 Charles Morris to James Fulton, March 26, 1787, MD, vol. 395, PANS.
62 Circular letter of R. Bulkeley, May 28, 1785, MD, vol. 137, PANS.
63 Bulkeley to Board of Agents, Shelburne, July 19, 1786, ibid.

CHAPTER FOUR

1 Parr to Shelburne, July 25, 1783, *Public Archives of Canada Report*, 1921, App. E.
2 Inglis was told this on his first episcopal visit in 1844 by some who had witnessed it. See A.W.H. Eaton, "The New York Loyalists in Nova Scotia," *The Grafton Magazine*, 176, Vertical file U, PANS.

3 Proclamation, January 10, 1784, MD, vol. 346, PANS; Diary of Captain W. Booth, March 27, 1789, Acadia University.

4 *Winslow Papers*, 192.

5 H.B. Brown to Jacob Bailey, June 29, 1783, MG 23, D1(1), vol. 72, PAC.

6 Charles Morris to Sneeden and Polhemus, November 16, 1785, MD, vol. 395, PANS.

7 Morris to Marston, 1784, MD, vol. 394, 149–50, and July 10, 1784, MD, vol. 394, PANS.

8 W.O. Raymond, "The Founding of Shelburne," *Coll. NBHS*, no. 8 (1909): 265.

9 Morris to James Clarke, September 4, 1784, MD, vol. 395, PANS.

10 H.C. Mathews, *The Mark of Honour* (Toronto 1965), 117.

11 Joseph Pynchon to Admiral Stanhope, December 27, 1783, Stanhope Letter Book, Royal Military College.

12 General Return, MG 23, D1(1), vol. 24, PAC.

13 Raymond, "Founding of Shelburne," 256.

14 Morse's Report, *Public Archives of Canada Report*, 1884, xlii.

15 Raymond, "Founding of Shelburne," 259.

16 Morse's Report, *Public Archives of Canada Report*, 1884, xxvii.

17 Charles Inglis Journal, August 3, 1790, MG 23, C6, PAC.

18 Morse's Report, *Public Archives of Canada Report*, 1884, xxvii.

19 Mathews, *Mark of Honour*, 117.

20 Ibid., 108.

21 Ibid., 118.

22 *Gazette*, March 7, 1786.

23 J.P. Edwards, "The Shelburne That Was and Is Not," *Dalhousie Review* 2, no. 2 (1922): 191.

24 *Port Roseway Gazetteer*, June 27, 1785.

25 *Royal American Gazette*, January 24, 1785.

26 J.P. Edwards, "Vicissitudes of a Loyalist City," *Dalhousie Review* 2, no. 3 (1922): 216.

27 *Royal American Gazette*, May 9, 1785.

28 Ibid., June 13 and 20, 1785; Shelburne Records, p. 100, PANS.

29 George Thomas to Admiral Stanhope, March 1, 1784, Stanhope Letter Book, Royal Military College.

30 Letter from Passamaquoddy, *Gazette*, January 31, 1786.

31 Parr to Sydney, December 31, 1785, CO 217, vol. 58.

32 Hugh Findlay to John Wentworth, February 27, 1784, Wentworth Papers, vol. 1, PANS.

33 Edward Winslow to John Wentworth, November 27, 1784, *Winslow Papers*, 251.

34 See Jacob Bailey's "Description of Nova Scotia," MG 23, D1(1), vol. 72, 12–13, PAC.

35 Sir A.S. Hamond to _____, 1782, MG 30, D62, vol. 15, PAC.

36 Bailey to Dr Morice, November 3, 1784, MG 23, D1(1), vol. 72, PAC.

37 Parr to _____, August 1, 1785, CO 217, vol. 57.

38 *Winslow Papers*, 264.

39 Petition of the Inhabitants of Ardois Hill, n.d. [c. 1785], Gillmore Saga, vol. 2, PANS.

40 T.H. Raddall, "Tarleton's Legion," *Coll. NSHS* 28 (1949): 33–4.

41 Commodore Douglas to the Captain, HMS *Observer*, MG 12, Admiralty 1, vol. 491, PAC.

42 Keats to Commodore Douglas, June 7, 1784, MG 12, Admiralty 49, vol. 2, PAC.

43 Parr to Dr Morice, June 27, 1785, MG 17, B-1, SPG-CII, no. 95, PAC.

44 Memorial of Lord Charles Montagu, December 20, 1783, CO 217, vol. 56.

45 A.C. Jost, *Guysborough Sketches and Essays* (Guysborough 1950), 120–1, 149–50, 127–30; Morris to Marston, October 29, 1783, MD, vol. 394, PANS.

46 Jost, *Guysborough Sketches*, 141.

47 Ibid., 173, 176, 141.

48 Five hundred and seventy-eight males and their dependents. General Return, MG 23, D1(1), vol. 24, PAC; Jost, *Guysborough Sketches*, 142.

49 Lt B. Meighen to Gideon White, August 24, 1784, White Collection, no. 307, PANS.

50 John McPherson to Gideon White, May 16, 1784, White Collection, no. 274, PANS.

51 R.F. Brownrigg to Gideon White, June 8, 1784, White Collection, no. 284, PANS.

52 McPherson, Surgeon, to _____, April 3, 1786, CO 217, vol. 58.

53 Charles Morris to Amos Chapman, December 10, 1784, MD, vol. 395, PANS.

54 Petition of the non-commissioned officers and privates of the Duke of Cumberland's Regiment to Robert Barrett, n.d., CO 217, vol. 57.

55 James Ballmer to Gideon White, September 26, 1784, White Collection, no. 317, PANS.

56 *Winslow Papers*, 271.

57 Petition of the 3rd and 4th Btln, 60th Regiment, to Sydney, March 31, 1785, CO 217, vol. 57.

58 G.A. Rawlyk, "The Guysborough Negroes: A Study in Isolation," *Dalhousie Review* 48 (Spring 1968): 26.

59 General Return, MG 23, D1(1), vol. 24, PAC.

60 Ibid.

61 *Gazette*, August 10, 1784.

62 Petition of Loyalists at Country Harbour to John Parr, November 15, 1785, Assembly Papers, vol. 1-A, PANS.

63 C. Stewart to Winslow, August 9, 1784, General Return, MG 23, D1(1), vol. 24, PAC.

64 C.J. MacGillivray, *Timothy Hierlihy and His Times* (Halifax 1935), 78–81.

65 Morris to Patterson, April 29, 1784, MD, vol. 394, PANS.

66 A.A. Johnston, *A History of the Catholic Church in Eastern Nova Scotia, 1611–1827* (Antigonish 1960), 1: 126.

67 C. Stewart to Winslow, August 9, 1784, General Return, MG 223, D1(1), vol. 24, PAC.

68 MacGillivray, *Hierlihy*, 115–16.

69 G. Patterson, *History of the County of Pictou* (Montreal 1877), 118.

70 Ibid., 119–22, 154–6.

71 General Return, MG 23, D1(1), vol. 24, PAC.

72 Morris to Major Milledge, June 20, 1784, MD, vol. 394, PANS.

73 Bailey to Samuel Peters, May 6, 1784, Peters Papers, 1–2, PANS.

74 General Return, MG 23, D1(1), vol. 24, PAC.

75 S.S. Blowers to Ward Chipman, November 8, 1784, MG 23, D1(1), vol. 1, PAC.

76 Letter from Annapolis Royal, July 25, 1785, MG 12, Admiralty 1, vol. 491, no. 204, PAC.

77 Bailey to Dr Morice, October 28, 1785, MG 17, B6, SPG, B1/1, vol. 1, PAC.

78 Eliza Cottnam to A.B. Howe, September 23, 1786, Howe Family Papers, vol. 3, PANS.

79 Bailey to Dr Morice, October 28, 1785, MG 17, B6, SPG, B1/1, vol. 1, PAC.

80 Bailey to Samuel Peters, June 20, 1785, Fort Anne Papers, no. 1, PANS.

81 Memorial of the Annapolis County Loyalists to John Parr, May 1786, CO 217, vol. 58.

82 Parr to Sydney, June 10, 1786, ibid.

83 Bailey to Samuel Peters, November 7, 1786, Peters Papers, 1–2, PANS.

84 John Robinson to Winslow, July 18, 1784, MG 24, D1(1), vol. 24, PAC.

85 Memorial of the Inhabitants of Digby to the SPG, August 1, 1785, MG 17, B6, SPG, B1/1, vol. 1, PAC.

86 John Robinson to Winslow, September 16, 1784, MG 23, D1(1), vol. 24, PAC.

87 Morris to Amos Botsford, April 6, 1784, MD, vol. 394, PANS.

88 General Return, MG 23, D1(1), vol. 24, PAC.

89 Stephen Jones to Gideon White, August 28, 1785, White Collection, no. 385, PANS.

90 Memorial of Adolphus Harris for the 84th Regiment, CO 217, vol. 58.

91 John Wentworth's certificate, June 5, 1784, MD, vol. 223, PANS.
92 T.F. Fraser, *Essays on the History of Hants County* (Windsor 1881), 74.
93 Return of G. Stewart, MG 23, D1(1), vol. 24, 327, PAC.
94 Ibid.
95 Quoted in G. Patterson, "Presbyterian Pioneers," chap. 9, Family Papers, PANS.
96 Memorial of Augustus Fricke, January 22, 1784, CO 217, vol. 35.
97 Charles Morris to Robert Morris, June 29, 1784, MD, vol. 394, PANS.
98 G. Stewart's Return, MG 23, D1(1), vol. 24, 327, PAC.
99 General Return, MG 23, D1(1), vol. 24, PAC.
100 Ibid.
101 Ibid. "A circumstance which must naturally affect the Settlers along this shore is the number of fishing vessels from the American States with which the whole Coast abounds and which ought if possible to be suppressed." William Shaw to Edward Winslow, June 5, 1784, ibid. Shaw found no loyalists in the bays from Sheet Harbour to Country Harbour, "But in all of them numbers of vessels from the States carrying on a very Advantageous Fishery." Shaw to Winslow, June 13, 1784, ibid.
102 *Gazette*, April 4, 1786.
103 General Return, MG 23, D1(1), vol. 24, PAC.
104 William Shaw to Edward Winslow, June 2, 1784, ibid.
105 See T.B. Akins, "History of Halifax City," *Coll. NSHS* 8 (1895): 103.
106 *London Chronicle*, May 11–13, 1784, 459.
107 Mrs. Wentworth to _____, October 5, 1784, Lady Wentworth's Letters, PANS.
108 Joseph Peters to Samuel Peters, August 27, 1784, Peters Papers, 1–2, PANS.
109 Overseers of the Poor to Parr, 1784, MD, vol. 301, no. 57, PANS.
110 *London Chronicle*, December 2–4, 1784, 541.
111 James W. Walker, *The Black Loyalists: The Search for a Promised Land in Nova Scotia and Sierra Leone, 1783–1870* (New York 1976), 3.
112 Robin W. Winks, *The Blacks in Canada: A History* (Montreal 1971), 33.
113 Walker, *Black Loyalists*, 12.
114 Winks, *Blacks in Canada*, 37.
115 Walker, *Black Loyalists*, 24.
116 Ibid., 25 and 27.
117 Winks, *Blacks in Canada*, 36.
118 Walker, *Black Loyalists*, 29.
119 Ibid., 31–2.
120 Extract, letter dated July 31, 1787, *Gazette*, August 7, 1787.
121 Parr to "My Lord," November 11, 1785, MG 11, NS-A, vol. 107, PAC.

CHAPTER FIVE

1 Harris Papers, vol. 19, Loyalists, no. 12 PANS.
2 Bailey to Samuel Peters, October 31, 1784, MG 23, D1(1), vol. 72, PAC.
3 Jonathan Sewell to Ward Chipman, April 22, 1782, MG 23, D1(1), vol. 2, PAC.
4 Jonathan Sewell to Ward Chipman, February 1783, MG 23, D1(1), vol. 2, PAC.
5 W.O. Raymond, "The Loyalists in Old Nova Scotia," in George U. Hay, *Canadian Historical Readings* (Saint John 1900), 1; 248–9.
6 Ibid.
7 Memorial of Mary Swords to Lord Sydney, April 18, CO 217, vol. 35.
8 John O'Donnell to Gideon White, July 2, 1758, White Collection, no. 375, PAC.
9 Ensign John Lindsay to Gideon White, April 4, 1784, White Collection, no. 268, PAC.
10 Nehemiah Strong to Amos Botsford, September 3, 1783, Botsford Papers, MG 23, D4, vol. 1, PAC.
11 Jonathan Ingersoll to Amos Botsford, July 31, 1783, ibid.
12 William Donaldson, to Thos. Newland, February 9, 1785, *Winslow Papers*, 266.
13 Rough notes of Captain W. Booth, RE, April 14, 1789, Acadia University.
14 Danice Rindge to John Wentworth, July 17, 1784, Wentworth Papers, vol. 2, D4, vol. 1, PANS.
15 New York agents to Botsford, Hauser, and Peters, May 25, 1783, Botsford Papers, MG 23, D4, vol. 1, PAC.
16 Thomas Hassara [?] to Fanning, July 20, 1785, Peters Papers, 1–2, PANS.
17 Samuel Andrews to Dr Morice, September 29, 1785, MG 17, B1/1, vol. 1, PANS.
18 Mary Peters to Samuel Peters, March 19, 1784, Peters Papers, 1–2, PAC.
19 Phelps Devenport to Samuel Peters, April 22, 1786, ibid.
20 Carleton to North, October 13, 1783, MG 11, CO 5, vol. 111, PAC.
21 Sydney to Parr, April 20, 1786, CO 218, vol. 27.
22 Petition of John Swift, 1784, Land Grant Petitions, vol. 5, PANS.
23 Carole W. Troxler, "The Migration of Carolina and Georgia Loyalists to Nova Scotia and New Brunswick" (PHD diss., University of North Carolina, 1974), 195–237.
24 Memorial of Daniel Mathews to John Parr, April 19, 1783, MD, vol. 248, PANS.
25 W.O. Raymond, "The Founding of Shelburne," *Coll. NBHS* no. 8 (1909): 214.
26 Jacob Bailey to Amos Bailey, n.d., Bailey Papers, vol. 14, PANS; Return of Captain Hunt's Company of Loyalists embarked for Annapolis Royal,

Botsford Papers, MG 23, D4, vol. 2, PAC; A.C. Jost, *Guysborough Sketches and Essays* (Guysborough 1950), 125–75; Memorial from Digby, August 1, 1785, MG 17, B1/1, vol. 1, PAC; J.W. Wilson, *A Geography and History of the County of Digby* (Belleville 1972), 51.

27 See Marion Gilroy, *Loyalists and Land Settlement* (Halifax 1937).

28 C.H. Van Tyne, *The Loyalists in the American Revolution* (New York 1902), 303.

29 Parr to Shelburne, October 9, 1789, *Public Archives of Canada Report, 1921*, App. 3; Raymond, "Founding of Shelburne," 214.

30 See Gilroy, *Loyalist and Land Settlement*, also Petition of Henry Purdy, November 3, 1784, Assembly Papers, 1–A, PANS.

31 J.R. Campbell, *A History of the County of Yarmouth, Nova Scotia* (Saint John 1870), 231.

32 Wilson, *History of Digby*, 51; Jacob Bailey to Peter Bochard, May 4, 1784, Bailey Papers, vol. 16, PANS.

33 Lawrence Collection, MG 23, D1(1), vol. 74, 54, PAC.

34 J.S. Macdonald states that many of those distressed Scots seeking relief in Nova Scotia were from Boston and Philadelphia. See his *Annals of the North British Society, 1763–1903* (Halifax 1903), 66.

35 Esther Clark Wright, *The Loyalists of New Brunswick* (Fredericton 1955), 29; Parr to Nepean, August 13, 1784, CO 217, vol. 59.

36 Troxler, "Migration," 1.

37 James W. Walker, *The Black Loyalists* (New York 1976), 5.

38 Most of the 300 freeholders in Clements township were ex-German soldiers and Dutch loyalist refugees from New York. See J.D. Wagner to SPG, April 6, 1786, MG 17, CII, no. 101, PAC. There were also Irish Catholics among the loyalists. See Jones to the Bishop of Quebec, April 27, 1781, Archepiscopal Archives of Quebec, NS 1. Munro, in his tour of the colony a decade after the loyalist arrival, was struck by the number of Scots among them. He noted that the Jordan River settlement had been settled by loyalists, "a good many of them Being scotch people," and in Digby, "tho they came from the States a good many of them are scotch people." *Public Archives of Nova Scotia Report, 1974*, 40. Concerning the Scottish loyalists, see also Macdonald, *North British Society*, H.C. Mathews, *The Mark of Honour* (Toronto 1965), chap. 8, R.A. Logan, "Highlanders from Skye in North America and Nova Scotia 1771–1881," *The Scottish Genealogist* 12, no. 4 (February 1966): 92–108.

39 Troxler, "Migration," 1.

40 Raymond, "Loyalists in Old Nova Scotia," 249.

41 Wright, *Loyalists of New Brunswick*, 164.

42 Charles Staynor, "The Sandemanian Loyalists, *Coll. NSHS* 29 (1951): 62.

43 E.R. Forbes, "The Loyalist Myth in Nova Scotia in the Nineteenth Century," seminar paper, Department of History, Queen's University, April 1969, n. 5.

44 R.S. Longley, "The Delancey Brothers, Loyalists of Annapolis County," *Coll. NSHS* 32 (1959): 55.

45 William Clarke to Samuel Peters, October 11, 1786, Peters Papers, 1–2, PANS.

46 Petition of Henry Bolton, Land Grand Petitions, vol. 3, PANS.

47 Mathews, *Mark of Honour*, 119.

48 Raymond, "Founding of Shelburne," 214.

49 Gilroy, *Loyalists and Land Settlement.*

50 W.S. MacNutt, *The Atlantic Provinces*, 94.

51 Rev. William Walter to Dr Morice, July 1783, MG 17, SPG, CII, PAC.

52 Raymond, "Founding Shelburne," 219, 242, 265.

53 G. Patterson, *History of the County of Pictou* (Montreal 1877), 120.

54 Raymond, "Founding of Shelburne," 205.

55 C.W. Vernon, *Bicentenary Sketches and Early Days of the Church in Nova Scotia* (Halifax 1910), 144.

56 Troxler, "Migration," 1.

57 John Sayre to Dr Morice, October 2, 1783, MG 17, SPG, CII, PAC.

58 Raymond, "Founding of Shelburne," 214.

59 Minute Book, Port Roseway Associates, MG 9, B6, pt. 1, 2–23, PAC.

60 Bailey to Captain Anthill, April 20, 1784, Bailey Papers, vol. 16, PANS.

61 Letter book of Rev. Jacob Bailey, 1784–5, Fort Anne Papers, 34–5, PANS. Sutherland, in his study of the area around Clements township, found the loyalists there were ordinary farmers and manual labourers. See I.M. Sutherland, "Clements Township: Its History and Its People, 1783–1870" (MA thesis, Acadia University, 1957), 29.

62 Return of Captain Hunt's Company of Loyalists bound for Annapolis Royal, Botsford Papers, MG 23, D4, vol. 2, PAC.

CHAPTER SIX

1 Isaac Browne to Dr Morice, September 26, 1783, MG 17, SPG, C1/1, PAC; C. Clopper to Charles Whitworth, April 18, 1783, White Collection, no. 193, PANS; Jacob Bailey, quoted in A.W.H. Eaton, *The History of King's County, Nova Scotia* (Salem 1910), 107.

2 Jonathan Sewell to Edward Winslow, *Winslow Papers*, 14.

3 Joseph Pynchon to Port Roseway Associates, Minute Book of the Port Roseway Associates, MG 9, B6, 60–1, PAC.

4 R.S. Longley, "An Annapolis County Loyalist," *Coll. NSHS* 31 (1957): 89.

5 Unsigned to Jacob Bailey, February 13, 1782, Bailey Papers, vol. 3, PANS.

6 Gen. Timothy Ruggles to Edward Winslow, Sr, July 17, 1783, *Winslow Papers*, 106–7; Gideon White to Thomas Melish, August 3, 1784, White Collection, no. 300, PANS; Edward Winslow to Ward Chipman, July 7, 1783, *Winslow Papers*, 97; James Courteney to Archibald Cunningham, July 1, 1783, White Collection, no. 210, PANS.

7 William Parker to Charles Whitworth, June 8, 1784, White Collection, no. 283, PANS.

8 Quoted in James S. Macdonald, "Memoir of Governor John Parr," *Coll. NSHS* 14 (1909): 51.

9 W.O. Raymond, "The Founding of Shelburne," *Coll. NBHS*, no. 8 (1909): 250.

10 Capt. Callbeck to Edward Winslow, November 21, 1783, *Winslow Papers*, 149.

11 Joshua Chandler to Amos Botsford, July 1783, MG 23, D4, vol. 1, PAC.

12 Edward Winslow to Sir John Wentworth, November 27, 1784, *Winslow Papers*, 251; Diary of an unnamed Loyalist, August 18, 1783, White Collection, vol. 15, no. 1539, PANS; *Winslow Papers*, 135.

13 Journal of Mather Byles III, Byles Papers, vol. 1, folder 2, PANS.

14 Edward Winslow to Ward Chipman, April 4, 1785, *Winslow Papers*, 291; Jacob Bailey to _____, May 4, 1789, Papers relating to the Rev. Jacob Bailey, Church Historical Society, Austin, Texas; Jacob Bailey to Mrs Rachel Barlow, November 8, 1779, Bailey Papers, vol. 13, PANS; John Garner, "The Electoral Franchise in Colonial Nova Scotia" (MA thesis, University of Toronto, 1948), 52.

15 Diary of an unnamed Loyalist, September 5, 1783, White Collection, vol. 15, no. 1539, PANS.

16 Minute Book of the Port Roseway Associates, MG 9, B6, 193–4, PAC; Macdonald, "Memoir of Governor Parr," 5.

17 Memorial of the Magistrates of Shelburne to Parr, January 3, 1784, *Public Archives of Canada Report*, 1894, 412.

18 Charles Morris to Amos Botsford, September 3, 1783, MG 23, D4, vol. 1, PAC; Mather Byles, Jr, to Edward Winslow, January 21, 1785, *Winslow Papers*, 264.

19 Charles Whitworth to Messrs Debloise, October 21, 1784, White Collection, vol. 3, PANS.

20 *Port Roseway Gazetteer*, June 19, 1789; *Royal American Gazette*, April 18, 1785.

21 Correspondence of Charles Inglis, MG 23, C6, pt. 1, 4, PAC; Memorial to Governor Parr, December 21, 1782, MG 9, B6, 34–5, PAC; *Royal American Gazette*, June 13, 1785.

22 Esther Clark Wright, *The Loyalists of New Brunswick* (Fredericton 1955), 35; W.S. MacNutt, *New Brunswick: A History, 1784–1867* (Toronto 1963), 34. This reference is to land in the St John Valley; Beamish

Murdoch, *A History of Nova Scotia*, 3 vols. (Halifax 1865–7), 3: 31; John McPherson to Gideon White, May 16, 1784, White Collection, vol. 3, PANS; Charles Morris to Robert Gray, January 2, 1785, MD, vol. 395, PANS.

23 Raymond, "Founding of Shelburne," 213.

24 Carleton to Parr, October 23, 1783, CO 5,vol. 111.

25 Charles Morris to Major Studholme, November 12, 1784, MD, vol. 394. PANS.

26 Charles Morris to Rev. Edward Brudenell, March 24, 1785, ibid.

27 *Port Roseway Gazetteer*, May 12, 1785.

28 Raymond, "Founding of Shelburne," 226, 235, 240.

29 Campbell to Sydney, April 20, 1784, June 24, 1785, *Public Archives of Canada Report*, 1894, 417, 433–4.

30 Charles Morris to Rev. Edward Brudenell, February 12, 1785, MD, vol. 395, PANS.

31 J. Aplin to Chief Justice Smith, March 6, 1784, MG 11, NS-A, vol. 104, PAC.

32 Antill Gallop to Jacob Bailey, December 19, 1783, Bailey Papers, vol. 3, PANS; Edward Winslow to George Leonard, October 5, 1784, *Winslow Papers*, 240; Jacob Bailey to Colin Campbell, March 17, 1785, Bailey Letterbooks 1784–5, Fort Anne Papers, PANS.

33 Joseph Peters to Samuel Peters, October 11, 1785, and May 2, 1791, Peters Papers, 1–2, PANS.

34 Thomas Barclay to John Wentworth, November 27, 1783, Wentworth Papers, vol. 1, PANS; Joseph Aplin to Chief Justice Smith, March 6, 1784, MG 11, NS-A, vol. 104, PAC; Joseph Peters to Samuel Peters, November 27, 1786, Peters Papers, 1–2, PANS.

35 Jacob Bailey to Dr Peter, November 16, 1785, Bailey Papers, vol. 14 PANS; Jacob Bailey to Thomas Brown, January 31, 1784, Bailey Papers, vol. 16, PANS.

36 Rev. Charles Mongan to Edward Winslow, March 23, 1784, *Winslow Papers*, 172.

37 Shelburne Records, Special Sessions, March 13, 1786, PANS; Raymond, "Founding of Shelburne," 234; Macdonald, "Memoir of Governor Parr," 64; Shelburne Records, Special Sessions, May 12, 1785, PANS; Phyllis Blakeley, "Boston King: A Negro Loyalist Who Sought Refuge in Nova Scotia," *Dalhousie Review* 48 (1968): 352–3; Raymond, "Founding of Shelburne," 265.

38 Mather Byles to his sister, February 20, 1784, Byles Papers, vol. 1, folder 1, 5a, PANS; same to same, February 6, 1784, ibid., 3.

39 Captain Brownrigg to Gideon White, January 24, 1784, White Collection, no. 345, PANS.

40 Sarah Winslow to Benjamin Marston, October 18, 1783, *Winslow Papers*, 141–2; same to same, October 29, 1783, ibid., 150; Penelope Winslow to Ward Chipman, April 2, 1785, ibid., 288; same to same, November 28, 1784, ibid., 252; same to same, April 2, 1785, ibid., 287.

41 Macdonald, "Memoir of Governor Parr," 54, 56; Parr to Lord North, January 15, 1784, *Public Archives of Canada Report*, 1894, 412; T.W. Smith, "The Loyalists at Shelburne," *Coll. NSHS* 6 (1888): 66.

42 J.R. Campbell, *A History of the County of Yarmouth, Nova Scotia* (Saint John 1870), 87; Thomas Raddall, "Tarleton's Legion," *Coll. NSHS* 28 (1949): 33; C.W. Vernon, *Bicentenary Sketches and Early Days of the Church in Nova Scotia* (Halifax 1910), 137; Isaac Browne to Dr Morice, December 31, 1783, MG 17, SPG, C1/1, PAC; *Gazette*, October 28, 1783.

43 Dr Walter to Secretary, MG 17, SPG, C1/1, PAC.

44 W.O. Raymond, "The Founding of the Church of England in Shelburne," *Coll. NBHS*, no. 8 (1909): 279–80; Dr Walter to the Secretary, July 1783, MG 17, SPG, C1/1, PAC.

45 Dr Walter to Secretary, October 17, 1783, MG 17, SPG, C1/1, PAC; J.L. Bumsted, "Church and State in Maritime Canada, 1749–1807," *Canadian Historical Association Report*, 1967, 50; *Royal American Gazette*, January 24, 1785.

46 Mr Panton to Governor Parr, December 24, 1785, Assembly Papers, vol. 1A, PANS; Bumsted, "Church and State," 50; *Royal American Gazette*, January 24, 1785.

47 For a thorough study of the difficulties of Bishop Inglis and his church, see Judith Fingard, *The Anglican Design in Loyalist Nova Scotia, 1783–1816* (London 1972).

48 H.C. Mathews, *The Mark of Honour* (Toronto 1965), 120; T.W. Smith, "Loyalists at Shelburne," 73.

49 S.D. Clark, *Church and Sect in Canada* (Toronto 1948), 49.

50 Blakeley, "Boston King," 352; George Cox, "John Alexander Barry and His Times," *Coll. NSHS* 28 (1949): 133–4; Joseph Tinkham to Gideon White, October 6, 1785, White Collection, vol. 3, PANS; Clarke, *Church and Sect*, 85.

51 Charles Morris to Jonathan Prescott, October 12, 1784, MD, vol. 394, PANS; Parr to Nepean, May 1, 1784, *Public Archives of Canada Report*, 1894, 418; Minutes of the Executive Council, MG 11, NS-B (18), 148, PAC.

52 White Collection, no. 308, PANS.

53 Memorial of William Martin to Governor Parr, Vertical Mss. file, Loyalists, PANS; Charles Morris to William White, March 24, 1785, MD, vol. 395, PANS.

54 Rev. Mongan's Remarks on Nova Scotia, March 10, 1784, CO 217, vol. 56.

55 Raymond, "Founding of Shelburne," 221.

56 Amos Botsford to Charles Morris, September 3, 1783, MG 23, D4, vol. 1, PAC.

57 Raddall, "Tarleton's Legion," 29–30, 34.

58 New York Agency to Botsford et al., January 24, 1783, MG 23, D4, vol. 1, PAC.

59 Brownrigg to Gideon White, June 8, 1784, White Collection, vol. 3, PANS; same to same, July 11, 1784, ibid.

60 Deposition of John Hooton, Digby, October 2, 1784, MG 23, D4, vol. 2, PAC; Deposition of B____, October 7, 1784, ibid.; Isaac Bonnell to Amos Botsford, October 7, 1784, ibid.; J.W. Wilson, *The Geography and History of the County of Digby* (Belleville 1972), 77.

61 Raymond, "Founding of Shelburne," 216, 220.

62 Pynchon to Wentworth, May 14, 1784, Wentworth Papers, vol. 1, PANS.

63 Raymond, "Founding of Shelburne," 265. Until and including July 22, the last entry before the riots, Marston's diary contains only the mundane details of the surveys.

64 Extract, letter from Halifax, August 1, 1784, *London Chronicle*, November 11–3, 1784, 472.

65 Scroll to Campbell, August 31, 1784, MD, vol. 221, PANS.

66 Parr to Sir Charles Douglas, September 2, 1784, MD, vol. 136, PANS.

67 Raymond, "Founding of Shelburne," 266.

68 That Marston might have been used as a recognized scapegoat was noted by both Gideon White and Charles Morris, although Morris did concede that there was some partiality in Marston's surveying. See White to Winslow, September 6, 1784, in Raymond, "Founding of Shelburne," 267. See also Charles Morris to Robert Gray, August 12, 1787, MD, vol. 395, PANS; Parr to Lord Sydney, April 29, 1785, CO 217, vol. 57.

69 Charles Morris to Amos Botsford, July 12, 16, and 21, 1783, MG 23, D4, vol. 1, PAC.

70 Charles Morris to Robert Gray, February 23, 1785, MD, vol. 395, PANS.

71 Raymond, "Founding of Shelburne," 213–4, 221. As late as 1787 Morris was asking Robert Gray at Shelburne to look into the case of "a Poor Soldier of the 30 Regt John Drury who alleged he had Built a Small House & a slaughter House on a lot assigned Him by Mr. Marston but afterwards taken from Him by the Board." Morris to Gray, March 6, 1787, MD, vol. 395, PANS.

72 Vernon, *Bicentenary Sketches*, 103; Mather Byles to his sister, February 20, 1784, Byles Papers, vol. 1, folder 1, 5c, PANS; James Gautier to Gideon White, August 10, 1784, White Collection, vol. 3, PANS; N. Ford to Gideon White, August 23, 1786, ibid.

73 Raymond, "Founding of Shelburne," 212–13, 219–20.

74 Mather Byles III to his aunt, n.d., Mather Byles Papers, vol. 2, 49, PANS;
   G. Townsend to Ward Chipman, January 25, 1786, MG 23, D1(1), vol.
   4, PAC; Memorial of Samuel Seabury, December 1783, CO 217, vol. 35.

75 Unsigned memorial to Lord Shelburne, October 1782, MG 23, A4, vol.
   67, 144, PAC.

76 *Winslow Papers*, 61–2; Mather Byles to his aunt, May 5, 1784, Byles
   Papers, vol. 1, folder 2, PANS; Memorial of Edward Liskman, September
   1785, Land Grand Petitions, vol. 14, PANS.

77 Memorial of Benvie, Lockwood, and Burns, Land Grant Petitions, vol.
   15A, PANS; Memorials of James Twaddle and Nathaniel Thomas, ibid.,
   vol. 10; Memorial of Stephen Skinner, August 28, 1783, ibid., vol. 2;
   New York Agents to Amos Botsford et al., May 25, 1783, MG 23, D4,
   vol. 1, PAC; *Gazette*, April 19, 1785; Charles Morris to Amos Botsford,
   July 2, 1783, MG 23, D4, vol. 1, PAC; Longley, "Annapolis County Loyalists,"
   91.

78 *Gazette*, April 19, 1785; Charles Morris to Amos Botsford, July 2, 1783,
   MG 23, D4, vol. 1, PAC; Longley, "Annapolis County Loyalists," 91.

79 Marion Gilroy, *Loyalists and Land Settlement in Nova Scotia* (Halifax
   1937), 146.

80 Parr to Secretary of State, March 4, 1784, *Public Archives of Canada
   Report*, 1894, 414.

81 Gilroy, *Loyalists and Land Settlement*, 148. Details of the bitter contest
   between the fifty-five and those opposing them are to be found in MG
   23, D1(1), vol. 75, PAC, and in CO 217, particularly vols. 56 and 59. The
   contest also led to a pamphlet war in 1784 and 1785 which saw the
   publication of the following: *Vindication of Governor Parr and his
   Council against the Complaints of certain Persons, who sought to engross
   275,000 Acres of Land in Nova Scotia* ... ; *Remarks on a Late Pamphlet
   Entitled a Vindication of Governor Parr and his Council ... by a
   Consistent Loyalist* [Charles Inglis]; J. Viator, *Reply to Remarks on a
   Late Pamphlet, entitled a Vindication of Governor Parr and his Council
   ...* ; Charles Inglis, *A Defence of his Character against certain false
   and malicious Charges contained in a Pamphlet entitled Reply to
   Remarks on a Vindication of Governor Parr ...* ; J. Viator, *An Answer
   to Dr Inglis' Defence of his character ....* By the time Viator's pamphlets
   appeared the affair had climaxed and the fifty-five's claims had been
   disallowed. The affair is an interesting illustration of the divisions among
   the loyalists and the opportunism existing in this unprecedented
   situation; the pamphlets leave the impression that deep divisions had
   existed, if only nascently, in New York. Perhaps equally important is
   the role of the affair in shaping the reputation of John Parr among
   the loyalists. It showed a hard core assiduously sowing seeds of
   discontent concerning his rule as early as 1784, at that time for the

practical purpose of obtaining 275,000 acres. After their failure, the resentment and the opposition to Parr would remain. Peleg Wiswall had assumed Samuel Peters was Viator, and warned him to remain anonymous. "Indeed if he ever hopes to be Bishop of N Scotia as it should not be suspected – Some of the 55 though not in place have influence and are strong." Peleg Wiswall to Samuel Peters, November 24, 1784, Peters Papers, 1–2, PANS.

CHAPTER SEVEN

1 William Knox, *Proposals*, quoted in Judith Fingard, *The Anglican Design in Loyalist Nova Scotia* (London 1972), 10; Lord Sheffield, *Observations on the Commerce of the American States*, 182n, quoted in ibid., 199.

2 Unsigned, n.d., CO 217, vol. 56, 348; Sydney to Parr, March 8, 1785, CO 217, vol. 57, *Royal American Gazette*, April 18, 1785.

3 *Public Archives of Ontario Report*, 1904, pt. 1, 12; W.S. MacNutt, *The Atlantic Provinces* (Toronto 1965), 97.

4 See, for example, Parr to "My Lord," October 17, 1785, MG 11, NS-A, vol. 107, PAC, and Parr to Sydney, November 11, 1784, CO 217, vol. 56.

5 Parr to Sydney, November 11, 1784, CO 217, vol. 56; Parr to Shelburne, March 22, 1784, *Public Archives of Canada Report*, 1921, App. E.

6 Charles Morris to Major Studholme, April 16, 1784, MD, vol. 394, PANS; Charles Morris to Edward Brudenell, February 12, 1785, MD, vol. 395, PANS.

7 Rev. Thomas Wood to the SPG, February 16, 1784, MG 17, SPG, CII, PAC.

8 Sydney to Parr, March 8, 1785, CO 217, vol. 57; Sydney to Parr, April 5, 1786, CO 217, vol. 60.

9 Joseph Peters to Samuel Peters, November 25, 1785, Peters Papers, 1–2, PANS.

10 Parr to Shelburne, June 16, 1784, *Public Archives of Canada Report*, 1921, App. E; Parr to Nepean, n.d. [fall 1784], CO 217, vol. 59; *Winslow Papers*, 146; Samuel Gould to G.H. Monk, October 1783, MG 23, GII 19, vol. 3, PAC.

11 Parr to Nepean, April 11, 1784, CO 217, vol. 59; Parr to Shelburne, May 1, 1784, *Public Archives of Canada Report*, 1921, App. E; Parr to Nepean, August 13, 1784, *Public Archives of Canada Report*, 1894, 423; Parr to Shelburne, August 17, 1784, *Public Archives of Canada Report*, 1921, App. E; Sydney to Parr, October 8, 1784, *Public Archives of Canada Report*, 1894, 427.

12 W.S. MacNutt, *New Brunswick: A History, 1784–1867* (Toronto 1963), 37.

13 Mrs Wentworth to Lady Fitzwilliam, October 5, 1784, Lady Wentworth's

Letters, microfilm, PANS; Parr to Shelburne, June 27, 1785, MG 23, A4, vol. 88, PAC.

14 Parr to the Magistrates of Shelburne, October 3, 1783, MD, vol. 136, PANS.

15 Parr to Shelburne, October 9, 1789, *Public Archives of Canada Report*, 1921, App. E; Bulkeley to McEwan and Pynchon, August 19, 1783, MD, vol. 136, PANS; Parr to Nepean, May 1, 1784, CO 217, vol. 59; Parr to "My Lord," May 12, 1784, ibid.; Parr to Nepean, August 13, 1784, ibid.; Parr to Shelburne, May 1, 1785, MG 23, A4, vol. 88, PAC.

16 For a summary of Parr's instructions to the surveyors, see Charles Morris to Brudenell, September 14, 1785, MD, vol. 395, PANS; Parr to Brig. Gen. Fox, October 31, 1783, ibid.; Petition of Jane O'Brien to Parr, March 14, 1785, MD, vol. 223, PANS; Thomas Miller to Nepean, November 17, 1784, CO 217, vol. 35.

17 Parr to Nepean, September 3, 1784, CO 217; Parr to Shelburne, October 6, 1784, *Public Archives of Canada Report*, 1921, App. E.

18 Parr to Shelburne, May 1, 1785, MG 23, A4, vol. 88, PAC; Parr to Shelburne, January 24, 1784, *Public Archives of Canada Report*, 1921, App. E; Parr to Nepean, April 10, 1784, CO 217, vol. 59.

19 Parr to Nepean, February 28 and August 13, 1784, CO 217, vol. 59; Parr to Shelburne, July 26, 1784, *Public Archives of Canada Report*, 1921, App. E. This reference to "nationalism" is interesting in that Joseph Peters often commented on the fact that the Halifax establishment, religious and political, was dominated by the Protestant Irish. Hamond, in a letter dealing with the controversy over the governor's farm, claimed that Parr had turned the chief justice and his clique against him, for they were all Irish, all "his countrymen." Hamond to _____, December 7, 1785, CO 217, vol. 57.

20 See, for example, Bulkeley to Perkins, November 20, 1783, D.C. Harvey, ed., *The Diary of Simeon Perkins, 1780–1789* (Toronto 1958), 207; Newton to Sydney, July 25, 1785, CO 217, vol. 57; L.F.S. Upton, *The United Empire Loyalists: Men and Myths* (Toronto 1967), 71 ff.; Campbell to Sydney, April 20, 1784, *Public Archives of Canada Report*, 1894, 417.

21 Charles Morris to Robert Morris, March 31, 1785, MD, vol. 395, PANS; Charles Morris to Thomas Milledge, August 13, 1784, ibid.; Charles Morris to Edward Brudenell, September 14, 1785, ibid.; Charles Morris to Botsford, July 12, 1783, MG 23, D4, vol. 1, PAC; Charles Morris to Studholme, May 3, 1783, MD, vol. 394, PANS.

22 Charles Morris to Marston, March 9, 1784, MD, vol. 394, PANS.

23 Charles Morris to Brudenell, March 24, 1785, and to Milledge, September 14, 1785, MD, vol. 395, PANS; Charles Morris to Burbidge, October 18, 1784, ibid.; Charles Morris to Milledge, December 5, 1785, ibid.; Charles

Morris to Robert Gray, January 2, 1785, ibid.; Charles Morris to Brudenell, February 12, 1785, ibid.

24 Carleton to North, October 26, 1783, CO 5, vol. 111; Parr to North, April 3, 1783, CO 217, vol. 56; Parr to Nepean, November 10, 1785, CO 217, vol. 57; Parr to Nepean, August 20, 1785, ibid.

25 JHA, October 6, 1783; *Gazette*, October 14, 1783, MG 11, NS-C, vol. 12, November 10, 1783, PAC.

26 Parr to Nepean, October 25, 1783, *Public Archives of Canada Report*, 1894, 408. Parr did eventually get an increase in salary from £500 to £1,000. See Parr to Nepean, November 30, 1785, CO 217, vol. 57; Memorial of the House of Assembly to Parr, November 22, 1783, CO 217, vol. 56; Beamish Murdoch, *History of Nova Scotia*, 3 vols. (Halifax 1865–7), 3: 22; MD, vol. 344, PANS.

27 Bailey to Rev. Mather Byles, November 5, 1779, Bailey Papers, vol. 13, PANS.

28 JHA, November 27, 1784; MG 11, NS-C, vol. 12, November 30, 1784; JHA, October 15, 1783; ibid., November 17 and 20, 1784.

29 List of Council Members, November 1781, CO 217, vol. 56; Parr to Sydney, June 11, 1785, CO 217, vol. 57; Bruce to Nepean, June 22, 1785, ibid.

30 Parr to Sydney, December 6, 1784, CO 217, vol. 57.

31 Bulkeley to James Robertson et al., February 18, 1785, MD, vol. 137, PANS.

32 Harvey, *Diary of Simeon Perkins*, 203.

33 T.W. Smith, "The Loyalists at Shelburne," *Coll. NSHS* 6 (1888): 56.

34 Bailey to _____, May 4, 1780, Bailey Papers, Annapolis, 1776–88 (Microfilm, Church Historical Society, Austin, Texas), PANS; Bailey to H.B. Brown, March 12, 1783, MG 23, D1, vol. 72, PAC; Bailey to Peter Fry, October 14, 1785, Bailey Papers, vol. 14 PANS.

35 Charles Morris to Amos Botsford, May 8, 1784, MD, vol. 394, PANS.

36 Jonathan Wiswall to Samuel Peters, May 29, 1787, Wiswall Papers, PANS.

37 Frank Patterson, *John Patterson, The Founder of Pictou Town* (Truro 1955), 11.

38 Deposition of James McCabe, February 15, 1784, CO 217, vol. 58.

39 Bailey Papers, vol. 10, 37–9, PANS; Extract from diary, MD, vol. 223, 7–7b, PANS.

40 Bulkeley to James Law, Christopher Harper, and Charles Dickson, August 2, 1783, MD, vol. 136. PANS.

41 See particularly G.A. Rawlyk and G. Stewart, "Nova Scotia's Sense of Mission," *Social History* 2 (1968): 5–17, and G.A. Rawlyk and G. Stewart, *A People Highly Favoured of God: The Nova Scotia Yankees and the American Revolution* (Toronto 1972).

42 Harvey, *Diary of Simeon Perkins*, 130, 139, 162.

43 Memorial of Samual Poole et al. to Parr, n.d. [c. 1783], MD, vol. 223, PANS; Memorial of David Jones and John Smith to Parr, October 28,

1783, ibid.; Land Petitions, vol. 14, no. 2, PANS; Memorial of George Smith, March 10, 1784, CO 217, vol. 35.

44 Included in Joseph Gray to Richard Bulkeley, October 31, 1785, MD, vol. 223, PANS.

45 *Gazette*, February 17, 24, and March 9, 23, and August 10, 1784.

46 A.C. Jost, *Guysborough Sketches and Essays* (Guysborough 1950), 143.

47 Carole Troxler, "The Migration of Carolina and Georgia Loyalists to Nova Scotia and New Brunswick" (PHD diss., University of North Carolina, 1974), 134; see also 117 and 184.

48 *Gazette*, March 1, 1785; H.L. Stewart, *The Irish in Nova Scotia: Annals of the Charitable Irish Society of Halifax, 1786–1836* (Kentville 1905), 37–8; *Gazette*, January 1, 1788, April 18, 1786; Troxler, "Migration," 134.

49 J.S. Macdonald, *Annals of the North British Society, 1763–1903* (Halifax 1903), 55; Stewart, *The Irish in Nova Scotia*, 88.

50 *Gazette*, July 3, 1787.

51 Harvey, *Diary of Simeon Perkins*, 378, 240–9.

52 Mentioned in Andrew Belcher to sister Betty, n.d. [c.1790], Byles Papers, vol. 1, folder 3, PANS; Journal of Charles Inglis, August 24, 1791, microfilm reel A 709, C9, PAC; Letter to the editor, *Nova Scotia Magazine*, February 24, 1791.

53 Bailey to Inglis, January 21, 1788, Bailey Papers, vol. 15, PANS; Murdoch, *History of Nova Scotia* 3: 99.

54 Jacob Bailey's Description of Nova Scotia, MG 23, D1(1), vol. 72, PAC.

55 Charles Morris to Richard Morris, November 8, 1786, MD, vol. 395, PANS.

56 A.A. Johnston, *A History of the Catholic Church in Eastern Nova Scotia* (Antigonish 1960), 125–7.

57 Parr to "My Lord," November 8, 1788, CO 217, vol. 61; extract, Robert Gray to Morris, March 5, 1785, ibid.

58 Bulkeley to John Crawley and Phineas Durkee, MD, vol. 137, PANS.

59 Charles Morris to Richard Bulkeley, December 8, 1784, MD, vol. 395, PANS.

60 Deposition of James McCabe, February 15, 1784, CO 217, vol. 58.

61 Richard Bulkeley to G.H. Monk, April 19, 1784, MD, vol. 136, PANS.

62 G.H. Monk to Parr, May 21, 1784, MG 23, G2, 19, vol. 3, PAC.

63 MD, vol. 430, no. 23 1/2, Indians: 1783, PANS.

64 Memorial of Solomon Taumaugh and Philip Bernard to Parr, February 1, 1786, MD, vol. 430, PANS.

65 Richard Bulkeley to Gilbert Totten, May 20, 1785, MD, vol. 137, PANS.

66 John Young to G.H. Monk, September 7, 1783, MG 23, GII, 19, vol. 3, PAC.

67 Parr to Nepean, December 7, 1783, CO 217, vol. 59; Memorial of Lt. Governor Fanning, November 2, 1783, CO 217, vol. 35; Bailey to Dr Morice, October 28, 1785, Bailey Papers, vol. 14, PANS; Harvey, *Diary of Simeon Perkins*, 184, 188, 189.

68 Memorial of the Magistrates, Grand Jury and principal inhabitants of King's County, MD, vol. 224, 47, PANS.

69 Parr to Sydney, September 29, 1784, CO 217, vol. 56.

70 Admiral Sawyer to Philip Stephens, July 23, 1785, MG 12, Admiralty 1, vol. 491, PAC.

71 Parr to Nepean, October 25, December 1783, CO 217, vol. 59; ibid., December 1783.

72 See Raymond, "Founding of Shelburne," 239, 262, and map, 212; Parr to Nepean, October 1 and January 23, 1783, CO 217, vol. 59; Charles Morris to P. Morris, June 27, 1787, MD, vol. 395, PANS (although correspondence exists concerning a similar amount of land for the Church of England, Charles Morris's letter does not seem to refer to the church land but rather to a more private undertaking by the governor); Jason Dole to Sir Guy Carleton, September 19, 1783, MD, vol. 369, PANS; Charles Morris to Major Studholme, April 16, 1784, MD, vol. 394, PANS.

73 John Breynton to Samuel Peters, May 3, 1785, Peters Papers, 1–2, PANS; Parr to Lords Commissioners of His Majesty's Treasury, June 15, 1784, CO 217, vol. 59; Parr to Nepean, n.d. [c. fall 1784], ibid.; Parr to Nepean, November 17, 1784, ibid.; Sydney to Parr, May 1, 1785, CO 218, vol. 25.

74 In an account of half-fees from June 1, 1784 to March 31, 1786, for grants of 1,299,164 acres, plus 3,339 acres of town lots, the governor's share came to £1,042.16.3, the secretary's share to £318.10.6, and the surveyor-general's to £273.12.6. See Parr to Nepean, August 7, 1786, CO 217, vol. 58.

75 Parr to Nepean, May 7, 1785, MG 23, A2, vol. 8, PAC; Parr to Sydney, December 6, 1784, CO 217, vol. 57.

76 R.J. Uniacke replaced him as solicitor-general. See Hamond to Germain, January 6, 1782, CO 217, vol. 56.

77 Hon. John Doull, "The First Five Attorney-Generals," *Coll. NSHS* 26 (1947): 41–2; *Sketches of the Attorney-Generals of Nova Scotia, 1750–1926* (Halifax 1964), 11.

78 Sydney to Parr, March 8, 1785, CO 217, vol. 57.

79 Unsigned, n.d., MG 23, A2, vol. 8, 131–3, PAC.

80 Parr to Nepean, May 7, 1785, MG 23, A2, vol. 8, PAC.

81 Carleton to Parr, October 23, 1783, CO 5, vol. 111.

82 Charles Morris to Robert Gray, February 6, 1785, MD, vol. 395, PANS; Petition of Arbraham Whillbanch and Nehemiah Field, CO 217, vol.

61; Charles Morris to Col. Glasiar, June 20, 1784, MD, vol. 394, PANS; Charles Morris to Jonathan Norwood, December 8, 1783, ibid.; Charles Morris to Amos Botsford, July 8, 1784, MG 23, D4, vol. 1, PAC.

83 Raymond, "Founding of Shelburne," 226, 233; Rough notes of Captain W. Booth, March 27, 1789.

84 Journal of Charles Inglis, October 15, 1790, reel A709, C4, PAC.

85 Col. Dundas to Earl Cornwallis, December 28, 1786, *Winslow Papers*, 337; R.W. Jeffery, *Dyott's Diary 1781–1785: A Selection from the Journal of Williams Dyott, Sometimes General in the British Army and Aide de Camp to His Majesty King George II* (London 1907), 1: 57.

86 Andrew Brown, "History of North America," Andrew Brown Papers, University of Edinburgh, 57.

87 Rough notes of Captain W. Booth, May 17, 19, and March 24, 1789.

88 "A Sketch of Shelburnian Manners," MG 9, B9(14). The description was apparently written by a Mr Fraser, formerly a district judge in New Brunswick, later a substantial merchant in Halifax, and probably a loyalist. See note at the end of the manuscript.

CHAPTER EIGHT

1 W.O. Raymond, "The Founding of Shelburne," *Coll. NBHS* 8 (1909): 268.

2 New York Agents to Amos Botsford et al., May 25, 1783, MG 23, D4, vol. 1, PAC.

3 Raymond, "Founding of Shelburne," 211.

4 Ibid., 213.

5 Ibid., 214.

6 Parr to Amos Botsford, July 12, 1783, MG 23, D4, vol. 1.

7 Charles Morris to Amos Botsford, July 12, 1783, ibid.

8 T.W. Smith, "The Loyalists of Shelburne," *Coll. NSHS* 6 (1888): 51, 67.

9 Memorial to B. Ross, C. Campbell, and A. Robertson, n.d., MG 9, B6(2), PAC.

10 Report of Joseph Pynchon, January 23, 1783, in Minute Book of the Port Roseway Associates, MG 9, B6, 63, PAC.

11 Memorial of the Magistrates of Shelburne, November 2, 1785, Assembly Papers, vol. 1A, PANS.

12 Shelburne Records, Special Sessions, September 15, 1785, PANS.

13 See C.B. Fergusson, *A Directory of the Members of the Legislative Assembly of Nova Scotia, 1758–1958* (Halifax 1958), 14. See, for Aplin's criticism, Joseph Aplin to Chief Justice Smith, March 6, 1784, MG 11, NS-A, vol. 104, PAC.

14 Joseph Aplin to Chief Justice Smith, March 6, 1784, MG 11, NS-A, vol. 104. PAC.

15 Memorial of B. Ross, C. Campbell, and A. Robertson, n.d., MG 9, B6(2), PAC.

16 John Garner, "The Electoral Franchise in Colonial Nova Scotia" (MA thesis, University of Toronto, 1948), 52.

17 Garner, "Electoral Franchise," 53.

18 JHA, November 2, 1784.

19 Garner, "Electoral Franchise," 53; Beamish Murdoch, *History of Nova Scotia*, 3 vols. (Halifax 1865-7), 3: 37.

20 Murdoch, *Nova Scotia* 3: 44.

21 Jacob Bailey to Mr Sower, November 25, 1785, Bailey Papers, vol. 14, PANS.

22 Minutes of the Council of the Whole House, December 6, 1785, Assembly Papers, vol. 1-A, PANS.

23 Jacob Bailey to Peter Fry, December 15, 1785, Bailey Papers, vol. 14, PANS.

24 JHA, June 23, 1786, PANS.

25 Ibid.

26 James Clark to Gideon White, March 1786, White Collection, no. 404, PANS.

27 A.C. Jost, *Guysborough Sketches and Essays* (Guysborough 1950), 184.

28 Fergusson, *Nova Scotia MLAs*, 163-4.

29 Marion Gilroy, *Loyalists and Land Settlement in Nova Scotia* (Halifax 1937), 147.

30 Jacob Bailey to Peter Fry, January 5, 1786, Bailey Papers, vol. 14, PANS.

31 Gilroy, *Loyalists and Land Settlement*, 147.

32 J.M. Beck, *The Government of Nova Scotia* (Toronto 1957), 29.

33 James Clarke to Gideon White, February 3, 1786, White Collection, PANS.

34 Margaret Ells, "Nova Scotia 'Sparks of Liberty'," *Canadian Historical Association Report*, 1934, 476n.

35 Ibid.

36 Elisha Lawrence to Secretary of State, August 6, 1790, MG 11, NS-A, vol. 20, PAC.

37 See JHA, December 17, 1785, June 23, 1786, November 20 and 28, 1787, March 12, 14, and 31, April 1 and 6, 1789, March 10, 20, and 29, April 6 and 8, 1790.

38 See ibid., June 20, 1786, December 8, 1787, March 18, 1789.

39 Ibid., June 23, 1786.

40 Ibid., March 12, 1789.

41 Ibid., March 14, 1789.

42 Ibid., June 20 and July 1, 1786.

43 On December 8, 1787, four loyalists were supported by four pre-loyalists; on March 12, 1787, six loyalists were supported by seven pre-loyalists,

and in another vote that day seven loyalists were supported by seven pre-loyalists; on March 20, 1789, five loyalists voted with eight pre-loyalists; on March 31, 1789, seven loyalists voted with five pre-loyalists; on April 1, 1789, seven loyalists voted with eight pre-loyalists, and in another vote that day six loyalists voted with four pre-loyalists.

44 On November 20, 1787, eight loyalists voted with five pre-loyalists; in each of two votes on December 17, 1785, the four loyalists were supported by at least ten pre-loyalists, and in another vote that day seven loyalists voted with fifteen pre-loyalists; on April 6, 1789, eight loyalists voted with ten pre-loyalists; on March 10, 1790, eight loyalists voted with nine pre-loyalists; on March 20, 1790, eight loyalists voted with ten pre-loyalists; on April 8, eight loyalists voted with nine pre-loyalists, and later in the day eight loyalists voted with ten pre-loyalists.

45 See Fergusson, *Nova Scotia MLAs*.

46 Ibid.

47 Ells, "Nova Scotia 'Sparks of Liberty'," 477. The efforts of the assembly to stimulate the economy through bounties and other incentives are examined in chap. 10.

48 Ibid. Despite their penchant for encouraging economic growth, the loyalists defeated Captain Howe's two motions to continue bounties on hemp and iron. One reason for this was that they were Howe's motions; another was that the bounties did not significantly affect the loyalists and other communities. See JHA, April 4 and 6, 1789.

49 On the influence of Halifax and the ties between council members see Beck, *Government of Nova Scotia*, 20–2.

50 Fergusson, *Nova Scotia MLAs*, 341.

51 Tonge to Nepean, June 28, 1786, *Public Archives of Canada Report*, 1894, 444.

52 C.B. Fergusson, ed., *The Diary of Simeon Perkins, 1790–1796* (Toronto 1961), xxvii.

53 Ibid., xxviii.

54 Tonge to Grenville, May 1, 1790, *Public Archives of Canada Report*, 1894, 464.

55 JHA, 1786, 54, quoted in Ells, "Nova Scotia 'Sparks of Liberty'," 484.

56 Ibid.

57 Ibid., 486.

58 JHA, March 30, 1790.

59 See Beck, *Government of Nova Scotia*, 57, and Ells, "Nova Scotian 'Sparks of Liberty'," 486–7.

60 Parr to Grenville, April 23, 1790, CO 217, vol. 62.

61 JHA, April 1, 1790.

62 Parr to Grenville, May 3, 1790, CO 217, vol. 62.

63 JHA, March 12, 23, and 31, 1789.

64 Ibid., March 12 and 23, 1789.

65 Ibid., March 31, 1789.

66 Beck, *Government of Nova Scotia*, 50. For the first election regulations, see Minutes of Council, May 20, 1758.

67 E.g., the elections in Shelburne and Annapolis.

68 *Gazette*, February 26, 1789.

69 JHA, March 31, 1789.

70 29 Geo. 3, C. 1 (1789).

71 JHA, April 1, 1789.

72 Ells, "Nova Scotian 'Sparks of Liberty'," 478–9.

73 Ibid., 479.

74 Parr to Nepean, December 5, 1787, CO 217, vol. 60.

75 Ibid., January 30, 1788.

76 Lt. Col. Delancey, "State of the Bench of the Supreme Court of Judicature in Nova Scotia," March 1, 1786, *Public Archives of Canada Report*, 1894, 440.

77 JHA, November 28, 1787.

78 Ibid., December 1, 1787.

79 Ibid., 1787, 64–5.

80 *Gazette*, February 2, 1788.

81 Ibid.

82 Ibid., January 29, 1788. See also SUL NARL's letter, February 12, 1788.

83 *Gazette*, February 19, 1788.

84 Ibid.

85 Ibid., February 26, 1788. Morris won the by-election, 415–274.

86 Proceedings of His Majesty's Council concerning the Conduct of the Justices, CO 217, vol. 60.

87 Ells, "Nova Scotia 'Sparks of Liberty'," 480.

88 Parr to Nepean, March 8, 1788, CO 217, vol. 60.

89 Ibid., April 18, 1788.

90 Parr to Sydney, April 20, 1788, CO 217, vol. 690.

91 Parr to Nepean, May 5, 1788, ibid. Parr mentioned hearing that Pemberton had been appointed chief justice. If someone had been appointed much earlier, according to Parr, "this affair of the Puisne Judges would not have happened."

92 JHA, March 12, 1789.

93 Ibid.

94 Ibid.

95 Ibid., March 14, 1789.

96 Ells, "Nova Scotia 'Sparks of Liberty'," 482.

97 *Weekly Chronicle*, March 21, 1789, from Murdoch, *History of Nova Scotia* 3: 67–9.

98 Ibid., 70.

99 JHA, March 14, 1789.

100 Parr to Nepean, April 20, 1789, CO 217, vol. 61.

101 Parr to Secretary of State, April 24, 1790, CO 217, vol. 62.

102 Ibid.

103 JHA, March 20, 1790.

104 Ibid., March 29, 1790.

105 Ibid., April 5, 1790.

106 Ibid.

107 Ibid., April 9, 1790.

108 Ibid.

109 Ibid.

110 Ibid.

111 Parr to Secretary of State, May 5, 1790, *Public Archives of Canada Report,* 1894, 464.

112 Parr to Nepean, June 12, 1790, CO 217, vol. 62.

113 Ells, "Nova Scotia, 'Sparks of Liberty'," 488–9.

114 Parr to Secretary of State, April 24, 1790, CO 217, vol. 62.

115 Parr to Nepean, April 24, 1790, ibid.

116 Ibid.

117 S.S. Blowers to Parr, February 21, 1788, published in *Halifax Journal,* CO 217, vol. 62.

118 See Haliburton to Nepean, April 20, 1788, *Public Archives of Canada Report,* 1894, 454, CO 217, vol. 62.

119 Ells, "Nova Scotia 'Sparks of Liberty'," 478.

120 Joseph Pynchon to the Committee of the Port Roseway Associates, February 1783, as quoted in T.W. Smith, "Loyalists at Shelburne," 67.

CHAPTER NINE

1 Jacob Bailey's Description of Nova Scotia, MG 23, D1(1), vol. 72, 10, PAC.

2 Andrew Brown, "History of North America," Andrew Brown Papers, University of Edinburgh, 105.

3 Parr to Nepean, January 27, 1788, CO 217, vol. 60.

4 Marston to Israel Manduit, August 8, 1784, MG 23, D1(1), vol. 21, PAC.

5 Parr to Shelburne, September 28, 1785, MG 23, A4, vol. 88, PAC; Parr to to Nepean, February 5, 1787, CO 217, vol. 60.

6 Letter of February 25, 1786, MD, vol. 301, no. 78, PANS.

7 Samuel Goldbury to Edward Winslow, March 1, 1785, *Winslow Papers,* 270–1.

8 A.T. Smith, "Transportation and Communication in Nova Scotia, 1749–1815" (MA thesis, Dalhousie University, 1936), 88, 11, 143.

9 Carole W. Troxler, "The Migration of Carolina and Georgia Loyalists

to Nova Scotia and New Brunswick"(PH D diss., University of North Carolina 1974), 125.

10 JHA, c. 8, 1786, from A.T. Smith, "Transportation and Communication," 148; Memorial, JHA, April 1, 1790.

11 A.T. Smith, "Transportation and Communication," 168–70.

12 *Gazette*, October 25, 1785.

13 A.T. Smith, "Transportation and Communication," 179.

14 *Royal American Gazette*, January 24, 1785; Petition of Wm. Black and Thomas Watson, June 14, 1786, Assembly Papers, vol. 2, PANS; Report of December 20, 1794, MD, vol. 48, no. 120, PANS.

15 Report of the Committee on Bounties, December 24, 1785, November 23, 1787, MD, vol. 301, PANS; JHA, March 21, 1789.

16 Troxler, "Migration," 123.

17 W.O. Raymond, "The Founding of Shelburne," *Coll. NBHS* 8 (1909): 269.

18 Memorial of Richard Townsend, Senior and Junior, July 16, 1785, MG 12, Admiralty 1, vol. 491, PAC.

19

1787	Fish Dried (quintals)	Fish Wet (barrels)
Newfoundland	732,216	3,865
Cape Breton	36,736	1,021
Quebec	2,080	328
PEI	186	10
Nova Scotia	44,723	13,363
New Brunswick	2,017	3,709
Total	817,958	22,296
Average quantities shipped, 1771, 1773, 1774		
Newfoundland, Canada, Nova Scotia	563,234	1,544
American Colonies	345,294	36,444
Total	908,528	37,990

Source: Irving's Report on American Fisheries, MG 23, A2, vol. 8, 89, PAC.

20 Beckles Willson, *Nova Scotia, The Province That Has been Passed By* London 1911), 122.

21 D.C. Harvey, ed., *The Diary of Simeon Perkins, 1780–1789* (Toronto 1958), 350.

22 Quoted in Mathews, *The Mark of Honour* (Toronto 1965), 114–15.

23 *Royal American Gazette*, June 20, 1785.

24 T.W. Smith, "The Loyalists at Shelburne," *Coll. NSHS* 6 (1888): 81.

25 Shelburne Records, General Sessions, April 10, 1786, PANS; CO 217, vol. 62, 257; Wm. Forsyth to John Wentworth, October 17, 1791, Wentworth Papers, vol. 2, PANS; JHA, July 1, 1786.

26 A.T. Smith, "Transportation and Communication," 47; JHA, December 27, 1785; Statutes at Large, c. 8 (1786), sec. 2; *Gazette*, August 29, 1786; CO 217, vol. 60, 286; *Gazette*, January 9, 1787.

27 *Gazette*, October 21, 1788, August 21, 1787; Journal of Charles Inglis, August 27, 1780, MG 17, A709, C5, PAC.

28 G.F. Butler, "Commercial Relations of Nova Scotia with the United States" (MA thesis, Dalhousie University, 1934), 48–9.

29 Campbell to Haldimand, October 16, 1783, MG 21, vol. B, 149, PAC; *Royal American Gazette*, April 18, 1785; see also January 31 and April 25, 1785.

30 Butler, "Commercial Relations," 48. See also Brook Watson to _____, August 26, 1785, MG 23, D1(1), vol. 72, PAC.

31 R. Cumberland to Committee of Correspondence, House of Assembly, February 25, 1786, MD, vol. 301, PANS.

32 Parr to "My Lord," September 2, 1787, MG 11, NS-A, vol. 108, PAC.

33 Henry Newton to Parr, January 26, 1788, CO 217, vol. 60.

34 JHA, July 1, 1786.

35 Parker to Whitworth, June 2, 1784, White Collection, no. 279, PANS.

36 *PANS Report*, 1947, 44; Harold Innis, *The Cod Fisheries: The History of an International Economy* (Toronto 1954), 427.

37 Innis, *Cod Fisheries*, 231.

38 *PANS Report*, 1947, 49.

39 Innis, *Cod Fisheries*, 231.

40 Willson, *Nova Scotia*, 122; T.W. Smith, "History of Shelburne," 124.

41 S. Hollingsworth, *An Account of the Present State of Nova Scotia* (Edinburgh 1786), 24.

42 Ibid., 130; from James W. Walker, *The Black Loyalists* (New York 1976), 42.

43 Walker, *Black Loyalists*, 46.

44 Butler, "Commercial Relations," 49, 50.

45 *PANS Report*, 1947, 35.

46 From A.T. Smith, "Transportation and Communication," 162.

47 W. Paine to John Wentworth, March 1, 1788, Wentworth Papers, vol. 2, PANS.

48 See Lt. Gov. Carleton to Lord Grenville, July 15, 1791, MG 23, D1(1), vol. 75, PAC.

49 *PANS Report*, 1947, 35.

50 Troxler, "Migration," 132.

51 Jonathan Wiswall to Samuel Peters, May 28, 1787, Peters Papers, vol. 3, PANS.

52 Gillmore Saga, vol. 2, 48, PANS.

53 I.M. Sutherland, "Clements Township: Its History and Its People, 1783–1870" (MA thesis, Acadia University, 1957), 55.

54 See M. Hutchinson to M. Mascarene, June 2, 1787, and August 9, 1791, Mascarene Papers, PANS.

55 Gillmore Saga, vol. 2, 48, PANS.

56 See, for example, *Nova Scotia Magazine* 1: 398–9, and 4: 75; see also *Gazette*, May 18, 1790, March 15, 1791.

57 Walker, *Black Loyalists*, 52.

58 Journal of Charles Inglis, July 29, 1788, reel A709, C5, PAC; Memorial to the King from the Magistrates and Vestry at Digby, August 15, 1789, Peters Papers, vol. 4, PANS.

59 Address of Anthony Kyst, 1789, MD, vol. 301, no. 58, PANS.

60 R.W. Jeffery, *Dyott's Diary* (London 1907), 1: 68; William Clark to Samuel Peters, April 7, May 24, 1787, Peters Papers, vol. 3, PANS; Memorial of the Refugees of Annapolis County to Parr, 1786, MD, vol. 223, no. 130, PANS; Beamish Murdoch, *History of Nova Scotia*, 3 vols. (Halifax 1865–7), 3: 53.

61 Judith Fingard, *The Anglican Design in Loyalist Nova Scotia* (London 1972), 93.

62 Jonathan Wiswall to Dr Morice, April 7, 1791, Wiswall Papers, PANS.

63 *London Chronicle*, December 4–7, 1784, 546.

64 Dr Walter to "My Lord," November 20, 1784, CO 217, vol. 57; Wm. Chew to Gideon White, August 23, 1784, MG 23, D1(1), vol. 23, PAC; Rough notes of Captain W. Booth, March 14, 1789, Acadia University; Nathaniel Whitworth to his brother Charles, March 15, 1784, White Collection, no. 264, PANS; Phyllis Blakeley, "Boston King," *Dalhousie Review* 48 (1968): 354.

65 T.W. Smith, "Loyalists at Shelburne," 81–2.

66 Memorial of the Leading Citizens of Shelburne, June 20, 1791, MD, vol. 221, PANS.

67 Ibid.

68 T.W. Smith, "Loyalists at Shelburne," 81.

69 Brown, "History of North America," 106–7; Thomas Milledge to Gideon White, September 4, 1784, White Collection, no. 310, PANS.

70 Charles Whitworth to George Parker, January 3, 1785, White Collection, no. 343, PANS.

71 S.S. Blowers to Ward Chipman, July 28, 1785, May 13, 1786, MG 23, D1(1), vol. 1 PAC.

72 *Gazette*, August 21, 1787; *Nova Scotia Packet*, August 24, 1786.

73 Shelburne Records, Shelburne Executions, PANS.

74 See Parr to Sydney, September 21, 1787, and March 8, 1788, CO 217, vol. 60; see also Parr to Grenville, July 20, 1790, CO 217, vol. 62.

75 MG 11, NS-C, vol. 14, 26, PAC.

76 From Mathews, *Mark of Honour*, 124.

77 Brown, "History of North America," 106–7.

78 White Collection, no. 343, PANS; Harvey, *Diary of Simeon Perkins*, 318–19; George Patterson, *A History of the County of Pictou* (Montreal 1877), 143; Jonathan Wiswall to Dr Morice, May 29, 1787; Wiswall Papers, PANS; Rev. George Gillmore to Mr Fuller [?], n.d. [c.1788], Gillmore Saga, vol. 2, PANS; Memorial to the Commissioners of Claims, May 25, 1789, ibid.; T.W. Smith, "History of Shelburne," PANS.

79 Mathews, *Mark of Honour*, 122.

80 Journal of Charles Inglis, August 23, 1791, MG 23, C9, A709, PAC.

81 White Collection, no. 560, PANS.

82 Blakeley, "Boston King," 353. The year 1792 was another year of drought and failed crops. See Journal of Charles Inglis, June 28 and July 3, 1792, MG 23, C9, A709, PAC.

83 Blakeley, "Boston King," 353.

84 James Moody, John Taylor, and Stephen Jones to John Parr, March 1, 1790, MD, vol. 286, PANS.

85 Charles Dickens, *David Copperfield*, Collins Library of Classics, n.d., 179: "Annual income twenty pounds, annual expenditure nineteen nineteen six, result happiness. Annual income twenty pounds, annual expenditure twenty pounds ought and six, result misery."

CHAPTER TEN

1 Memorial of the inhabitants of Digby, August 1, 1785, SPG, MG 17, B1/1, vol. 1, PAC; C. Clopper to Chas. Whitworth, April 18, 1783, White Collection, PANS; J. Alptharp to John Wentworth, February 20, 1788, Wentworth Papers, vol. 2, PANS; Jacob Bailey to Capt. Benjamin Palmer, August 2, 1784, Bailey Papers, vol. 15, PANS; N. Ford to Gideon White, August 23 and June 8, 1786, White Collection, PANS.

2 Cited in W.H. Nelson, *The American Tory* (London 1961), 169; B. Watson to E. Winslow, August 26, 1785, *Winslow Papers*, 312; *Gazette*, October 18, 1785.

3 Jacob Bailey to Moses Badger, July 1, 1779, Bailey Papers, vol. 13, PANS; Jacob Bailey to Charles Inglis, August 22, 1783, MG 23, D1(1), vol. 72, PAC.

4 George Deblois to _____, May 1785, MG 23, D1(1), vol. 20, 12, PAC.

5 *London Chronicle*, August 25–27, 1785; N. Ford to Gideon White, August 23, 1786, White Collection, PANS; Gideon White to Charles _____,

June 22, 1787, ibid.; Benjamin Marston to Edward Winslow, September 8, 1787, *Winslow Papers*, 347.

6 *Nova Scotia Packet*, January 1, 1787, Wm. Parker to Chas. Whitworth, June 8, 1784, White Collection, PANS.

7 *Nova Scotia Packet*, July 13 and October 5, 1786.

8 *Royal American Gazette*, February 7, April 18, and August 1, 1785.

9 *Nova Scotia Packet*, November 9 and December 14, 1786.

10 The *Royal American Gazette* and the *Port Roseway Gazetteer* had both ceased publication in Shelburne by September 1787, while the *Nova Scotia Packet* existed as late as February 1789. See Marie Tremaine, *A Bibliography of Canadian Imprints* (Toronto 1952), 612–17.

11 *Nova Scotia Magazine* 1: 105 ff., 199 ff., 204, 364 ff.

12 J.S. Macdonald, *North British Society* (Halifax 1905), 55.

13 M. Hutchinson to M. Mascarene, September 6, 1783, Mascarene Papers, PANS; Andrew Belcher to his sister, Betty, n.d. [c.1790], Byles Papers, vol. 1, f. 3, PANS; R. Altman to Miss Byles, June 19, 1790, ibid.

14 Gideon White to Chas. _____, June 22, 1787, White Collection, PANS; F.W. Geyer to Ward Chipman, June 12, 1786, MG 23, C1(1), vol. 2, PAC; G. Townsend to Ward Chipman, November 19, 1787, Chipman Papers, PAC; same to same, May 10, 1788, ibid.

15 Mather Byles III to his aunts, August 26, 1788, Byles Papers, vol. 1, f. 2, PANS; Journal of Mather Byles, July-September 1790, Byles Papers, vol. 1, f. 2, 29c–i, PANS.

16 M. Hutchinson to M. Mascarene, October 20, 1783, Mascarene Papers, PANS; same to same, October 3, 1786, ibid.

17 See, for example, Bailey's journal of the flight from New England, Bailey Papers, vol. 5, PANS.

18 Jacob Bailey to Rev. John Gardiner, December 8, 1787, Bailey Papers, vol. 15, PANS.

19 William Clark to Samuel Peters, May 12, 1787, Peters Papers, vol. 4, PANS.

20 Roger Viets to Samuel Peters, October 12, 1787, Peters Papers, vol. 3, PANS.

21 Andrew Brown, "History of North America," Andrew Brown Papers, University of Edinburgh, 103.

22 Charles Morris to Major Studholme, November 12, 1784, MD, vol. 394, PANS; Jacob Bailey to _____, November 12, 1787, Bailey Papers, vol. 13, PANS; quoted in William Clark to Samuel Peters, June 23, 1789, Peters Papers, vol. 4, PANS; J. Peters to Samuel Peters, November 17, 1788, Peters Papers, vol. 3, PANS.

23 Sarah Winslow to Benjamin Marston, April 10, 1783, *Winslow Papers*, 87.

24 William Clark to Samuel Peters, May 12, 1790, Peters Papers, vol. 4, PANS.

25 William Clark to Samuel Peters, September 4, 1790, ibid.; quoted in William Clark to Samuel Peters, June 23, 1789, ibid.; *Gazette*, December 23, 1791.

26 Some loyalists who entered the establishment in Nova Scotia retained a rhetoric of contempt and hostility. What is interesting in Nova Scotia is that the establishment, chiefly non-loyalist under Parr, managed to usurp the image of loyalism and to brand some of the loyalist reformers as suspect.

27 C.H. Van Tyne, *The Loyalists in the American Revolution* (New York 1902), 301. For an informative study of British thought, policy, and action regarding the loyalists, and of the fate of the loyalists in Britain, see Mary Beth Norton, *The British-Americans: The Loyalist Exiles in England, 1774–1789* (Boston 1972).

28 "In the whole course of their work, they examined claims to the amount of forty millions of dollars and ordered nineteen millions to be paid . . . If, to the cost of establishing the Loyalists in Nova Scotia and Canada, we add the compensations granted in money, the total amount expended by the British government for their American adherents, was at least thirty millions of dollars." Van Tyne, *Loyalists in the Revolution*, 303.

29 See, for example, *Gazette*, November 11, 1783.

30 Deputy Attorney J. Pendrey [?] to John Wentworth, December 17, 1783, Wentworth Papers, vol. 1, PANS; unsigned, Whitehall, to Parr, June 4, 1784, CO 217, vol. 56; H.C. Mathews, *The Mark of Honour* (Toronto 1965), 120.

31 Unsigned to Samuel Peters, November 10, 1783, Peters Papers, vol. 1, PANS.

32 *Gazette*, March 2, 1784; *Royal American Gazette*, April 21, 1785.

33 *Royal American Gazette*, April 21, 1785.

34 Beamish Murdoch, *History of Nova Scotia*, 3 vols. (Halifax 1865–7), 3: 45. On the following day fifty-three loyalists presented the commissioners with a complimentary address. See *Gazette*, November 22, 1785; Mathews, *Mark of Honour*, 100. On the parliamentary debates, see *Gazette*, March 28 and October 3, 1786; see also *Nova Scotia Packet*, August 17, 1786.

35 *Gazette*, February 7, 1787; Parr to Col. Balfour and John Stranger, East Florida Claims Office, June 28, 1789, MD, vol. 137, PANS; Petition of the House of Assembly to the king, March 16, 1790, CO 217, vol. 62.

36 Commissioner's Statement, June 10, 1789, White Collection, no. 497, PANS.

37 C.J. MacGillivray, *Timothy Hierlihy and His Times* (Halifax 1935), 124; Mathews, *Mark of Honour*, 120.

38 Rough notes of Captain W. Booth, June 25, 1789, Acadia University; Roger Viets to Samuel Peters, August 11, 1789, Peters Papers, vol. 4, PANS; Rev. Gillmore to Samuel Peters, September 22, 1791, Gillmore Saga, vol. 2, PANS.

39 Paul Maylor to Gideon White, July 2, 1787, White Collection, PANS; Jacob Bailey to _____, November 12, 1787, Bailey Papers, vol. 15, PANS; Roger Viets to Samuel Peters, August 11, 1789, Peters Papers, vol. 4, PANS.

41 See, for example, Joseph Peters to Samuel Peters, Peters Papers, May 5, 1790, vol. 4, no. 79, PANS.

42 Margaret Ells, "Settling the Loyalists in Nova Scotia," *Canadian Historical Association Report*, 1934, 107.

43 George Patterson, *History of the County of Pictou* (Montreal 1877), 118.

44 Douglas Lawson to Parr, n.d. [c.1784], MD, vol. 223, 104, PANS; Charles Morris to Rev. Brudenell, October 6, 1788, MD, vol. 395, PANS; Charles Morris to Thomas Milledge, October 6, 1788, ibid.

45 MacGillivray, *Hierlihy*, 116; Patterson, *History of Pictou*, 188; I.M. Sutherland, "Clements Township: Its History and Its People, 1783–1870" (MA thesis, Acadia University, 1957), 52–4; John Wentworth to Parr, March 5, 1788, Wentworth Papers, vol. 49, PANS.

46 *Royal American Gazette*, April 28, 1785; Wardens and Vestry of the Church of England, Shelburne, to Dr Morice, June 28, 1785, MG 17, A170, SPG, CII, PAC; Shelburne Records, General Sessions, April 19, 1786, PANS.

47 R.W. Jeffery, *Dyott's Diary* (London 1907), 1: 55–6; Rough notes of Captain W. Booth, March 24, 1789; *Nova Scotia Magazine* 4: 633.

48 Charles Inglis to Dr Morice, March 7, 1791, MG 23, C6, vol. 1, PAC; General Meeting of St Patrick's and St George's in Christ Church, October 1, 1790, Shelburne Records, PANS; Journal of Charles Inglis, August 3, 1790, MG 23, C6, A709, PAC.

49 General Meeting of St Patrick's and St George's in Christ Church, October 1, 1790, Shelburne Records, PANS.

50 Rev. Munro's estimate, *PANS Report*, 1947, 43.

51 T.W. Smith, "Loyalists at Shelburne," 86; Brown, "History of North America," 107, 109; Rough notes of Captain W. Booth, June 13, 1789, Acadia University.

52 Murdoch, *Nova Scotia* 3: 73.

53 Charles Inglis to Parr, January 6, 1789, MG 23, C6, vol. 7, PAC; see, for example, Bailey to Inglis, March 10, 1788, Bailey Papers, vol. 15, PANS.

54 MD, vol. 223, no. 155, PANS; Charles Inglis to Dr Morice, July 7, 1790, MG 23, C6, vol. 7, PAC; John Wiswall to Dr Morice, April 7, 1791, Wiswall Papers, PANS; Sutherland, "Clements Township," 54–5.

55 Roger Viets to Samuel Peters, September 20, 1786, Peters Papers, 1–2, PANS; Viets to Peters, November 27, 1789, Peters Papers, vol. 4, PANS; Church Wardens and Vestry at Digby to Charles Inglis, September 21, 1790, Digby Vestry Journal, PANS; Roger Viets to Samuel Peters, September 16, 1786, Peters Papers, 1–2, PANS.

56 James W. Walker, *The Black Loyalists* (New York 1976), 96.

57 Ibid., 101.

58 Ibid., 116–17, 129, 137.

59 *Gazette*, October 20 and December 1, 1789; Richard Bulkeley's letter to the sheriffs, August 13, 1790, MD, vol. 137, PANS.

60 William Black's letter of September 17, 1804, *Methodist Magazine* 5 (1805): xxvii; Joshua Marsden, *Narrative of a Mission in Nova Scotia, New Brunswick and the Somers Islands* (London 1816), 22n; Rev. James Munro's "History and description and state of the Southern and Western Townships of Nova Scotia in 1795," *PANS Report*, 1947, 43, 48, 51; Judge Savary to Arthur G. Bradley, n.d. [c.1917], Fort Anne Papers, reel 3, sec. 32, PANS.

61 Parr to "My Lord," November 8, 1788, CO 217, vol. 61; J.R. Campbell, *A History of the County of Yarmouth, Nova Scotia* (Berwick 1903), 304; D.C. Harvey, ed., *The Diary of Simeon Perkins, 1780–1789* (Toronto 1958), 435, 442; Sutherland, "Clements Township," 56; Jonathan Wiswall to Dr Morice, November 22, 1785, Wiswall Papers, PANS; Assessment Records (microfilm), no. 443, 26, PANS.

62 Macdonald, *North British Society*, 61.

63 Peter McMahon to Charles Bready, November 29, 1784, White Collection, no. 333, PANS; Eliza Byles to her aunts, January 13, 1790, Byles Papers, vol. 1, folder 3, PANS; Byles Papers, vol. 1, folder 2, PANS; Captain Brownrigg to Edward Winslow, June 29, 1785, *Winslow Papers*, 308–9; Ward Chipman to Edward Winslow, January 4, 1786, ibid., 323; Eliza Cottnam to A.B. Howe, September 23, 1786, Howe Collection, vol. 3, PANS.

64 Rough notes of Captain W. Booth, May 27, 1789, Acadia University; Philip Jarvis to Gideon White, July 5, 1789, White Collection, no. 501, PANS.

65 H.C. Hart, *History of the County of Guysborough, Nova Scotia* (Windsor 1895), 60; Mason Wade, *The French Canadians, 1760–1967*, 2 vols. (Toronto 1968), 1: 124; Mathews, *Mark of Honour*, 123.

66 Parr to Nepean, September 8, 1784, CO 217, vol. 59; Parr to Shelburne, September 28, 1785, MG 23, A4, vol. 88, PAC.

67 Parr to Grenville, May 25, 1791, CO 217, vol. 63; Roger Viets to Samuel Peters, September 16, 1786, Peters Papers, 1–2, PANS; Minutes of St George's, Shelburne, March 31, 1791, PANS; Joseph Peters to Samuel Peters, n.d. [c. December 24, 1791], Peters Papers, vol. 4, PANS; William Clark to Samuel Peters, December 7, 1789, ibid.; same to same, March 29, 1791, Peters Papers, vol. 5, PANS; Macdonald, *North British Society*, 55; William Clark to Samuel Peters, July 5, 1788, Peters Papers, vol. 3, PANS; Wm. Shipman to Gideon White, White Collection, no. 545, PANS.

68 Jacob Bailey to Samuel Peters, November 12, 1787, Bailey Papers, vol. 15, PANS; Jacob Bailey to Dr Morice, November 12, 1787, ibid.; Jacob Bailey to Charles Inglis, March 10, 1788, Peters Papers, vol. 4, PANS.

69 William Clarke to Samuel Peters, July 16, 1790, Peters Papers, vol. 4, PANS; Charles Morris to John Grehen, October 19, 1788, MD, vol. 396, PANS; Roger Viets to Samuel Peters, August 11, 1789, ibid.

70 Colonel Dundas's letter from Nova Scotia, 1786, *Public Archives of Ontario Report*, 1904, 21; Parr to Shelburne, October 9, 1789, *Public Archives of Canada Report*, 1921, App. E; Magistrates and Grand Jury of Shelburne to Charles Inglis, January 12, 1793, Shelburne Records, 56, PANS; White Collection, no. 464, PANS; Rev. Munro's "History and Description," *PANS Report*, 1947, 43.

71 Charles Inglis to Grenville, September 8, 1790, CO 217, vol. 72; Roger Viets to Samuel Peters, October 12, 1787, Peters Papers, vol. 3, PANS.

72 Charles Morris to John Fraser, August 9, 1791, MD, vol. 396, PANS.

73 Journal of Charles Inglis, September 10, 1791, MG 23, C6, A709, PAC; Murdoch, *Nova Scotia* 3: 84; Parr to Dundas, August 13, 1791, CO 217, vol. 63; same to same, September 27, 1791, ibid.; Charles Morris to J. Harris, October 13, 1791, MD, vol. 396, PANS; Charles Morris to _____, November 20, 1791, ibid.; Charles Morris to John Fraser, August 9, 1791, ibid.

Note on Sources

It would be of little value to list all the material read in preparing this study. The most relevant primary sources are indicated by the use made of them throughout the text. Some of the sources were very influential in shaping one's impressions, insights, and conclusions. Other material, although requiring much time to comb through, offered only marginal insights or sparse if confirming support for the more revealing material. It may be of use, then, to mention here at least some of the richer sources.

One obvious fact about the period had a significant impact on the value of some sources, surprising in their insights into a remarkable period and people: this was an age of slow, cumbersome post, when a writer's thoughts, views, arguments, and justifications often had to be expressed over long distances and at lengthy intervals. It was therefore necessary to express them clearly and, if not necessarily succinctly, then often both frankly and forcefully, even in official correspondence. And this is one of the most attractive features of reading the documents of the age: the researcher is brought so intimately into a sense of the period and its players, their concerns and conflicts.

The Carleton Papers (MG 23, B1), in the Public Archives of Canada were one of the most important sources for the evacuation period. MG 11 contains the very important Colonial Office 217 series, consisting of original correspondence between the Colonial Office and Nova Scotia and Cape Breton. The Admiralty Papers in MG 12 give important if irregular insights into the difficulties and dangers of those first years of settlement, and the role played by the navy in ensuring that the loyalists survived. Occasional reflections on the new communities are also to be found in the papers of the Society for the Propagation of the Gospel in MG 17. In MG 23 are to be found the papers of such significant British politicians as Dartmouth, Sydney, and Shelburne. The series also contains several collections essential for understanding affairs in Nova Scotia, such as the Inglis Papers, those of Edward How(e), the Botsford, Sewell, and James Monk papers, the Lawrence Collection (Ward Chipman), and an assortment of papers on the loyalists in the first years of settlement.

Material at the Public Archives of Nova Scotia is, of course, essential for any study of the loyalists in that province. Concerning official business, there can be found assembly papers, minutes of both councils, official correspondence between the governors and White-all, letter books of the governor and provincial secretary, letter books of Charles Morris, the surveyor-general, and John Wentworth, the surveyor-general of the woods, papers relating specifically to the American Revolution and loyalist immigration, muster rolls of loyalist settlements in Nova Scotia, and much other essential material.

The family papers at the PANS are also a rich source. It is difficult, for example, to imagine attempting a study of the loyalists without the comments and insights found in the Jacob Bailey Papers, the Byles Papers, and the White Collection. On microfilm at the PANS, the Andrew Brown Papers, the Fort Anne Papers, the Mascarene Papers, the Samuel Peters Papers, and Lady Wentworth's Letters are all very useful. The archives also contains a wealth of printed sources ranging from contemporary pamphlets to the Journals of the House of Assembly.

One important source found in most university libraries is W.O. Raymond's edition of *The Winslow Papers, A.D. 1776–1826*. Raymond also edited Benjamin Marston's diary, an important source of inforation on early Shelburne, which appeared in the *Collections of the New Brunswick Historical Society*, no. 8.

Although newspapers varying from the *Quebec Gazette* to *The Times* of London were read for this study, the most useful were those of Nova Scotia, particularly the three Shelburne papers, *The Nova Scotia Packet*, the *Port Roseway Gazetteer and Shelburne Advertiser*, and the *Royal American Gazette*. These were particularly useful in revealing life in Shelburne, the progress and decline of the settlement, and the attitudes of its inhabitants towards their new home, the new empire, and the new nation to the south.

Most of the major theses and secondary sources used in this study are described in a recently published guide by Robert S. Allen, *Loyalist Literature: An Annotated Bibliographic Guide to the Writings on the Loyalists of the American Revolution* (Toronto: Dundurn Press

1982). Another reference work that had not yet appeared when this study was undertaken is *The Loyalist Guide: Nova Scotia Loyalists and Their Documents*, compiled by Jean Peterson and published by the PANS.

Index